CULTURE IN HISTORY

D0217187

CULTURE IN HISTORY

Production, consumption and values in
historical perspective

Edited by Joseph Melling and Jonathan Barry

University of Exeter Press

First published 1992 by
University of Exeter Press
Reed Hall, Streatham Drive
Exeter, Devon EX4 4QR
U.K.

British Library Cataloguing in Publication Data
A catalogue record of this book is
available from the British Library

ISBN 0 85989 380 4

Typeset in 10/12 Sabon by Exe Valley Dataset, Exeter
Printed and bound in Great Britain by Short Run Press, Exeter

Contents

Contributors

Jonathan Barry is Lecturer in History at the University of Exeter.

Dario Castiglione is Lecturer in Politics at the University of Exeter.

Philip Corrigan is Professor of Applied Sociology at the University of Exeter.

Iain Hampsher-Monk is Senior Lecturer in Politics at the University of Exeter.

Eric L. Jones is Professor of Economics (Economic History) at La Trobe University, Melbourne.

Paul Keating is Lecturer in Sociology at the University of Exeter.

Joseph Melling is Lecturer in Economic and Social History at the University of Exeter.

Stephen Mennell is Professor of Sociology and Social Anthropology at Monash University, Melbourne.

Sidney Pollard was the Professor of Economic History at Bielefeld University and Visiting Professor at the University of Exeter.

Roy Porter is Senior Lecturer in the Social History of Medicine at the Wellcome Institute for the History of Medicine, London.

Robert Witkin is Senior Lecturer in Sociology at the University of Exeter.

Preface

This collection arose out of a series of seminars and colloquia at the University of Exeter. These were supported intellectually by colleagues from many departments within the Faculties of Arts and Social Studies and we would like to thank them all: many of their ideas are reflected in the essays published here. Financial support for these meetings was provided by the Departments of Economic and Social History and History and Archaeology. Further funds to support this publication have come from the departments of Economics, Geography, Politics and Sociology, the Faculty of Social Studies, and the Centres for South-Western Historical Studies, European Studies and Management Studies. Their generosity reflects the spirit of interdisciplinary cooperation within the University personified in Michael Havinden, to whom the collection is dedicated.

The editors would like to thank their fellow-contributors for their speed in preparing their pieces for publication and their patience thereafter. We would also like to thank the secretarial and technical staff in our two departments for their assistance. Finally, we thank Elizabeth, Harriet, Maria and Ross for their understanding.

Joseph Melling and Jonathan Barry
University of Exeter
April 1992

An Appreciation of Michael Havinden

Jonathan Barry, Eric Jones and Joseph Melling

The opportunity is being taken to dedicate this volume to Michael Havinden, economic historian, former Dean of the Faculty of Social Studies, and one of the best-liked and most energetic members of staff the University of Exeter can ever have had. Characteristically, he was one of the most supportive and stimulating participants in the seminar series and colloquia from which the book arose, and we hope that its contents reflect a little of his breadth of interests.

Michael Ashley Havinden was born in 1929 and educated first at Dartington School, in its experimental days. His history master's opening lesson on the Middle Ages was held against the vast Dartington manorial fireplace, impressing Michael for ever with a sense of the physical reality behind the abstractions of the past. When these halcyon surroundings became a-buzz with the Second World War, Michael was packed off to the United States. He came back aged fifteen, stopping over at Lisbon, RAF officers at one end of the aerodrome bar, Luftwaffe at the other.

A similar privileged evacuee's sojourn is recounted in Anthony Bailey's *England First and Last*. Both Bailey and Havinden report the democratizing effect of America; they liked it. The experience clearly lifted Michael once and for all out of the mental confines of English society. On the other hand, American educational laxities did not make for a painless return to English schooling. Michael then entered Harrow and, despite starting with no Latin at all, he succeeded in learning enough of this and of arcane English lore to win a History Scholarship to Magdalene College, Cambridge.

For seven years after coming down from Cambridge he farmed, thus appearing unusually practical among the chairbound agricultural history profession he was afterwards to join. When he left farming it was to be a research student, this time at Magdalen College, Oxford, under the supervision of W.G. Hoskins. He met Eric Jones in 1958 when Michael was starting a series of evening classes and struggling to convince a village audience that local history was an exercise in the understanding of place, not an excuse to gossip about the not-so-long dead. His thesis was devoted to the early modern agriculture of Oxfordshire, using the probate inventories. Subsequently he edited a volume of the county's inventories, a labour of love spent deciphering the quirks of forgotten spellings and even less decipherable lost tools. But the prime product was what became a classic paper, 'Agricultural Progress in Open-field Oxfordshire' (1961) which demonstrated the extent to which cropping improvements were adopted before enclosure. Economists may now say they expected as much, but thirty years ago it was heresy.

The next stage was a move to Ardington, near Wantage. This was a village where 'every stick and stone' belonged to the squire. Michael and Kate Havinden lived there for a year or two and Michael wrote a much-cited historical and sociological study, *Estate Village.*

After this came his move to the University of Exeter, as the early modernist and agricultural historian in the Department of Economic History. Michael's contribution to teaching for the Department and the Faculty of Social Studies was particularly wide-ranging and touched on most of the themes which are sketched in this collection. His courses on peasant societies, African agriculture and colonialism were both innovative and popular with the many students who passed through the Department. The British courses he presented traced the growth of industrialization and the spread of consumer taste in the early modern period. Throughout, his teaching emphasized the interdependence of economy, society and culture rather than the primacy of any particular set of historical forces. This is also a feature of his forthcoming book (written with David Meredith) on British colonialism.

His interest in the economic and social history of West Africa (the subject of another popular course) grew from his personal experience as a teacher at Fourah Bay in Sierra Leone. *La fièvre Africaine* took hold. He also spent a productive time as a teacher at La Trobe University in Melbourne, where his contacts with Eric Jones were strengthened. He has always made friends among those from other cultures and has long taught and researched on their histories as well as that of the English.

His contacts and interests are international but he has developed a strong interest in the history of the South West. He edited several volumes of *Exeter Papers in Economic History*, based on the Department's regular research symposia on regional themes and then in 1981 published his book on the Somerset landscape, in the series inspired by Hoskins. He has been one of the most active amongst the group of academics across the University who came together to establish the Centre for South-Western Historical Studies, which came into being formally in 1986. The Centre reflects Michael's breadth of interests in its inter-disciplinary brief, encompassing all aspects of the region's past. He is also committed to its aim of bringing together professionals and amateurs, from higher education, archives, libraries, museums, local and county history and archaeology societies and many other backgrounds, in a sharing of ideas and resources. Michael acted as Chair of what was first an Executive Committee and then a Board of Management of the Centre until 1991, presiding over its steady growth with vigour, tact, flair and unfailing good humour. Even his regional interests, however, have an international dimension, through his collaboration with colleagues at the University of Haute-Bretagne (Rennes II). Joint work on issues of de-industrialization and the problems of peripheral regions culminated in the publication of a bilingual study, *Centre and Periphery: Britanny and Devon and Cornwall Compared* (Exeter, 1991), co-edited by Michael with Jean Queniart and Jeffrey Stanyer. Michael is still very involved in the further development of all these regional projects.

Within the University he has played an influential role as President of the Association of University Teachers and Dean of the Faculty of Social Studies (as well as leading his own department) at a period when the University was undergoing trying times as it struggled with limited resources and the need for internal reorganization within the Faculty. Outside the University he has given his time unselfishly to many scholarly bodies such as the Agricultural History Society and the Economic History Society.

We wish both Michael and Kate Havinden a long and comfortable semi-retirement and offer these essays as a gesture of thanks for their contribution to the life of the University and of their many friends at Exeter and abroad.

Part I
The Problem of Culture

The Problem of Culture: An Introduction

Jonathan Barry and Joseph Melling

I

These essays are presented as a contribution to the discussion on the place of culture in historical explanation. The authors review distinct debates on the role of culture in social explanation and each provides a fresh insight into a specific example. They share a particular concern with the relationship between 'the economic' and 'the cultural'. Whilst 'production' and 'consumption' provide the organizing themes for this text, the essays suggest that the boundaries of production and consumption are themselves cultural constructs, formed by changing conceptions of economic and cultural explanation. This introduction seeks to draw out some of these general themes and establish a context and vocabulary for what follows.

The relationship between culture and historical developments in production and consumption has become a strongly contested question in recent years. The issues involved are inherently complex and controversial—problems of definition and causal direction abound, and disputes inevitably occur as scholars from different disciplines meet on common territory. This collection brings together colleagues working in departments of history, economic history, politics and sociology, and arises out of inter-disciplinary seminars and colloquia which attracted teachers from a wide range of academic departments. The success of such an enterprise indicates the growing significance accorded to cultural factors in historical change, but it would be naive to ignore the great differences that remain between disciplines—and within them—about what needs to be explained, and what is likely to provide a good explanation. If the term culture, with its inherent ambiguity, helps to blur these differences enough to get people talking, then it soon becomes imperative that they begin to define terms and recognize their varied interests and pre-suppositions. This book arises out of such a process and we hope that it will prove useful to others engaged in a similar exercise, for example in the growing area of 'cultural studies'.

The essays and commentaries contained here do not offer a common approach, but rather a self-critical exploration of some of the issues associated, both with invoking culture as a factor in economic and social change (a particular theme of Part II) and with seeking to correlate cultural trends—whether in art or the history of ideas—with social and economic developments (in part III). The case-studies offered are comple-mented by the general observations, both of this introduction and of the essays by Iain Hampsher-Monk and Stephen Mennell. Hampsher-Monk offers a polemical review of 'economic-type' causal explanations in history and a defence of 'actors' reasons' explanations, while Mennell seeks to justify the study of long-term processes in history, with particular emphasis on Norbert Elias' account of 'the civilizing process'. Through-out the book, but particularly in Part I, we hope to show how both cultural studies and economic analysis can be enriched through an historical approach.

The concern to offer an account of the past in which *meaning*—contemporaries' understanding of their actions and their significance—is given priority, has been a leading trend in recent decades across a range of disciplines concerned with the past.[1] In history it has been associated with the expansion of social rather than economic history, the so-called 'revival of narrative' (but narrative now intended to uncover broad social patterns, not the behaviour of a narrow male elite) and a new sensitivity to language, symbolism and the reconstruction of meaning in past societies.[2] Here historians have followed in the footsteps of social anthro-pology as its focus shifted from functionalism to hermeneutic or meaning-centred accounts, as exemplified by such scholars as Clifford Geertz and Mary Douglas.[3] In sociology, too, functionalist and present-centred analysis has lost ground, with a revival of interest in the kind of historical sociology found in Marx, Durkheim, and, in particular, Weber. More recent models of social action by Giddens and Elias have also stressed the importance of meaning in any explanation of agency.[4] Within the Marxist tradition of historical sociology there has been an equally interesting (and contested) move towards social and experiential emphases, notably through the influence of E.P. Thompson and in the work of such groups as those contributing to *History Workshop Journal*.[5] Political theorists and historians of political thought have generally become much more sensitive to the establishment of intellectual and linguistic context, an enterprise offered theoretical justification, as well as exemplary practice, by John Pocock and Quentin Skinner. Underlying Skinner's work has been the impact of analytic philosophy, notably Wittgenstein and Austin, while Pocock invokes structural linguistics.[6] In this respect, at least, they share something with recent developments in literary criticism, such as the so-called 'new historicism', where the interface between language (and cultural exchange more broadly) and past societies has become a key issue once again.[7]

It would be misleading to present all these changes as moving in harmony and in a single intellectual direction. For example, there is a clear tension between the emphasis laid by some, notably literary critics, on the autonomous power of the text and language, compared to the interest of others in recovering the intentions of historical actors. Put crudely, the former are seeking to 'deconstruct' the identity and rationality of historical actors, while the latter strive to 'reconstruct' them. To some extent we are seeing, *within* the concept of 'culture' as a basis of historical explanation, a revival of the standard sociological debate between 'structure' and 'action'. Should culture be conceived of as a given system or structure within which past actors are predestined to operate? Or does the emphasis on culture place higher priority on human creativity, on self-conscious action by the individual or society to change their condition? The two contrasting assumptions can be seen in the essays by Jones and Hampsher-Monk respectively.

It would be ironic should this false dichotomy become too well-entrenched, since the notion of culture has in many ways been invoked precisely to avoid the need to choose between structure and action, but the danger remains, if concealed by the inherent ambiguity of 'culture' as an explanation. Stephen Mennell presents Norbert Elias' notion of a 'civilizing process' as a means of avoiding this false dichotomy,[8] but for others, including Philip Corrigan in his comments on Mennell, the notion of a process is itself too redolent of a passive yet ineluctable necessity—one in which both the responsibility of human actors for change and their ability to respond creatively is underestimated, even discouraged. Scholars within this other tradition are inclined to see culture less as a monolithic or determining factor and more as a fragmented area of contention, offering a set of resources available to many different social groups, and Melling's essay points to this conclusion. A key term in this context has become the notion of 'appropriation', as used for example by the French historian Roger Chartier.[9] Yet, as Corrigan again reminds us, all such cultural resources tend to disempower as well as enable, usually establishing boundaries of the acceptable, even the imaginable, which often reinforce the most fundamental divisions of power within society and exclude certain groups from the means of expression.[10]

The most important contribution on this theme has been made by feminist scholars; the absence of both women contributors and (by and large) gender themes from this collection are linked (and regrettable) omissions. Too many debates on culture have ignored the massive contribution of women to production, consumption and culture in human history. As Eric Hobsbawm has noted, women were largely responsible for two seminal innovations in production—the invention of agriculture and the spread of pottery-making. Recent feminist studies of capitalist production and class relations have generally emphasized the need to break down the traditional (and gendered) distinction between paid (male) employment and domestic (female) consumption.[11] Some of the most powerful critical work concerning the concepts of production and consumption, and their rooting in specific historical and cultural contexts, has thus come from work concerned primarily with gender issues.

Male-centred approaches to production and class have been historically strengthened by the division of labour within academic life between male theorists and female researchers, which has widened the 'epistemological gap' in social science.[12] Only now is it becoming clear that women's labour in the household—largely hidden and usually unpaid— has been a vital means of sustaining output under capitalism as well as under earlier modes of production.[13] Our understanding of the politics generated within the sphere of production has been shaped by traditional cultural assumptions about the dignity of male labour and the reliance on physical prowess within the working-class world. The reproduction of patriarchy within the workplace has formed the basis of recent studies of women's work in mass production, showing, for example, that Fordism was as concerned with the maintenance of masculine authority as with the exploitation of labour.[14] Such writers have attacked sociologists such as Goldthorpe for their heavy concentration on the experience of male workers under capitalism and their masculinist conception of class relations and class politics.[15]

The relevance of gender-base studies to issues of consumption has always been recognized, at least implicitly, given the assumptions about women's role in domestic life. The most important developments here have perhaps been to break down the stereotypes that divide this world of 'private' consumption from the worlds of work and public life more generally. Central to this has been a dialectic between those studies which have established the historical processes that led to the construction of the notion of separate 'public' and 'private' spheres and, equally importantly, those which have demonstrated the ideological character of this division and its failure to coincide with the experiences and interests of most women (and, perhaps, men).[16] Some of the most important work has concerned itself with middle-class and professional groups, but working-class experience has not been neglected. To pick up an earlier example again, Goldthorpe's path-breaking analysis of the transition among Luton car workers from traditional collective loyalties to a 'privatized' era of personal consumption now appears very dated, since the analysis operates almost wholly without reference to women's participation in both the labour force and the household economy.[17] More recent work on the politics of labour has attempted to reappraise the importance of gender in the dynamics of class politics and to shift the focus away from production and towards areas of consumption (such as housing) in the making of class identities.[18] At the same time, other studies are making clear the political character of the plethora of 'cultural' products designed for female consumption. Here, as elsewhere in cultural history, a debate is developing between those who see these cultural forces as working hegemonically to control and limit female (and male) capacities and those studies which emphasize the capacity of women and men to 'appropriate' these materials and use them as resources within their own lives.[19]

II

What impact have these developments in cultural history had on the discipline of economic history?[20] Arguably, they have served only to reinforce the divergence between economic history, eager to achieve the rigour of an econometric science, and the rising star of social history, which has embraced the meaning-oriented trend described above. Famous controversies, such as that over the causes and consequences of English industrialization, have been dogged by the mutual incompatibility of quantitative and qualitative approaches, in each case involving not merely rival methodologies but, at the same time, rival ideologies. Cultural history could with justification be seen as a threat to the traditional self-image of economic history, as Sidney Pollard demonstrates in his response to Hampsher-Monk.

In the first place, cultural history has tended to question the universality of the economic motivations that have normally been assumed in accounts of economic history, as part of a wider onslaught on the 'natural foundations' of contemporary disciplines. Since the 1960s studies of the social and cultural construction of academic disciplines (the sciences in particular) have sought to expose the cultural assumptions behind the modes of explanation used by each discipline.[21] In particular, they have *historicized* our understanding of, for example, economics, by showing the social and ideological conditions within which the paradigms of modern economics were established.[22] Some of the essays here contribute to this process. Thus both Castiglione and Porter show that in the eighteenth century—the century of Adam Smith and the 'origins of economics'—debates about economic change, in particular the roots of consumption, could be formulated within a number of disciplines, with medical and political discourses as significant as classical economics.

From this emerges the conclusion, hinted at by both Castiglione and Hampsher-Monk, that we should view the postulation of 'economic man' as the product of a particular historical moment, embedded in a specific cultural setting. Conventionally this setting has itself been resolutely economic, namely the changes in productive capacity and market penetration associated with the 'industrial revolution'. But as historians have stressed the pre-industrial assumptions of Smith and the embedding of his economic ideas within a broader moral philosophy, so it becomes plausible to see the decision to treat mankind as 'economic man' not as an inevitable response to economic change, nor simply as a methodological choice of an ideal type, but as an ideological choice, reflecting the break-down of a cultural consensus about how to explain and direct human actions.[23] Far from being the 'base' of human actions, with other factors as a mere cultural superstructure, the economic was merely the lowest common denominator about which people might agree, instrumentally, when cultural agreement on the traditional grounds of religion, politics or morality were in question. Furthermore the ideas of a writer like Smith or, as Castiglione shows, Mandeville are then subject to creative adaptation—appropriated—according to the changing needs of subsequent generations. Mennell argues that Marxist emphasis on the priority of economic factors stems from just such an appropriation of the assumptions of classical economics, turned, of course, to very different purposes. We are thus alerted to consider critically our own reasons for seeking to explore these past thinkers and issues; a point to which we shall return.

Underlying both Marxist and classical economic theory was the search for natural laws. In this respect 'economic' theories, in the sense of theories that give priority to such factors as price and scarcity in explanation, are part of a broader type of social explanation working on the 'covering law' principle, though they differ sharply in the respective weights placed on inductive and deductive procedures. For Hampsher-Monk, the problem lies in the extension of such 'economic models' of social explanation from the limited spheres of market conditions, where they are subject to a degree of falsifiability or at least to rigorous formulation, into spheres of social explanation where, he maintains, the model of market choices is merely a mystifying metaphor concealing the *a priori* attribution of motives (often themselves economic in the mundane sense) by the analyst. Thus the cultural prestige of contemporary economics and its place in explaining modern social action is appropriated for analysis of the past, at the expense of genuine study of the actual motivations of past actors. At the same time, however, the provision of explanations of the past in terms of our own motivations may be seen as a necessary and comforting way of legitimating the 'naturalness' of our own culture and its values.

Yet, paradoxically, the *rise* of economic modes of explanation might be seen as involving just the reverse of this process. Economic explanations of social change developed, via writers such as Mandeville, the French physiocrats and the Scottish Enlightenment conjectural historians, from a modern natural law tradition which had developed in post-Reformation Europe. This movement, catalyzed by the collapse of old certainties caused by the discoveries of New World societies and by religious and political upheaval after the Reformation, had sought a solution to social disorder, to scepticism about the possibilities of human knowledge and to disbelief in tradition, by developing ideal-type accounts of human development based on an *economical* (but not necessarily *economic*) set of basic assumptions about human psychology and needs. The most famous English exponents of this tradition are of course Hobbes and Locke, both deeply indebted to the natural law theories of Grotius. For these thinkers, however, *economic* motivations and considerations played a distinctly secondary role. Rather they offered a functionalist account based on such notions as self-preservation.[24] Thus, when students of long-term social change now employ economic-style models to proffer functionalist explanations, but without privileging specifically economic factors, their work is often strikingly reminiscent of the 'pre-economic' theories of these earlier thinkers.[25]

Such historians also face a paradox often noted in natural law theorists, but which Hampsher-Monk strikingly identifies in current exponents of such functionalist approaches. That is an ambivalence between an 'evolutionary' view, namely that natural laws are 'natural' because divergence from them, though humanly possible, will result in failure, and the stronger claim that what are being described are natural laws which actually determine human motivation. In natural law theory such a paradox centres on the character of a supposed 'contract' whereby the people are seen to act consciously to will the ends they require—has such a thing ever occurred, or is a contract merely a thought experiment, to bring out the hidden functions of social actions? Similarly, we may ask, are economic explanations really imputations of conscious human motivation—of reasons for action—or merely a description of the conditions for successful action and its functions? Sidney Pollard's defence of economic history rests essentially on the latter position, and he points to Paul Keating's essay on Ireland's economic malaise as evidence that, when other cultural factors block economic motivations, failure results. Eric Jones recognizes the power of culture in producing a 'lagging' effect due to the conservatism of human institutions, yet regards adaptation to economic needs as inevitable in the long-term. The evident danger with this evolutionary approach is that it combines both prescriptive and descriptive analysis: the language of failure implies that the goals of economic growth are primary, while the identification of 'obstacles' to growth, such as the state, can easily be taken to imply now, as in Smith's day, a contemporary justification for the unshackling of natural economic forces from the restrictions imposed by the state or, indeed, by an anti-entrepreneurial cultural ethic.[26]

III

As the essays in parts I and II are concerned with models of long-term and large-scale historical change and the space allowed for cultural values and actors' reasons in such studies, it may be helpful to outline the three dominant kinds of explanation of long-term historical change which can be found in various forms in much of the recent literature, and which inform the subsequent essays. The first are various individual choice and rational preference studies which underpin many of the neo-classical economic explanations of historical change. The second can be termed social structure and society-centred explanations which focus on changes in economic and social structures as the driving force of historical transitions. Thirdly, there are different kinds of state-centred and neo-institutionalist explanations of broad historical change. Some writers draw from all three schools of writing, while combinations of rational choice and institutionalist analyses are common. The purpose of these introductory comments is not to offer a sustained critique of these approaches to historical interpretation but to demonstrate that each of them has understated the important of culture in explaining the history of society. It is significant that each of these models has emphasized the fundamental impact which changes in the mode of production and the level of economic growth have upon the development of societies, at the expense of the role of consumption.

Rational choice explanations of historical change, derived from the neo-classical economic and political literature on public choice (itself drawing on the natural law theorists mentioned above), has been developed by Olson and others. The rational choice model focuses on the deliberate calculations made by rational individuals seeking to maximize their own satisfaction (or utility), whilst incurring the minimum costs possible.[27] This reliance on 'methodological individualism' to explain behaviour has been widely adopted by social theorists in recent years, including some Marxists, but the most celebrated historical application is provided by Douglas North. He has elaborated neo-classical utility theory and the literature on transaction costs to explain the strategic calculations which historical actors made in choosing between different opportunities.[28] This has the powerful advantage of appearing to explain structural change in terms of individual choices. There remain problems of deciding just how these choices are expressed and the role of structural and institutional factors in providing the context for such choices. For even markets themselves are dependent upon particular institutional arrangements rather than a natural state where contracts or institutions are chosen. Rational choice theorists have struggled with this problem and some acknowledge that it is not possible to explain the existence of states in terms of rational choice.[29]

There are also other assumptions which rational choice theorists have to make for the 'game' of calculated preferences to hold. The actors must be acting in their own interest, have reasonable information and stable preferences, and derive satisfaction from the goals rather than the playing of the game.[30] In this sense, the actors are engaged in a contract which they can consent to or withdraw from as they perceive their individual interests being affected. Margaret Levi, in a sophisticated and careful study of rulers and taxation policy in historical perspective, suggests that the most cost-effective and politically efficient kind of compliance in many different regimes is that established on a quasi-voluntary basis, rather than by coercion or ideological management. Even subjects in ancient societies could withdraw tacit consent from a contract with their rulers which they perceived as unfair.[31] A major constraint on both rulers and ruled is the imperfect information available to the individual actors, and the strict bounds on rational choice, which Tversky's work has emphasized (discussed in a different context by Hampsher-Monk in this collection).[32] Other writers have attempted to ground the workings of rational choice in the material relations of society, emphasizing the basis of reciprocity which exists in peasant societies and the framework of rational choice which is provided in such societies for collective (rather than individual) action.[33] Levi has also attempted to demonstrate that rational choice models are not incompatible with an historical approach that recognizes the power of social classes and institutions, since her whole emphasis is upon the rent-seeking behaviour of rulers and their concern to maximize their revenues according to the limits of their bargaining power with their constituents and subjects, as well as upon the transaction costs and discount rates which obtain for particular kinds of revenue policies.[34]

This literature provides a frame for reading the essays by Eric Jones and Iain Hampsher-Monk. Jones considers the question of economic growth in east Asia in the long term, suggesting that neither cultural nor ecological explanations of growth levels are adequate. He draws on neo-classical principles to develop a subtle account of rent-seeking by rulers and landowners in a 'political' analysis of economic development. Jones illuminates the key role of the powerful in the pattern of develop-ment, where entrepreneurs were able to foster extensive (though rarely intensive) growth levels when the visible hand of the rent-seeker was relaxed. This argument bears comparison with Weber's discussion of rent-seeking in oppressive feudal regimes, though Jones views rent-seeking as endemic amongst landed elites (rather than urban traders) in pre-modern society.[35] Jones also shares with the rational choice theorists a robust scepticism as to the significance of culture and the influence of non-rational preferences in the behaviour of actors. He rightly criticizes some culturist models for their lack of theoretical power and weak sense of specific historical conditions, notably in posing a timeless 'Eastern' culture. In place of the relativity of culture, Jones proposes to see human actions as following certain general paths or 'elemental human strategies', which drive history towards extensive or intensive economic growth.[36]

Human culture becomes much more flexible and malleable as human beings search for the means to survive rather than being fixed by their own belief systems. An implicit neo-Darwinian conclusion is also evident: that those who do not so adapt fall behind more innovative people who develop the cultural means to promote survival and efficiency.

In his essay, Iain Hampsher-Monk provides a sustained critique of the neo-classical economic paradigm and offers an alternative hermeneutic model of actors' reasons. He rejects price and marginal cost analyses as formal theories which have no real purchase on empirical reality until they are substantiated by knowledge gained from the culturally determined perceptions of the actors whose own activity is being 'explained'. Drawing on psychology and decision theory, Hampsher-Monk argues that the neo-classical assumptions of consistent behaviour and risk-aversion by optimizing individuals are not capable of being sustained by experimental evidence. The growing number of experimental economists working on risks, prospects and regrets in decision-making is an acknowledgement of the weakness of standard utility assumptions.[37] Such work also raises the question of the satisfaction which individuals receive from playing games and the cultural boundaries of such games.

Having questioned the cogency of the formal application of neo-classical theory, Hampsher-Monk criticizes North and others for their use of such methods in the interpretation of historical evidence. He suggests that the meanings which people give to their actions and the reasons for their behaviour offer a more realistic approach to understanding historical experience than the formal assumptions of price and utility theories. This can be achieved by examining human culture and discourse, since language is the shared property of society and one which gives any action public meaning. In this sense, the cultural defines the limits of human capacities within that society. By retrieving the shared language of the social actors we can discover the real reasoning of historical actors.

Hampsher-Monk does, however, endorse the methodological individualism of rational choice theory; for him, too, a satisfactory social explanation must be grounded in individual intention, formed though that may be by collective cultural forces. He does not, therefore, deploy the common critique in terms of 'unintended consequences' or underlying structures. Rather than yield such primacy to 'the intending, reasoning agent', Anthony Giddens has suggested that we should recognize *both* the theorem of knowledgeability and the existence of social processes which work beyond our perception 'affecting what we do in ways of which we are unaware'.[38] Many of the most vigorous criticisms of rational choice explanations have been made by Marxist writers who argue for a 'real' historical analysis of distinct modes of production, insisting that such structures define the boundaries of choice.[39] Within the Marxist analysis the emphasis is upon production, property rights and the mobilization of social actors behind class interests which struggle for control of the state and other social institutions. In a prescient comment on Marxist theory (noted in Mennell's essay), Elias suggested that Marx and Engels were originally concerned with economic phenomena which could be rigorously explained, rather than seeking to reduce all social action to economic fundamentals. Later Marxists, such as E.P. Thompson, have sought to integrate an analysis of culture within their accounts of historical change, sacrificing some analytical clarity as a result.[40] Gramscian historians have also enriched the Marxist analysis by focusing on the political and cultural factors in the building of the state, for example in Italy, and in explaining workers' politics. These are explored in the essay by Melling later in the collection, and since this set of arguments is probably the best-known, they will be passed over rapidly here.

Other society-centred explanations of historical change *do* emphasize the centrality of cultural values and here the work of Norbert Elias has been particularly influential. Scholars in the Eliadic school have drawn on the model of the 'civilizing process' to historicize the rational choice paradigm. Abram de Swaan, for example, has offered an ambitious account of the rise of the welfare state in Europe and North America which argues for the growing interdependence and ties of mutuality amongst the major social interests of urbanized industrial capitalism.[41] It is also within this framework that Stephen Mennell has developed his analysis of food and manners and of civilizing processes.[42] In his present essay Mennell extends the analysis of growing interdependence within history and introduces the fresh concept of momentum, which is combined with that of historical process. His criticisms of both Durkheim's and Marx's analysis of the division of labour and production is elaborated in a discussion of the relationship between competition and culture. He argues that the distinction between the competition of the market and the repose of the cultural, assumed by Jones in his essay, is a false dichotomy which should be abandoned. Mennell draws attention back to the psychological experiences of the individual as well as the growing rationalization in modern society and state management.

Elias seeks to historicize rational choice on two different levels. Firstly, he shares with Giddens and Marxists the view that individual choices are always structured by compelling processes—though he stresses that these need not be primarily economic. In particular, growing social interdependence renders individual actions less and less free; our capacity for rational and effective action depends upon recognition of this, and hence the abandonment of egocentric views of the world in which unrealistic estimates of human intentionality and willpower are fostered, in favour of recognition of impersonal processes. At the same time, however, Elias offers a cultural explanation of the importance to our society of 'actor's reasons', as well as 'covering law' explanations. Within the 'civilizing process' he emphasizes that growing human interdependence renders us more sensitive to the needs and feelings of others, as well as more conscious of our own dependence. If correct, such an analysis would explain why modern society has simultaneously generated both very powerful theories of 'scientific objectivity' and yet also a strong tradition of hermeneutic understanding, based on recovering the motives of others. Thus, it might be argued, our society has permanent need of the tension between the two modes of explanation being analysed here, a tension itself implicit within rational choice theory.

Of course, the 'civilizing process' and ties of interdependence have not reached all societies at the same pace or in similar ways. It is illuminating to consider the Irish case documented by Paul Keating in the light both of Elias' work and the Weberian model elaborated by Keating himself. The traditional cultural values of the Irish Republic have undermined the programme of economic modernization during the twentieth century. Keating offers us the perspective of those who have internalized the values identified by Weber and Elias: that successful participation in the modern capitalist world order requires acceptance of a set of rules for behaviour, which relate not just to economic entrepreneurship but to moral issues such as keeping one's word and respecting the value of money (not the same as enjoying its expenditure!). Farmers who inject illegal steroids or business people evading their taxes are not just free-riding on others: they have learnt from the long historical experience of their ancestors, who are still celebrated in folklore and political life. Keating's research supports Weber's argument that cultural values provide a direction for material interests to follow. This analysis is recast in a different form by Sidney Pollard, who suggests a larger role for the Irish state and the ingrained habits of resistance to the tax-collecting authorities in both rural and urban areas. For it is not only cultural values but the institutions which promote them which are historically important.

Keating's essay thus introduces us to the state-centred and institutionalist explanations of long-term historical change that form our
third set of ideas to be explored. Rather than focusing on changes in the
mode of production or the rational choices which individuals make,
state-centred theorists stress the impact of changes in the structure of
political institutions. A powerful case for the role of such state structures
in the development of society is made in Skocpol's study of modern
revolutions.[43] Here the emphasis is upon the distinctive interests and
innovations of the state, which is managed by actors within the state who
represent the interests of the state rather than any particular social group.
It is the relationship of the state with their population and with other
states which is regarded as the vital determinant of historical change.
Other neo-institutionalist writers have confirmed the emphasis on the
internal dynamics and external contacts of the institution as the motor of
history.[44]

In this light, the impact of cultural values is treated as marginal to the
main drama of structural change in state and society. This analysis has
been criticized for putting the state back into history and taking the
people out. Philip Abrams has taken this case furthest, by questioning the
very existence of 'the state' as a meaningful subject of social analysis, as
opposed to the social interests of those involved in specific political
institutions and the role played by 'the idea of the state' in legitimating
particular power relations; for him the state has meaning chiefly as a
cultural resource in specific historical contexts.[45] Norbert Elias also
portrays state formation as an inescapably cultural process, a perspective
shared, despite many differences of substance, by Philip Corrigan in his
contribution here and his other work, which builds on a Marxist analysis
of the capitalist state as heavily dependent on the moral and cultural
regulation of those living under its control.[46]

The neo-institutional approach has also been challenged by the rational
choice theorists. Levi insists that the state is no more than an institution
composed of human beings, and that its actions are merely 'the end
result of concrete human action'.[47] Michael Taylor has also argued that
revolutions occurred in peasant rather than industrial societies because
the relations of reciprocity and shared values which exist in the peasant
community provides a practical basis for mobilization which is broken up
by industrialization. It is human agency rather than the logic of state
structures which determined the progress of revolutions in pre-industrial
societies.[48] Such a critique is persuasive but is itself limited by the absence
of any sustained discussion of culture. For the rational choice perspective

usually allows the intrusion of culture only as part of the normative rules in the game of self-interest.

Turning again to Keating's essay on modern Ireland, we can find evidence both for and against the neo-institutional approach. Certainly, the 'traditional' values which have been so resilient in Irish society have been cultivated and periodically refabricated by strategic groups who have an interest in retaining the mythologies of Celtic innocence which Keating portrays so well. It is not that acquisitiveness is prohibited in Irish society, but rather it is directed into private vices and public virtues which are sanctioned by the powerful institutions of church and state. The absence of ethical discipline and scrupulous behaviour in business life can be attributed to the power of institutions which do not value economic activity for its own sake, but rather as a means to validate pre-capitalist values. Economic growth has been caught in the ruts of rural Ireland, whilst the political legacy of the independence struggle against Britain was a romanticized and deeply conservative appraisal of Irish history and culture. The Irish education system, family and Gaelic organizations are vital to the maintenance of the peculiar constituency of the Irish parties and the Catholic priesthood. It is these institutions which compel the financial arm of the state to tolerate a native capitalism which is poorly managed and weakly regulated. Even the predatory inclinations of the revenue collectors are blunted by the resistance of the Irish business community.

Yet, as this last point indicates, the state is itself the result of a particular cultural matrix and torn between its 'rational' interests in modernization and financial stability and its commitment to an anti-Weberian ethic. Sidney Pollard adds the suggestion that an important reason for the absence of responsible compliance amongst the Irish is to be found in the historical antagonism between the native population and a central state constructed by the British colonizers. The political revolutionaries of 1916–22 allied with the conservative institutions of Irish society to promote a social order which constrains the modernizers in both the economy and the state. The appropriate nationalist culture is a political construction maintained by rulers in many post-colonial societies, where powerful coalitions may sustain values which deprive the economy (or the state itself) of vital resources.

The relationship between economy, culture and politics is also the focus of Melling's essay on employers' welfare schemes and socialist politics in industrial Britain. Drawing on the work of Burawoy and Levi, Melling argues that 'compliance' is a more useful conceptual tool in explaining the welfare contract between capital and labour than the model of industrial paternalism offered by other writers. In developing a political analysis of workplace culture, Melling argues that the authority relations which are essential in capitalist production are sustained by various forms of compliance on the shop floor. This compliance is secured by the political settlements which are reached between capital, labour and the state at strategic moments in the development of industrial society. The cultural resources of labour were invested in the articulation of a particular kind of masculine craftsmanship during the middle decades of the nineteenth century, providing labour with one peculiar form of 'gendered subjectivity' which other writers have documented in modern capitalist production.[49] The emphasis on practical experience and learning-by-doing was one thread in the industrial culture which tied workers to employers who relied on apprenticeship and working foremen to achieve output, rather than theoretical knowledge and detailed administration of production. Industrialists were able to impose welfare regimes on women and younger workers who were excluded from the benefits of the craft societies, whilst the unions pressed for legislation to tighten accident and truck laws in a drive to exclude company schemes.

The struggle against business welfarism formed a significant part of the contest for citizenship on the shop floor of industry at this period. Employers found their customary authority under threat as women and the less skilled organized themselves in the workplace and the industrial districts, weakening the hold of employers on local labour markets as well as addressing the need for political solutions to poor working conditions and irregular employment. Faced with the evidence of continuing conflict in production, the state assumed the initiative in introducing legislation for the insurance of workers in industry and directed the energies of working-class institutions to the autonomous administration of welfare funds. The account documents the competing rationalities which were available to actors who engaged in prolonged discursive struggles around national insurance reforms, indicating the weaknesses of analyses which couple self-evident interests to a simple rational choice as well as casting doubt on neo-institutionalist studies which emphasize the primacy of state actors.

Thus Melling's essay encapsulates the argument that culture has to be taken seriously in any broad historical analysis. We should see culture not as a residual factor—as another 'black box' of historical change to which we can attribute whatever is not otherwise explicable. Rather, culture should be seen as a fundamental part of the distribution of resources and the relations of power in society. Cultural values inform the strategic calculations which people make about their interests. On the evidence of these essays, it is misleading to restrict our explanation of human action to the pursuit of self-evident interests by rational individuals. Indeed, it may be more useful to talk in terms of *needs* rather than interests and of the psychological and emotional (as well as material) concerns of individuals and societies. And lest needs too be considered a timeless or acultural entity (for example the hierarchy of needs outlined by Maslow), Goldthorpe and others have rightly noted that needs can only be defined in the context of a culture which defines which needs should be met or even tolerated.[50]

IV

To turn from interests to needs is consonant with the shift in attention, within economic history, from an emphasis on the means of production and class interests in relation to them towards a concern with consumption, and hence both the creation and the satisfaction of consumer needs. Many factors have combined to generate this shift in interest, including a re-evaluation of our own capitalist society. As we shall see, the contemporary ambiguities of this vision of our society has its implications for historical analysis. But in simple terms, renewed interest in consumption has clearly paid its part in forcing the economic historian to consider cultural factors. Consumer choice requires cultural explanation. Such analysis is now attracting renewed attention as historians begin to rediscover the 'demand-side' of, for example, the industrial revolution in Britain.[51] This specific episode is itself now seen in the much broader context of a transformation in the world economy generated by the European traffic in a set of key commodities—spices, tobacco, sugar, tea, coffee, chocolate and cotton textiles—and the consequent growth of European imperialism. This trade rested on the fragile basis of European consumer demand for new or luxury products, converted into everyday commodities during the early modern centuries. The demand thus unleashed is itself now credited with far-reaching changes in domestic economic patterns which played a vital part in economic growth and industrialization. The global process thus set in train is still clearly in operation in today's world.[52]

The essays in part III of this collection enable us to consider the cultural significance of this process from a number of perspectives. Each, in its way, problematizes a situation which we have perhaps come to take for granted (as we have the notion of 'economic man'), namely the idea that the consumption of material goods (or material culture) is a normal and culturally neutral experience. In this respect they, like the earlier essays, challenge the premise that consumption is a natural process, driven simply by the availability of goods at affordable prices.[53] As a consequence, they also serve to undermine the notion of a simple dichotomy between production and consumption. The desire to consume, both material goods in general and specific items in particular, is itself produced, as are the images we hold and the values we invest in consumption, whether it be of the art objects analysed by Robert Witkin or of the petticoats that Mandeville credited with such a momentous effect. Furthermore, in consuming objects, we are ourselves producing our own culture, though not always on our own terms.

Both Castiglione and Porter's essays bring out the anxiety generated in pre-industrial society by the rise in consumption, particularly of the kinds of products described above, demand for which was taken to rest not on natural needs, but on artificial desires. As Castiglione shows, Mandeville created uproar by emphasizing the cultural ambiguities created by this situation, which found a resonant summation in the notion that the public good depended on private behaviour unchecked by the standards of virtue and morality that the public culture required. It was in responding to this challenge, both practical and ideological, Castiglione suggests, that modern notions of public good as the inevitable result of private self-interest were forged. Yet if Castiglione detects, by the late eighteenth century, a new complacency about this state of affairs, Porter's account of Thomas Trotter reminds us that, outside the sphere of political economy, concerns about the pathology of consumption remained rife. For Trotter, Porter notes, the consumption of material goods, and above all drinks, had become the central feature of an artificial society in which, through material culture, man invented himself as a creature of culture rather than nature. The chain of consequences thus unleashed may profitably be compared to the 'compelling processes' discussed by Mennell, since what ensued was a growing chain of dependence and interdependence, of people dependent on each other and on material goods, which deprived them of the liberty which was traditionally associated with self-sufficient virtue. Porter's account could indeed easily be integrated with Elias' vision of the civilizing process—married perhaps with Freud's insights into civilization's discontents.

Thus Porter and Castiglione each draw attention to one side of that paradoxical consequence of economic growth noted above, namely the simultaneous growth of the impulse to analyse our society objectively and subjectively. Faced with the task of interpreting consumer choice, the social analyst could either adopt the tautologies of self-interest and price theory, substituting regularity of occurrence for an understanding of motive, or else turn, as the Romantic movement and German historicism did, towards a grasp of inner meaning and intentionality.[54] Thus we may trace to the culture of consumption itself part at least of that troublesome dialectic with which this collection is constantly grappling. Castiglione's analysis of Mandeville's subsequent career throws a fascinating light on this ongoing process, notably in the writings of Weber and his colleagues, who each strove to discover a rationality within modern society's propensity to consume beyond necessity. It is interesting to note that Weber was of all these writers the least inclined to find in simple consumption the key to capitalism; like Keating, in his observations on Irish conspicuous consumption, Weber drew a clear distinction between such involvement in material culture and the ascetic spirit of capitalism which entailed a mastery over the immediate lure of goods for the sake of rational investment and productivity.

Witkin's examination of the relationship between realist art and bourgeois society takes us directly again to the question of the natural (or realistic) and the way in which bourgeois man uses the natural, in this case images of nature, to understand and express social relationships. Drawing on Durkheim's sociology in his critical reworking of Hauser's theories on art,[55] Witkin explores the idea that a realistic style of art emerges in societies whose complexity and interdependence encourages its participants to understand and express their understanding of the world around them as one not given by God or tradition but as created by man. Yet in classic bourgeois societies, unlike our own, this process of individuation also involved a relatively successful process of socialization, whereby the public values of the culture and the private ones of the individual were seen as broadly consonant. Within such a society, Witkin argues, perceptual-realist art flourished because natural objects, like social relationships, could be valued for their immanent rather than their transcendental values and yet also be placed with a coherent system of social meanings. For Witkin twentieth-century society has seen the collapse of that coherence between public and private, represented in the changing styles of modern art.

This approach is a valuable complement to the other pieces, not least because of its insistence that art, like natural and social sciences, must be seen as representing social relationships, a point taken up by Philip

Corrigan. Yet, as with any analysis of one cultural form, problems arise in relating its specific genre history to broader social movements. Here it may help to ask a cruder question about the consumption of art: who consumed this art and for what purposes? Witkin's analysis does not seek to distinguish the role of artist and viewer in engaging with his works of art, nor how the process of consumption changes over time and according to social circumstance. Yet without such analysis, can we be certain that a specific cultural form is still playing the same role in representing that society to itself as it had before? May not Hauser be right, for example, to shift his attention from paintings to film and photography, which may well be said to capture modern man's relation to the worlds of goods he has created more centrally than paintings can ever aspire to do? Why, if it is indeed the case, did modern art take until the twentieth century to register a crisis between public and private senses of self, when already faced by the eighteenth century with that divergence between public and private described above, a crisis clearly reflected in Romantic culture more generally? As Witkin observes, the meaning of perceptual-realism was doubtless itself constantly being revised, both by successive generations of artists and successive consumers of that art. We, in turn, are the latest generation to find the need to define ourselves in relation to that culture.

This brings us back, finally, to the ambivalence of interest in consumption within our own society. We noted above the ideological implications of choosing to privilege the economic as natural. Equally, the decision to emphasize non-economic explanations and hermeneutic approaches itself carries specific ideological implications in the modern context. The collapse of Marxist, economic-centred alternatives to capitalism has, as Castiglione indicates, led to a shift in the grounds on which capitalism can be criticized and a renewed interest in critiques of consumption as a means to this end. Many modern scholars have shared the feelings which Porter so graphically describes in Thomas Trotter, namely a deep distrust for the cultural processes of consumerism as somehow 'unnatural', as part of a social disease.

Yet ambivalence, rather than outright rejection, has tended to be the response to consumer culture, even from those critical of its implications. For social critics, despair at the addictive qualities of consumer culture, as manipulated by commercial and establishment interests, has coexisted with the need to appeal to that same consumer power and to believe that consumers might be re-educated, not least by an understanding of their history as consumers, to use their power to consume differently (or not at all) so as to bring about social change. Equally, as Corrigan emphasizes, those in control have never found dependence on the public as consumers an easy situation to accept, since they too are aware of that potential power to change the private meaning of consumption. At the same time, it has often suited capitalist interests and ruling groups to draw attention away from the means of production, and people's relationship towards them, and focus instead on people's position as consumers, theoretically sovereign within the free market but in practice limited by their specific location as consumers of varied wealth, social standing and so on. The political agenda of the 1980s revealed quite clearly the ambiguities involved in a concept that can be central to the ideologies of laissez-faire conservatives, reformist social democrats and radical ecologists.

V

As indicated at the start, this introduction has been concerned to clarify issues and highlight problems, very much in the spirit of the essays that follow. It has argued that, like any important concepts, those of history and culture, production and consumption are inherently contested and contestable, and that our interests in these issues are bound to be connected to contemporary concerns, both about the demarcation of disciplines and in wider ideological issues. Yet we have also identified within the essays that follow, despite their variety of approach and conclusion, a common epistemological theme. What kind of an explanation of large-scale economic and social change is it appropriate for us to offer? We have seen that the answers (for there are many) to this question have themselves been formed, and are still being formed, by the historical processes that they seek to explain. In turn, the outcome of those processes will depend on our understanding of their history. For that reason alone the debates to which this collection seeks to contribute will never reach a conclusion, but for that reason too, it is vital that the debate continue through cordial yet critical analysis. We hope this collection will exemplify and enhance such an exchange.

Notes

1. Q. Skinner (ed.), *The Return of Grand Theory in the Human Sciences* (Cambridge, 1985); L. Hunt (ed.), *The New Cultural History* (Berkeley, 1989); J.H. Pittock and A. Wear (eds), *Interpretation and Cultural History* (Basingstoke, 1991).

2. L. Stone, 'The Revival of Narrative', *Past and Present* 85 (1979), pp. 3–24; P. Burke and R. Porter (eds), *The Social History of Language* (Cambridge, 1987); P. Corfield (ed.), *Language, History and Class* (Oxford, 1991); P. Joyce (ed.), *The Historical Meanings of Work* (Cambridge, 1987). Lawrence Stone is now warning against the dangers of 'the linguistic turn' for historians, provoking a response from Patrick Joyce and others: see, 'History and Post-Modernism', *Past and Present* 131 (1991), pp. 217–18 and 133 (1991), pp. 204–13.

3. C. Geertz, *The Interpretation of Cultures* (New York, 1973); M. Douglas, *Natural Symbols* (rev. edn., Harmondsworth, 1973); id., *Implicit Meanings* (1975).

4. P. Abrams, *Historical Sociology* (Shepton Mallet, 1982); A. Giddens, *Capitalism and Modern Social Theory* (Cambridge, 1971); id., *Central Problems in Social Theory* (1979); id., *The Constitution of Society* (Cambridge, 1984); N. Elias, *The Civilising Process* 2 vols (Oxford, 1978–82). Cf. also, W.G. Runciman, *A Treatise on Social Theory*, 2 vols to date (Cambridge, 1983–9) and M. Mann, *The Sources of Social Power*, vol. 1 (Cambridge, 1986).

5. E.P. Thompson, *The Making of the English Working Class* (Harmondsworth, 1968); id., *The Poverty of Theory* (1978); R. Johnson, 'Culture and the Historians' and 'Three Problematics', in J. Clarke, C. Critcher and R. Johnson (eds), *Working-Class Culture. Studies in history and theory* (1979); H.J. Kaye and K. McClelland (eds), *E.P. Thompson: Critical perspectives* (Cambridge, 1990); R. Samuel and G. Stedman Jones (eds), *Culture, Ideology and Politics* (1982); G. Stedman Jones, *Languages of Class* (Cambridge, 1983).

6. Q. Skinner, *The Foundations of Modern Political Thought* 2 vols (Cambridge, 1978); J. Tully (ed.), *Meaning and Context: Quentin Skinner and his critics* (Cambridge, 1988); J.G.A. Pocock, *Virtue, Commerce and History* (Cambridge, 1985).

7. H. Aram Veeser (ed.), *The New Historicism* (New York, 1989). The British pioneer in this field was Raymond Williams in, e.g., *Keywords* (rev. edn, 1983) and *Marxism and Literature* (Oxford, 1977).

8. Elias, *The Civilising Process*; S. Mennell, *Norbert Elias* (Oxford, 1989).

9. P. Corrigan, *Social Forms/Human Capacities* (1990); R. Chartier, *Cultural History* (Cambridge, Polity Press, 1988); id., 'Culture as Appropriation' in S. Kaplan (ed.), *Understanding Popular Culture* (Berlin, New York and Amsterdam, 1984). A similar approach to 'cultural determinism' is offered by G.E.R. Lloyd, *Demystifying Mentalities* (Cambridge, 1990).

10. B. Anderson, *Imagined Communities* (1983) is the most influential example.

11. E.J. Hobsbawm, contribution to conference 'Back to the Future', South Bank Polytechnic, 1988.

12. H. Kay, 'Constructing the Epistemological Gap: Gender Divisions in Social Research', *Sociological Review* 38 (1990), pp. 344–51; J.W. Scott, *Gender and the Politics of History* (New York, 1988)

13. N. Hart, 'Gender and the Rise and Fall of Class Politics', *New Left Review* 175 (1989), pp. 19–47.

14. P. Willis, 'Shop Floor Culture, Masculinity and the Wage Form' in Clarke *et. al.* (eds), *Working-Class Culture*; M. Glucksmann, *Women Assemble* (1990).

15. J.H. Goldthorpe, D. Lockwood, F. Bechhofer & J. Platt, *The Affluent Worker in the Class Structure* (Cambridge, 1969), discussed in Hart, 'Gender and the Rise and Fall of Class Politics', pp. 21–3.

16. S. Burman (ed.), *Fit Work for Women* (1979); J.B. Elshtein, *Public Man, Private Woman: Women in Social and Political Thought* (1981); M. Vicinus (ed.), *A Widening Sphere: Changing roles of Victorian women* (1982); E. Gomarnikow *et al.* (eds), *The Public and the Private* (1983); C. Steedman *et al.* (eds), *Language, Gender and Childhood* (1985); L. Davidoff and C. Hall, *Family Fortunes: Men and Women of the English Middle Class 1780–1850* (1987).

17. Goldthorpe *et al.*, *The Affluent Worker*.

18. J. Rendell (ed.), *Equal or Different: Women's politics 1800–1914* (Oxford, 1987); M. Savage, *The Dynamics of Working-Class Politics* (Cambridge, 1988); B. Harrison, 'Class and Gender in British Labour History', *Past and Present* 124 (1989), pp. 121–58.

19. Contrast N. Armstrong and L. Tennenhouse (eds), *The Ideology of Conduct: Essays on the literature and history of sexuality* (1987) with, e.g., C. Lucas, *Writing for Women: The example of women as readers in Elizabethan romances* (Milton Keynes, 1989). An excellent analysis is given in M. Shiach, *Discourse on Popular Culture: Class, gender and history in cultural analysis, 1730 to the present* (Cambridge, 1989).

20. For two recent reviews of the discipline by leading proponents see: C. Cipolla, *Between History and Economics: An introduction to economic history* (Oxford, 1991); D.C. Coleman, *History and the Economic Past* (Oxford, 1987).

21. T. Kuhn, *The Structure of Scientific Revolutions* (2nd edn, Chicago, 1970); B. Barnes and S.Shapin (eds), *Natural Order: Historical studies of scientific culture* (1970); R. Blackburn (ed.), *Ideology in Social Science* (1972). A major influence has been French philosophy, above all M. Foucault, *The Order of Things* (1970); id., *The Archaeology of Knowledge* (1973) and P. Bourdieu, *Distinction: A social critique of the judgement of taste* (Cambridge, Mass., 1984).

22. J. Appleby, *Economic Thought and Ideology in Seventeenth-Century England* (Princeton, 1978); K. Tribe, *Land, Labour and Economic Discourse* (1978).

23. E.A. Wrigley, 'The Classical Economists and the Industrial Revolution' in his *People, Cities and Wealth* (Oxford, 1987); I. Hont and M. Ignatieff (eds), *Wealth and Virtue: The shaping of political economy in the Scottish Enlightenment* (Cambridge, 1983).

24. Skinner, *Foundations of Modern Political Thought*; R. Tuck, *Natural Rights Theories* (Cambridge, 1979); Hont and Ignatieff (eds), *Wealth and Virtue*.

25. J. Goudsblom, E.L. Jones and S. Mennell, *Human History and Social Process* (Exeter, 1989).

26. For example M.J. Wiener, *English Culture and the Decline of the Industrial Spirit 1850–1980* (Cambridge, 1981); Corelli Barnett, *The Audit of War* (1986).

27. M. Olson, *The Logic of Collective Action. Public goods and the theory of groups* (Cambridge, Mass., 1971). Such theories are reviewed at greater length in J. Melling, 'Industrial Capitalism and the Welfare of the State', *Sociology* 25 (1991), pp. 219–39.

28. D.C. North, *Structure and Change in Economic History* (New York, 1981); Ellen M. Wood, 'Rational Choice Marxism', *New Left Review* 177 (1989), pp. 41–88.

29. G.M. Hodgson, *Economics and Institutions* (Cambridge, 1988); J.Y. Lin, 'An Economic Theory of Induced Change: Induced and imposed change', *Cato Journal* 9 (1989), pp. 1–33.

30. M. Taylor (ed.), *Rationality and Revolution* (Cambridge, 1988).

31. M. Levi, *Of Rule and Revenue* (Los Angeles, 1988), pp. 49–50, 54–6, 68.

32. Ibid., p. 17.

33. Taylor (ed.), *Rationality and Revolution*.

34. Levi, *Of Rule and Revenue*, pp. 2–4.

35. M. Weber, *From Max Weber* ed. H.H. Gerth & C. Wright Mills (1991), pp. 165–6.

36. E.L. Jones, 'Recurrent Transitions to Economic Growth', in Goudsblom *et al.*, *Human History and Social Process*, pp. 53–7.

37. For example G. Loomes, 'Further Evidence on the Impact of Regret and Disappointment in Choice under Certainty', *Economica* 55 (1988), pp. 47–62.

38. A. Giddens, *A Contemporary Critique of Historical Materialism. Power, property and the state* (1982), p. 16.

39. Wood, 'Rational Choice Marxism'.

40. Thompson, *Making of the English Working Class*, pp. 14, 781–2; cf. Johnson, 'Three Problematics', pp. 215, 221.

41. A. de Swaan, *In Care of the State* (Cambridge, 1988); cf. Melling, 'Industrial Capitalism'.
42. Mennell, *Norbert Elias*; id., *All Manners of Food* (Oxford, 1985).
43. T. Skocpol, *States and Social Revolutions* (New York, 1979).
44. S. Skowronek, *Building a New American State: The expansion of national administrative capacity, 1877–1920* (Cambridge, 1982); P.B. Evans *et al.*, *Bringing the State Back In* (Cambridge, 1985).
45. P. Abrams, 'Notes on the Difficulty of Studying the State', *Journal of Historical Sociology* 1 (1988), pp. 58–89.
46. Elias, *The Civilising Process*; P. Corrigan and D. Sayer, *The Great Arch: English state formation as cultural revolution* (Oxford, 1985).
47. Levi, *Of Rule and Revenue*, pp. 38–9.
48. Taylor (ed.), *Rationality and Revolution*, pp. 68, 81–3, 92.
49. M. Burawoy, *Manufacturing Consent. Changes in the labour process under monopoly capitalism* (Chicago, 1979); Levi, *Of Rule and Revenue*; P. Willis, *Learning to Labour* (1977), p. 95; id., 'Shop Floor Culture', p.194; Glucksmann, *Women Assemble*, pp. 15–16.
50. Goldthorpe *et al.*, *The Affluent Worker*.
51. B. Fine and E. Leopold, 'Consumerism and the Industrial Revolution', *Social History* 15 (1990), pp. 151–8 offers a critique of, amongst others, N. McKendrick, J.H. Plumb and J. Brewer, *The Birth of a Consumer Society in Eighteenth-Century England* (Cambridge, 1980).
52. For the international setting see: F. Braudel, *Capitalism and Material Life* (1974); P.D. Curtin, *Cross-Cultural Trade in World History* (Cambridge, 1984); C. Mukerji, *From Graven Images: Patterns of modern materialism* (New York, 1983); I. Wallerstein, *The Modern World System* 3 vols (New York, 1974–89). For the impact on European societies: S. Schama, *The Embarrassment of Riches* (1987); L. Weatherill, *Consumer Behaviour and Material Culture in Britain 1660–1760* (1988); C. Shammas, *The Pre-Industrial Consumer in England and America* (Oxford, 1990); J. Brewer and R. Porter (eds), *Consumption and the World of Goods* (1992).
53. M. Douglas and B. Isherwood, *The World of Goods: Towards an anthropology of consumption* (Harmondsworth, 1980); A. Appadurai (ed.), *The Social Life of Things: Commodities in cultural perspective* (Cambridge, 1986); D. Miller, *Material Culture and Mass Consumption* (Oxford, 1987); G. McCracken, *Culture and Consumption: New approaches to the symbolic character of consumer goods and activities* (Bloomington, Indiana, 1988).
54. F. Meinecke, *Historism* (1972); C. Campbell, *The Romantic Ethic and the Spirit of Modern Consumerism* (Oxford, 1987).
55. A. Hauser, *The Social History of Art*, 4 vols (1989).

Momentum and History

Stephen Mennell

The three decades after the Second World war witnessed a headlong 'retreat of sociologists into the present',[1] and sociologists were not alone in their flight. Political scientists, economists and anthropologists also backed away from any concern with longer-term processes of social development. Even historians, paradoxically, shared in the retreat—if not into the present, then into strictly delimited segments of the past.[2] Relatively few writers, with the exception of Marxist scholars, withstood the trend.

There were many reasons for the retreat.[3] As so often in intellectual history, it is hard to say whether the writings of prominent authors were causes or merely symptoms of the retreat into the present. At any rate, three prominent authors may be mentioned as—at the least—providing intellectual justification for a trend already in train: the philosophers Sir Karl Popper and Sir Isaiah Berlin, and the sociologist Robert Nisbet.[4]

The kernel of Popper's argument was that, because the course of history is influenced by the growth of human knowledge, and because we cannot predict future knowledge (otherwise we would already know it), history cannot be predicted and therefore no 'laws' can be discovered governing general historical processes. Popper's books were intended to constitute a logical, moral and political knockout blow against any belief—especially Marxist belief—in 'inexorable laws of historical destiny', or indeed any form of 'inevitability' in long-term social development.[5] Because Popper's case centres on the corpus of shared knowledge, it is particularly relevant to the question of whether long-term trends can be discovered in cultural change. Berlin, who appeared to advocate the writing of history in terms of the intentions of individuals, revived ancient arguments about human 'free will' and its incompatibility with any broader explanation of historical trends. Nisbet in turn revived the arguments about social 'evolution', attacking what he called 'developmentalism' and any principle of 'immanence' in social change. He largely avoids the word 'evolution' because the neo-Darwinian principle of random change selected and reinforced in specific environments would be acceptable to him as a social analogy; by 'developmentalism', on the other hand, he meant any belief—the Marxist belief most obviously—in sequential 'stages' of development where the seeds of a later stage are immanent in an earlier stage.

This essay seeks to show that it is possible to investigate and to theorize about the structure of social processes, to discover sequential order within change, without resorting to any notion of inevitability or immanence. The issue is best dealt with in terms of the momentum which social changes can acquire, while remaining historically contingent. I shall also argue that this applies as much to cultural change as to socio-economic development (if indeed that distinction is meaningful). Mechanical analogies are often misleading in the social sciences, but this one does not seem too dangerous: momentum is defined by physicists as mass multiplied by velocity, velocity being speed in a given direction, and it is clearly understood that bodies moving with momentum can be stopped or deflected if they encounter other bodies with sufficient mass.

A *metaphysical red herring and a realist solution*

The question of whether a sequence of social development can ever be said to be 'inevitable' has tended to become entangled with the philosophers' metaphysical antithesis of 'determinism' and 'free will'. The muddle is then further compounded when, as in Berlin's arguments, 'free will' is linked to 'freedom' in the sense of social and political liberty, and 'determinism' to the lack of liberty. Arguments of this type have constantly been resurrected even after repeated and forceful rebuttal.[6] No rebuttal is pithier than Norbert Elias'. Philosophical discussions of 'free will' and 'determinism' have always tended, he remarks, to overlook the simple fact that 'there are always simultaneously many mutually dependent individuals, whose interdependence to a greater or lesser extent limits each one's scope for action.'[7] That simple sentence cuts across centuries of metaphysical debate. The point can be illustrated in a simple way by considering the everyday problem of motorists joining a three-lane motorway on which there is a significant amount of traffic: none is entirely 'free' to choose the speed at which he or she will drive. Both Berlin's freely choosing individual and the opposite, Louis Althusser's *Träger* utterly devoid of choice ('There are no subjects except by and for their subjection'[8]), are metaphysical abstractions constructed by philosophers, and nowhere met with in the real social world.

Having thus set aside 2,500 years of futile philosophical disputation, we are left with the sociological problem of understanding how the activities of individuals who are acting in pursuit of their own particular objectives—objectives in part shaped through experience in interdependence with other people from birth, and pursued by means more or less constrained by their interdependence with other people—interweave to produce more or less long-term processes which, though 'blind' and unplanned, nevertheless possess a structure and direction of their own. Such processes build up momentum, but are still contingent: if they encounter obstacles or other processes with sufficient momentum of their own, they can be stopped, deflected, or reversed.

The late Philip Abrams[9] drew particular attention to the solution proffered by Norbert Elias to the issue of prediction and the false polarity between 'inevitability' and 'indeterminacy' in sequences of social development. Elias proposed that we think of such development as a continuum of changes, or figurational flow. Within the flow, we can identify a sequence of figurations, which we can label A, B, C, D; these are not static, discontinuous stages of development, but points inserted in a flow—various figurations of people, each figuration flowing from the previous one as the development takes its course from A to D. The kernel of Elias' argument is then as follows:

> Retrospective study will often clearly show not only that the figuration is a necessary precondition for D, and likewise B for C and A for B, but also why this is so. Yet, looking into the future, from whatever point in the figurational flow, we are usually able to establish only that the figuration at B is one possible transformation of A, and similarly C of B and D of C. In other words, in studying the flow of figurations there are two possible perspectives on the connection between one figuration chosen from the continuing flow and another, later figuration. From the viewpoint of the earlier figuration, the earlier one is usually a necessary condition for the formation of the later.[10]

There is, then, an asymmetry in the two time-perspectives. The reason is that figurations vary greatly in their pliability, plasticity, potential for change (or, conversely, their rigidity). Retrospective investigation will usually show that the possible outcomes have to be thought of in terms of probabilities; moreover, as a particular figuration changes into another, and a scatter of possible outcomes narrows down to single ones, another range of possible outcomes, once more with differing probabilities, hoves into view in the next phase of development.

The question of probabilities, of pliability, rigidity, potential for change is in no way metaphysical: it is a matter for empirical investigation by historians and social scientists. Elias' 'Game Models' are useful in drawing attention to the kinds of evidence that need to be examined. They draw attention to more or less unequal, changing and fluctuating power ratios as a characteristic of all bonds of interdependence between humans, from the most micro-level face-to-face interaction between individuals to the most macroscopic balances and conflicts between social groups and states. Particularly relevant in the present context, they draw attention to the way in which the more multipolar and multilevel power ratios between many people and groups are involved, and the more relatively equal the ratios become, the less can the course of events be adequately interpreted as the outcome of particular actors' intentions. This is reflected, slowly and imperfectly, in the consciousness of the people actually caught up themselves in the process:

> instead of players believing that the game takes its shape from the individual moves of individual people, there is a slowly growing tendency for impersonal concepts to be developed to master their experience of the game . . . Metaphors are used which oscillate constantly between the idea that the course of the game can be reduced to the actions of individual players and the other idea that it is of a supra-personal nature.[11]

In other words, human beings are caught up in 'compelling processes' which, though they do not 'determine' the actions of individuals, are not steered by the intentions of even the more powerful players either; and threading their way through such processes involves countless players (not just the social scientists studying them) in striving for the conceptual and discursive means of understanding the processes through which they seek to thread their own way.

Compelling trends

The classic case of a process with considerable momentum through much of history is the division of labour. Of course, the process has sometimes gone into reverse; a surprisingly large number of complex societies have collapsed in the course of history, with a decline in the division of labour as a principal symptom of collapse.[12] But in very long-term perspective, the division of labour—or more generally the division of social functions—has been one of the most sustained trends in human society since its origins.

Adam Smith's *The Wealth of Nations*, generally seen as the starting point of modern economics, is the benchmark discussion of the division of labour. Sociologists, however, tend to make much of Emile Durkheim's *The Division of Labour in Society*.[13] Durkheim, that founding father of sociology whose characteristic circularity of argument has left such a profound mark on the discipline, mounted a polemic against Herbert Spencer. In direct line of descent from Smith, Spencer had explained the process of the division of labour in terms of individuals' pursuit of their own advantage in competitive interdependence. Durkheim, in contrast, emphasized the necessity of trust, order and consensus before people felt able to put themselves in others' hands by dividing their labour—'all that is in the contract is not contractual.' Here, as also when he sets up the famous dichotomy between 'mechanical' and 'organic solidarity', Durkheim is indulging in process-reduction[14]—reducing the process of the division of labour to a static contrast between more and less. In fact both Durkheim's and Spencer's views can safely be discarded as one-sided, as a false and static polarity. What is involved in the process is not a circular causal relationship between two static entities (call them 'specialization' and 'trust' for short) but a spiral process of causality, in which for example pacification of territory creates the greater security necessary for the growth of trade, towns and specialization, which in turn generate the taxes to support administration capable of raising the level of security and calculability over still wider territory. And so on. The process is historically contingent. Not much more elucidation can be achieved by conceptual cogitation; what is required is historical investigation of actual cases.

Nor is there any need to resort to psychologistic assumptions of individual acquisitiveness or selfish impulses to explain the progression of the division of labour. Simple problem solving and learning by doing (within the framework of the settled social conditions of a stable state, to which Adam Smith drew attention, but which is also in part the product of earlier phases of specialization) are enough to explain why ten men may choose to divide their labour to make pins. Smith and Spencer were not wrong in thinking that the vast multiplication of the per capita output of pins gives individuals incentives to divide their labour (even if the price per pin on the market then falls dramatically). But what needs to be stressed for present purposes is the compellingness of the process once it is set in train: once groups of ten men are dividing their labour to make pins, the market ensures that the idiosyncratic individualist who prefers to produce the whole, hand-crafted pin will not be able to make his living by it. Karl Marx was to stress that point, of course.

Base and superstructure yet again

The division of labour, even if redescribed more generally as the division of social functions, is to a considerable extent an 'economic' process in which the constraints of competition and market forces play a large part. The idea of long-term compelling economic processes with a discernible structure and sequence of their own is not especially controversial. There has, however, for a long time been more dispute over whether any long-term processes of cultural development can be observed with comparable structure and compellingness. Later writers, such as Elias and some of the contributors to the present volume, have considered the distinction artificial: economic behaviour, after all, is cultural. But these issues were much discussed among sociologists in the early decades of the twentieth century. Alfred Weber presents a particularly clear distinction between what he calls 'civilizational processes', which do exhibit trend and direction, and 'culture movements' which do not. In his usage,[15] 'civilizational process' is the domain of material development, of the natural sciences and technology, of the rational and systematic conquest of the forces of nature. He had no difficulty in identifying a long-term trend, even 'progress' in this sphere. 'Culture', in contrast, was peculiar to its individual and social creators; it was laden with history and could only be conceived historically. It was not transferable from one historical entity to another, it was embedded in a unique situation, and there were no generally valid laws or trends in the world of culture. Alfred Weber was here following the distinction between nomothetic and idiographic disciplines laid down in the previous generation of Dilthey, Rickert, and Windelband.

As against this Karl Mannheim, in a paper entitled 'Competition as a Cultural Phenomenon'[16] argued that competition as a structured process was not confined to the economic sphere, but could also be observed in the competition between rival ideas. Apart from the limiting case of consensus, in which competition is simply absent, he discussed three models of how a public interpretation of reality could come about. They were through 'atomistic competition' (competition among many groups), through one group holding a monopoly position, and through the gradual concentration around one view of formerly atomistically competing groups. These fairly clearly correspond to economists' models of perfect competition, monopoly, and imperfect or monopolistic competition.

The roots of the debate, however, lie a century earlier, in Karl Marx's reaction to the ideas both of Hegel and the liberal economists. It is worth looking again at this familiar territory, in order to call in question whether it is useful still to think in terms of economic, political and cultural 'spheres' or 'factors' in explaining historical trends.

By the mid-nineteenth century, economics had emerged as the first of the relatively autonomous social sciences.[17] It was a short step from a theoretical demonstration of how market forces would apparently optimize the allocation of resources in a law-like way to arguing that the economy was and should be an autonomous 'sphere' of society. The 'laws' of that sphere would operate best if there was minimal interference in them from the other major 'sphere' of society, the state. The state itself was not seen as functioning according to impersonal, law-like regularities. This was how the nascent science of economics came to provide the intellectual foundation for liberal ideology. At the kernel of the ideology in its most extreme form was the advocacy of the 'night-watchman state'; the state, it was argued, should do no more than provide the framework of basic security within which entrepreneurs pursued their activities with minimal restrictions. Economics seemed to show that this was to the advantage of all; there is little doubt that it was to the advantage of the businessmen.

It is Elias' contention that Marx 'simply took over the basic conceptual scheme of the liberal ideology, but infused it with negative values'. In his hands, a short-term economic theory was transformed into a long-term sociological theory. The liberal view that the state ought not to interfere in the autonomous play of economic forces was transmuted into the view that the economic sphere did in fact have throughout history a high degree of autonomy in relation to other spheres. And the liberal view that the state ought to serve the interests of entrepreneurs had its counterpart in Marx's conception of the state as a mere 'superstructure' actually serving the economic interests of that class.

As to how Marx really saw the relationship between 'base' and 'superstructure', it is possible to present many contradictory texts. That he placed special emphasis on economic forces in social development there is no doubt; whether he saw them as simple one-way causal determinants of everything else is much more questionable. Elias sidesteps that old issue and points to a possibly more fundamental assumption in Marx's thinking. Marx and Engels, he argues, do not reach their hypothesis about the long-term importance of the economic basis from an investigation of the power of groups performing specialist economic functions in relation to the power of other groups. It comes instead from their conviction that 'laws' and 'regularities' can be discovered only in the 'economic' aspects of society. This assumption, shared with the liberal economics of the time, is mostly implicit, and needs to be teased out through careful reading. In a letter to Bloch, however, Engels made explicit that he regarded the 'economic basis' as structured, and all other aspects of social relationships as unstructured: 'as a host of accidents (i.e. of things and events whose inner connection is so remote or so impossible to prove that we regard it as absent and can neglect it)'.[18] If only the economic aspects of social relations were structured, they alone would be a possible subject for a science of society.

This limitation is ironic, for it was the tools of economics that enabled Marx to break away from the old philosophical modes of thought, and he extended the use of these tools far beyond the economics of his day. Yet this achievement was partly vitiated, Elias argued, by Marx's trying to conceptualize any structured, non-accidental, aspect of social relations as economic. On the one hand, as is well-known, Marx broke away from the thought of Hegel, and indeed the whole German philosophical tradition, in which concepts like 'spirit' and 'consciousness' were reified so that they seemed to refer to non-human moving forces in human history; he replaced them with concepts like 'relations of production' which much more clearly express the relationships and interdependencies of human groups. On the other hand, he himself—perhaps unwittingly —reinforced these same reifying tendencies on a new level by introducing concepts like 'base' and 'superstructure' which also give the impression of referring to things quite separate from the networks of groups people form with each other. The impression is strengthened by Marx and Marxists representing the base/superstructure dichotomy as a structural characteristic of all societies, irrespective of the stage of development in each case to which economic activities have become specialized as such.

The reason for the persistence of an overly reified dualism of base and superstructure in Marx's thought seems to be that in one respect he did not break sufficiently with the philosophical tradition. Hegel had made intellectual activity, developing in an autonomous sphere of 'spirit', the primary moving force in history. Marx instead made the production and distribution of goods for the satisfaction of the necessities of life the motive force. But, in identifying this with social 'Being' (*Sein*), and opposing it to 'Consciousness' (*Bewußtsein*) identified with the non-economic 'superstructure', he gave the impression that 'economic' activities are without consciousness and went too far towards an equally one-sided view. That was because he never broke away from the philo-sophical conception of 'consciousness' as representing a high intellectual, or ideological, level of thinking and knowledge. In his theorizing, he paid insufficient regard to what would no doubt have been obvious to him: that 'consciousness' is not something inhabiting a separate sphere. Consciousness plays a part in all human social activity—in a mother's feeding her child, in a farmer's ploughing his field, in workers making cotton in a nineteenth-century mill. Knowledge is as essential to human life as food. Different levels of consciousness certainly can be distin-guished: the consciousness of workers carrying heavy loads is not the same as that of learned people pronouncing on the nature of society, but the differences are only degrees along a continuum. Marx's notion of consciousness is too exclusively modelled on the latter.

This helped to create the false polarity of economy and culture, technology and ideology, as well as the equally false dichotomy of the economic versus the political and military. Elias always argued that the means of protection (including the means of attack) and the means of orientation are as important as the means of production, to which they are not reducible. They interweave with each other and thus contribute to 'momentum'. More recently, Michael Mann has argued much the same case, in *The Sources of Social Power*.[19]

Cultural momentum

When Elias discussed the problem of 'inevitability' and the nature of compelling processes, he always had in mind his own controversial theory of civilizing processes, first worked out through a very detailed theoretical-empirical study of European history since the Middle Ages.[20] Civilizing processes can be taken as a test-case of 'cultural' processes that build momentum and direction, but remain historically contingent and are in no way 'inevitable'. (Still less do they represent 'progress'.) They also demonstrate the futility of trying to separate a 'cultural' component from political, economic and other strands in a spiral process.

Elias in fact spoke of civilizing processes on two levels.[21] The first is the individual level, and is rather uncontroversial. Infants and children have to acquire through learning the adult standards of behaviour and feeling prevalent in their society; to speak of this as a civilizing process is more or less to use another term for 'socialization' (though the process of learning social standards, Elias always emphasized, always also simultaneously involves a process of individuation of the social standards being learned), and that this process has a typical structure and sequence is not disputed. But the second level is more controversial. Where did these standards come from? They have not always existed, nor always been the same. Elias argues it is possible to identify long-term civilizing processes in the shaping of standards of behaviour and feeling over many generations within particular cultures. Again, the idea that these standards change is not controversial; what generates controversy is that the changes take the form of structured processes of change with a discernible—though unplanned—direction over time. This problem of direction is crucial to the problem of 'momentum' for, as we have remarked, that word implies a direction of movement.

The basic idea, and the basic link between the two volumes of Elias' *magnum opus*, is that there is a connection between the long-term structural development of societies and long-term changes in people's social character or typical personality make-up. In other words, as the structure of societies becomes more complex, manners, culture and personality also change in a particular and discernible direction, first among elite groups, then gradually more widely. This is worked out with great subtlety for Western Europe since the Middle Ages. By the time Europeans had begun to use 'civilization' as a badge of what they supposed to be their superiority over other, non-European peoples, they had almost entirely forgotten that their own ancestors had passed through this process of development.

Implicitly Elias begins from Max Weber's definition of the state as an organization which successfully upholds a claim to binding rule-making over a territory, by virtue of commanding a monopoly of the legitimate use of violence,[22] but he is more interested in the process through which a monopoly of the means of violence and taxation (the means are at once 'political' and 'economic') is established and extended. One of Elias' central arguments is that if, in a particular region, the power of central authority grows, and people are forced to live at peace with one another, the moulding of the emotions is very gradually changed as well.[23] Elias does not put all his eggs in the state formation basket. State formation, he argues, is only one process interweaving with others to enmesh individuals in increasingly complex webs of interdependence. It interweaves with the division of labour, the growth of trade, towns, the use of money and administrative apparatuses, and increasing population in a spiral process. Internal pacification of territory facilitates trade, which facilitates the growth of towns and division of labour and generates taxes which support larger administrative and military organizations, which in turn facilitate the internal pacification of larger territories and so on—a cumulative process experienced as a compelling force by people caught up in it.

Furthermore, according to Elias, the gradually higher standards of habitual self-restraint engendered in people contribute in turn to the upward spiral—being necessary for example to the formation of gradually more effective and calculable administration. Equally, the loss of certain learned 'psychological' capacities could contribute to a downward spiral. But it is not so much a matter of identifying single causal factors as of tracing how various causal strands interweave over time to produce an overall process with increasing momentum.

Elias puts forward an elaborate theory of changing personality formation. He argues that as webs of interdependence become denser and more extensive, there gradually takes place a shift in the balance between external constraints (*Fremdzwänge*—constraints by other people) and self-constraints (*Selbstzwänge*), in favour of the latter. His book on time and timing[24] brings out particularly clearly the link between social and personality changes arising from the necessity of coordinating more and more complicated sequences of activities. The pressures on individuals to exercise greater foresight take various forms: Elias discusses especially the processes of rationalization, 'psychologization', and the advance of thresholds of shame and embarrassment.[25]

Psychologization is linked to the idea that spreading webs of interdependence tend to be associated with relatively more equal power ratios and 'functional democratization', meaning more and more reciprocal controls between more and more social groups. Less abstractly: 'more people are forced more often to pay more attention to more other people'.[26] This produces pressures towards greater consideration of the consequences of one's own actions for other people on whom one is more or less dependent, and there tends in consequence to be an increase in 'mutual identification'. This idea has a very direct bearing on matters of violence and cruelty. The advance of thresholds of shame and embarrassment also involves increased foresight, in the sense of greater vigilance in anticipating social dangers, especially the transgression of various social prohibitions.

Rationalization, warns Elias, has no absolute beginning in human history. Just as there was no point at which human beings suddenly began to possess a 'conscience', there is none before which they were completely 'irrational'. Still more misleading is it to think of rationality as some kind of property of individual minds in isolation from each other. What actually changes is the way people are bonded with each other in society, and in consequence the moulding of personality structure. Elias' argument is that the forms of behaviour we call 'rationality' are produced within a social figuration in which extensive transformation of external compulsions into internal compulsions takes place:

> The complementary concepts of 'rationality' and 'irrationality' refer to the relative parts played by short-term affects and long-term conceptual models of observable reality in individual behaviour. The greater the importance of the latter in the delicate balance between affective and reality-orientated commands, the more 'rational' is behaviour.[27]

The notion of momentum in long-term cultural processes is further clarified by Elias' account of the growth of scientific knowledge—this time couched not in solely European terms, but in the broadest terms of world history. Elias tries to show how the first steps are the most difficult in the acquisition of the kinds of 'reality-adequate' concepts and knowledge—adequate, that is, to enhancing human control over the forces of nature as well as over social forces—and the process only gradually builds up momentum.

In industrial societies, most people use concepts and explanations of natural events based on the idea of a course of events independent of any specific group of human observers, without being aware of the long struggle that was necessary to develop these modes of thinking. To illustrate this difficulty, Elias tells the amusing story of a nineteenth-century French general whose African troops refused to march after seeing an eclipse of the moon, which to them was an omen sent by the prophet. They listened patiently to the general's 'scientific' explanation of eclipses, accepted its truth—but still refused to march, because it was still a warning from the prophet. Unlike most twentieth-century anthropologists, however, Elias is not satisfied to say that some human beings see the world one way and others see it in another. He sets out to explain why they do.

He argues that the two modes of explanation typified by the general and his troops—usually called 'scientific' and 'animistic'—correspond to two types of personality structure which also correspond to very different social circumstances. The clue to animism lies in the higher level of involvement and emotionality of experience and thinking, and the more limited scope of knowledge, which in turn are linked to a more limited capacity for controlling dangers, which in turn again helps to maintain a high level of involvement and emotionality. This characteristic vicious circle or double-bind (a concept prominent in many of Elias' later writings) operated to impede the growth of human knowledge for very long periods of the species' existence. Extreme insecurity and hazard to life in the face of uncontrollable natural forces prevents people making the detour via detachment necessary to develop knowledge and explanations of the impersonal technical type that can be used in increasing the controllability of natural forces. Their knowledge remains innocently egocentric and emotionally involved and, as long as it does, impersonal causal explanations remain meaningless to them, because they do not meet their emotional and cognitive needs. The method people use in acquiring knowledge is interdependent with the substance of the knowledge they already possess, and especially with their basic image of the world. Where the world is experienced—according to a corpus of knowledge and modes of thinking transmitted from earlier generations—as a world of spirits and willful acts, then the aim is to discover knowledge of hidden aims and intentions behind events. In this context, relevant knowledge may comprise principally tales, proverbs and practical prescriptions passed on from generation to generation, interpreted by and expressed through priests, witches, oracles and so on.

That for the greater part of its existence humankind has been entrapped in this double-bind explains why knowledge in the past grew immeasurably more slowly than in industrial-scientific societies. Much the largest part of that existence was passed in the long ages of the palaeolithic era. In emphasizing the force of the double-bind in the extreme insecurity which prevailed then, Elias observes that 'Humans at that stage lived like the wild animals they hunted, always on the alert'.[28] Even much later there was only a very gradual changeover from animistic to causal modes of thought, the two co-existing for long periods. Nevertheless, though vestiges of magical-mythical thinking persist, it has steadily lost ground as a mode of experience during the development of industrial scientific societies.

Elias sums up the argument about knowledge and long-term social development in the idea of the triad of basic controls.[29] The stage of development attained by a society, he contends, can be identified and measured in relation to:

(1) the extent of its capacity for exerting control (Elias uses the term 'control-chances') over non-human forces and events—the 'forces of nature' as they are often called;

(2) the extent of its capacity for control over interpersonal relationships and events, or 'social forces';

(3) the extent to which each of the members of a society has control over him or herself as an individual.

These three kinds of control develop and function in interdependence with each other and with the development of knowledge but, Elias emphasizes, this interdependence is not to be understood in terms of simple parallel increases of all three in step with each other.

The first type of control, which corresponds broadly to technological development, has tended gradually to increase in the course of the overall long-term development of human societies, though there have often been setbacks. Again, in very long-term perspective, the second type of control-chances—human control over social processes—has tended gradually to increase. But the connection between the two is not simple and direct.

Paradoxically, says Elias, the gradual increase in human beings' capacity for taking a more detached view of natural forces and gaining more control over them—a process which has also accelerated over the long term—has tended to increase the difficulties they have in extending their control over social relationships and over their own feelings in thinking about them. The reason for this paradox is that as humans have gradually come to understand natural forces more, fear them less and use them more effectively for human ends, this has gone hand in hand with specific changes in human relationships. More and more people have tended to become more and more interdependent with each other in longer chains and denser webs. (If this sounds rather abstract, think of the example of the early 'hydraulic civilizations' of Mesopotamia and Egypt where, as archaeologists and historians have long been aware, the harnessing of the waters for irrigation and the control of hitherto disastrous floods necessarily went hand in hand with the emergence of much more elaborate political and economic organization.) The growth of the web of social interdependence tends to outstrip people's understanding of it. The same process which diminishes dangers and feelings of

insecurity in the face of natural forces tends also to increase the dangers
and feelings of insecurity in face of 'social forces'—the forces stemming
from people's dependence on each other for the satisfaction of their needs
and for their security. Elias puts the point vividly:

> It is as if first thousands, then millions, then more and more
> millions walked through this world with their hands and feet
> chained together by invisible ties. No-one is in charge. No-one
> stands outside. Some want to go this way, others that way. They
> fall upon each other and, vanquishing or defeated, still remain
> chained to each other. No-one can regulate the movements of the
> whole unless a great part of them are able to understand, to see
> as it were from the outside, the whole patterns they form together.
> And they are not able to visualize themselves as part of these
> larger patterns because, being hemmed in and moved uncom-
> prehendingly hither and thither in ways which none of them
> intended, they cannot help being preoccupied with the urgent,
> narrow and parochial problems which each of them has to face
> . . . They are too deeply involved to look at themselves from
> without. Thus what is formed of nothing but human beings acts
> upon each of them, and is experienced by many as an alien
> external force not unlike the forces of nature.[30]

These seemingly alien forces bring about, among other things, frequent
and unforeseen gains for some and losses for others, so they go hand in
hand with tensions and frictions between interdependent groups. And
'tests of strength and the use of organized force serve often as costly
means of adjustment to changes within this tangle of interdependencies;
on many of its levels no other means of adjustment exist.'

The bearing of this problem on the growth of human knowledge
becomes clear if the third of the triad of controls—people's differing
capacity for control over themselves as individuals—is brought into the
picture. Elias argues that, on the one hand, when people are in a situation
of vulnerability and insecurity, it is difficult for them to control more fully
their own strong feelings about events deeply affecting their lives, and to
approach those events with more detachment, as long as they have little
ability to control the course of events. On the other hand, it is also
difficult for them to extend their understanding and control of these
events so long as they cannot approach them with greater detachment
and gain greater control over themselves. This double-bind can obstruct
the growth of knowledge in respect of all three levels of the triad—the
always interconnected levels of the 'technological', the 'social' and the

'psychological' to put it perhaps too simply—even at later stages of social development.

Conclusion

The aim of this essay has been to rebut the old philosophically-based arguments which deterred many social scientists in the previous generation from concerning themselves with longer-term processes of social development. The renewed interest in such processes now widespread among sociologists and historians has not on the whole brought with it any renewed anxiety about whether the processes are 'inevitable'. Yet it is hard to avoid the conclusion that developmental processes are structured, that they exhibit sequential order, and that they acquire momentum in particular directions.

In understanding how such momentum develops, it is often misleading to think in terms of abstract economic, political and cultural 'spheres', or of base and superstructure, linked by simple unidirectional causal arrows. Much more complex patterns of spiral causality are involved. The principles have been illustrated by reference to Norbert Elias' theory of civilizing processes and his later, but related, theory of the long-term development of human knowledge. Neither process is 'inevitable', and though both build up momentum they remain historically contingent. If the long-term trend of the European civilizing process is fairly clear, beneath the overall trend line there have been many counter-spurts, fluctuations and reversals. Why they happen is the subject of much empirical research and theoretical debate.[31] The same applies to the long-term development of human knowledge and its relation to the technological, social and psychological dimensions of control. As Elias writes:

> Nothing in our experience suggests that part-processes of this kind must always work in the same direction. Some of the phases in which they went into reverse are known from the past. Increasing social tensions and strife may go hand in hand with both a decrease of people's ability to control, and an increase in the fantasy-content of their ideas about, natural as well as social events.[32]

Understanding both of how long-term social processes acquire momentum and how nevertheless their direction comes to be modified or reversed, however, is not advanced by philosophizing *in vacuo*. It is dangerous for the wheels to grind without corn (as Norbert Elias used to be fond of remarking), and these are questions not for philosophers but for theoretically-informed empirical investigation by working sociologists and historians.

Notes

1. The phrase is Elias': see Norbert Elias, 'The Retreat of Sociologists into the Present', *Theory, Culture and Society* 4 (1987), pp. 223–47.
2. Stephen Mennell, 'Introduction: Bringing the very long term back in', in Johan Goudsblom, E.L. Jones and Stephen Mennell, *Human History and Social Process* (Exeter, 1989).
3. Stephen Mennell, 'The Sociological Study of History: Institutions and social development', in Christopher G. Bryant and Henk A. Becker (eds), *What has Sociology Achieved?* (1990).
4. Sir Karl Popper, *The Open Society and its Enemies*, 2 vols (1945); id., *The Poverty of Historicism* (1957); Sir Isaiah Berlin, *Historical Inevitability* (Oxford, 1954); Robert A. Nisbet, *Social Change and History* (New York, 1969). For a more recent statement of Popperian views by one of Britain's most distinguished sociologists, see John H. Goldthorpe, 'The Uses of History in Sociology: Reflections on some recent tendencies' (T.H. Marshall Lecture, University of Southampton, 1988).
5. Popper, *Poverty of Historicism*, pp. v–vi. Cf. Eric Dunning's critique of Popper from the point of view of the work of Auguste Comte and Norbert Elias: 'In Defence of Developmental Sociology: A critique of Popper's "Poverty of Historicism" with special reference to the theory of August Comte', *Amsterdams Sociologisch Tijdschrift* 4 (1977), pp. 327–49.
6. A classic discussion can be found in E.H. Carr, *What is History?* (1961). Interestingly, Carr and Elias apparently discussed these issues at some date prior to Carr's G.M. Trevelyan lectures which formed the basis of that book. Elias remarked later that Carr had privately acknowledged his debt to Elias, which I think can be detected especially in ch. 2, 'Society and the Individual' and ch. 4, 'Causation in History'.
7. Norbert Elias, *What is Sociology?* (1978), p. 167.
8. Louis Althusser, 'Ideology and Ideological State Apparatuses', in *Lenin and Philosophy and Other Essays* (1971), p. 169.
9. Philip Abrams, *Historical Sociology* (Shepton Mallet, 1982), pp. 162–3.
10. Elias, *What is Sociology?*, p. 160.
11. Ibid., p. 91, and, more generally, ch. 3, 'Game Models', pp. 71–103.

See also Stephen Mennell, '"Individual" Action and its "Social" Consequences in the Work of Norbert Elias', in P.R. Gleichmann, J. Goudsblom and H. Korte (eds), *Human Figurations: Essays for Norbert Elias* (Amsterdam, 1977), pp. 99–109, and id., *Nobert Elias: Civilisation and the Human Self-Image* (Oxford, 1989), pp. 258–64.

12. Joseph A. Tainter, *The Collapse of Complex Societies* (Cambridge, 1988).

13. Emile Durkheim, *The Division of Labour in Society* [1893] (1984).

14. Elias, *What is Sociology?*, pp. 111 ff.

15. Alfred Weber, *Kulturgeschichte als Kultursoziologie* (Munich, 1950). Note that Alfred Weber's use of the terms 'civilization' and 'culture' is radically different from that of Norbert Elias, who was briefly his student.

16. Karl Mannheim, 'Competition as a Cultural Phenomenon' [1927], in *Essays on the Sociology of Knowledge* (1952).

17. This argument is drawn from Norbert Elias, 'On the Sociogenesis of Sociology', *Sociologisch Tijdschrift* 11 (1984), pp. 14–52; id., 'Sociology of Knowledge: New perspectives', *Sociology* 5 (1971), pp. 149–68, 355–70; id., 'Zur Gundlegung einer Theorie Sozialer Prozess', *Zeitschrift fur Soziologie* 6 (1977), pp. 127–49.

18. Friedrich Engels, letter to Josef Bloch in Königsberg, 21 September 1890, in *Marx-Engels Selected Works* (1968), pp. 692–3.

19. Michael Mann, *The Sources of Social Power*, vol. 1 (Cambridge, 1986).

20. Norbert Elias, *The Civilising Process*, vol. 1, *The History of Manners* (Oxford, 1978); vol. 2, *State-Formation and Civilisation* [US title: *Power and Civility*] (Oxford, 1982).

21. In fact, in his later work (such as his theory of the long-term development of knowledge, discussed below) Elias spoke of civilizing processes on a third level, that of humanity as a whole: see Mennell, *Norbert Elias*, pp. 200–24.

22. Max Weber, *Economy and Society* [1922] (Berkeley, 1978), vol. 1, p. 54.

23. Elias, *Civilising Process*, vol. 1, p. 201.

24. Id., *Über die Zeit* (Frankfurt, 1984).

25. For more detailed discussion, see Mennell, *Norbert Elias*, ch. 4.

26. J. Goudsblom, 'Stijlen en Beschavingen', *De Gids* 152 (1989), pp. 720–2.

27. Norbert Elias, *The Court Society* (Oxford, 1983), p. 92.

28. Id., *Involvement and Detachment* (Oxford, 1987), p. 66.

29. Id., *What is Sociology?*, pp. 156–7.

30. Id., 'Problems of Involvement and Detachment', *British Journal of Sociology* 7 (1956), p. 232 (my italics).

31. See Mennell, *Norbert Elias*, ch. 10, 'Civilisation and Decivilisation'; id., 'Decivilising Processes: Theoretical significance and some lines of research', *International Sociology* 5 (1990), pp. 205–23; and Zygmunt Bauman, *Modernity and the Holocaust* (Oxford, 1989).
32. Elias, 'Problems of Involvement and Detachment', p. 231.

Prices as Descriptions: Reasons as Explanations[1]

Iain Hampsher-Monk

The aim of this chapter is partly scene-setting: to provide an airing for patterns of explanation used in the study of history and the social sciences and in particular two modes of explanation intimately associated with the ideas of culture and economics which form the topic of this volume. By economic explanation I refer to that family of explanatory devices spawned by the notion of man as a rational economic calculator, variously specified. Cultural explanation embraces many possibilities, but the focus will in particular be on those explanations that take as central to understanding an action, the reasons, beliefs, and intentions of the actor(s). To remind the reader of this I shall refer to these as actor's reasons explanations.[2]

However, in the interests of debate a fairly extreme thesis will be pursued. This is that a logical analysis of economic-type explanations reveals them to be incapable of functioning as explanations in any strong sense at all, and the only way they can be made to do so is by feeding in other information about actor's reasons. Effective economic explanations are, I claim, logically parasitic on actor's reasons explanations. The relationship is parasitic and not symbiotic: actor's reasons explanations, I shall argue, are capable of forming a complete and self-sufficient mode of explanation in their own right. Clearly this is an easier case to argue with some than with other social phenomena. Explanation of the very long-term social processes discussed by Eric Jones and Stephen Mennell tests the limits of actor's reasons explanations—neither economic growth itself, nor the development of civility are the direct result of individuals' intentions. Still, I shall argue, explanations even at this level of generality must be integrated at some point with agents' perceptions and beliefs, since it is these, after all, that produce the actions which individually or

47

cumulatively constitute social and political phenomena. Whilst sketching the patterns of argument necessarily involves wide generalization, arguing the thesis requires a detailed analysis of crucial parts of some versions of the explanations under discussion; as a result there will be some unevenness of treatment, for which apology is made in advance.

What makes a good explanation? In a rough and ready way, to explain something is to render the unfamiliar, or the unaccountable, familiar or lucid. There is a primitive sense in which a successful explanation is a matter of subjective experience: if the explanation satisfies you, it evidently explained. On these grounds, even a fuller description of an event counts as an explanation, and I would not at all want to underrate the importance of such enterprises. However, if we are interested in going beyond mere subjective satisfaction to some level of formality, we must have in mind two rather *minimal criteria as to what is to count as a satisfactory explanation.*

The first is that the explanation must be capable of being specified independently of the *explanandum* (or phenomenon to be explained). Why this must be so was indicated four hundred years ago by Thomas Hobbes in prose I could not hope to emulate. Speaking of the peddlers of bogus explanations then operating in the universities he wrote:

> if you desire to know why some kind of bodies sink naturally downwards toward the Earth, and others goe naturally from it; the Schools will tell you out of Aristotle, that the bodies that sink downwards, are *Heavy*; and that this Heaviness it is that causes them to descend. But if you ask what they mean by *Heaviness*, they will define it to bee an endeavour to goe to the center of the Earth: so that the cause why things sink downward, is an Endeavour to be below: which is as much as to say that bodies descend or ascend, because they doe.[3]

The second criterion cannot, I fear, be so elegantly expressed. Most explanatory theories operate under *ceteris paribus* conditions. That is to say that the explanation will only hold under certain conditions. These conditions are not themselves strictly part of the theory. Galileo's theory about the behaviour of falling bodies specified the conditions under which it would be true: i.e. in a vacuum. There is no problem about specifying what we mean by a vacuum independently of the theory of falling bodies, nor any problem about knowing when we have one which might obscure the meaning or application of the terms used in the theory. In the social sciences, much economic explanation consists of purely mathematical formulations, in which, in order for the explanation to be applied, the terms of the formulae have to be specified as descriptions of the utility functions, incomes, outputs etc. of individual (or corporate) economic actors.[4]

A successful explanatory theory must be capable of discriminating between outcomes which are the property of the explanation, and outcomes which are merely entailed by a combination of the theory and the specifying conditions for its application. Failure, in principle, to meet this criterion will mean that the theory is unfalsifiable over the range of phenomena specified by the conditions for its application, and the explanations it is capable of generating will therefore be fundamentally equivocal. This is necessarily a little abstract at the moment but will be made clearer when we see the theory applied.

Economic explanation

The kind of economic explanation I have in mind comes in a number of forms, price theory, rational or social choice theory, social exchange theory.[5] One problem about trying to mount a generalized attack on it is precisely the variety of forms it takes. Let me take the plunge and try to characterize it generally before looking at some of its more closely specified variants.

One general way of characterizing the economic theory of human behaviour supposedly underpinning such explanations is that human beings simply buy cheap and sell dear. This has the virtues of conformity both to observation and (for most of us) introspection. The intuition that human beings are, in the broadest sense, economizers, is the driving notion behind all of the attempts to make this kind of explanation stick, and it clearly has a lot going for it.

However, 'buying cheap and selling dear' simply will not do as a way of characterizing economic explanation. The reason being that whilst in money markets we know what 'cheap and dear' mean (because we have a public medium to measure them by), in the case of other forms of activity or choice we do not. It is precisely when economic modes of explanation are extended to areas outside a normal money market that they start to get interesting for social theorists, and it is precisely at that point that the notion of 'cost' loses the generalizability that gives the explanations their clout. For the problem is—and it is a problem even within market forms of exchange, as economic theorists themselves acknowledge—that we must not make the mistake of assuming that only those objects traded, and their money values, enter into the equation. People set a value on all sorts of things—which come broadly under the category of the cultural—which may be affected by, although not formally part of, a financial transaction: friendship, rest and leisure, pride, patriotism, religious observances—all of which can affect whether an object is traded at a particular price, or at all. People may not trade because it infringes some cultural taboo, or simply because it's too much bother (the transaction costs are too high), as well as because the price is not right. It is in the attempt to model and explain these very kinds of choices that economic modes of explanation are extended beyond the marketplace in which they originated. And to do so we need some way of expressing the non-monetary value which actors place on these things too.

The classic way of getting round all this, and including search costs, leisure, pride, religious commitment and whatever else might lead us to trade or not to trade, do or not to do an action, is to postulate some psychological equivalent of money, some universal and standardized unit of satisfaction as the object of consideration whenever action is contemplated. There are various ways of trying to formulate what this 'utility' might be. Martin Hollis recently mischievously characterized it as a 'micro watt of inner glow'.[6] This catches some of the problem. Utility starts its life as pleasure and pain (which Bentham insisted 'are real things'), but even if utility can be regarded as, in some kind of sense, a real psychic unit, it is one which is directly accessible only to the person who experiences it.

However, stated like this the theory is in danger of running foul of the considerations advanced concerning explanation: since we do not know in advance what it is people find utility in, utility is revealed—or presumed to be revealed—only in the choices people actually make, and can only be inferred back from their choices. But then the notion that people are economizers because they are economizing on their utils becomes a truism. Economizing on your utils is doing what you do: if your actions (definitionally) reveal your preferences, and your preferences (definitionally) express your utilities, it could never be true that you failed to maximize your utilities, as long as you acted from choice.

This, it seems to me, remains the general difficulty for economic explanations. However, it cannot be dismissed by such a simplistic presentation of the objection as that stated above, and we shall have to pursue more disciplined formulations of the problem.

The next move in the step to prolong the life of economic man (it interestingly always is *man*) is to reject the latent psychologism in the notion of utility. The great philosophers of economics almost consistently pursue this line. Von Mises, Hayek and Friedman all, in slightly different ways it is true, nevertheless agree that the idea that the axioms of the economic model in some sense offer putative descriptions of individuals' psychological processes is a mistake. As Friedman puts it:

> To suppose that hypotheses have not only 'implications' but also 'assumptions' and that the conformity of these assumptions to 'reality' is a test of the validity of the hypothesis . . . is fundamentally wrong and productive of much mischief . . . the relation is almost the opposite of that suggested . . . in general the more significant the theory the more unrealistic the assumptions.

In support of this Friedman draws attention to his own critique of empirical studies designed to find out whether, as a matter of fact, businessmen were motivated by the concerns suggested by marginalist theories of the firm: studying (or at least seeking information on) the shape of the demand curve facing them, for example. Such studies he insisted, were a waste of time. Economic hypotheses, properly understood, do not purport to be descriptions of individuals' behaviour. Indeed, he goes further:

> To be important, a hypothesis must be descriptively false in its assumptions . . . the relevant question to ask about the assumptions of a theory is not whether they are descriptively realistic for they never are, but whether they are sufficiently good approximations for the purpose in hand. And this question can only be answered by seeing whether the theory works, which means whether it yields sufficiently accurate predictions.[7]

And most major theorists agree. The interesting exception to this position is Samuelson, who argues that as a matter of logic, hypotheses whose consequences are fully specified, realistic and confirmed must rest on assumptions which are realistic. Of course not all, in fact very few, hypotheses' consequences can all be specified, and even fewer are all confirmed, so the force of the logical point is somewhat blunted. Nevertheless he falls back on a remarkably chauvinistic gut feeling that realism in hypotheses *is* important, which underscores why the models are always models of 'rational economic *man*'. In what must be a classic footnote he writes: 'All economic regularities that have no commonsense core that you can explain to your wife will soon fail.'[8] Despite the male chauvinism there is, it seems to me, a grain of truth in this. For the methodological postulates of Friedman, Hayek and Von Mises cut us adrift completely from commonsense perceptions of reality, and would have us trying out hypotheses in a random way (since there is no sense in which they are supposed to model psychology) until we get one that chances to produce accurate deductions. We seem to be in a world of meaningless events looking for a conceptually random 'fit' for our hypothesis, like the covering law model of explanation in the natural sciences, which makes a brief appearance elsewhere in this volume and to which I shall come later.

Nevertheless, one might say, with Friedman *et al.*, the proof of the pudding is in the eating: if the method works, if 'fits' are indeed found between theories and data, if predictions are correctly made, the theory is confirmed. In that case then, surely retrospective explanations of a similar kind can be correctly asserted, explanation being, in some sense an analogue of confirmation?[9] I am not at all sure that this follows, for I believe there is a price to be paid for the desertion of realism, and of the theory's lowly psychological origins, and I shall next try to exact it by offering a critique of economic theory.

The rejection of realism in exchange for successful predictability throws the spotlight on the circumstances under which successful predictions are made. Those words liberally inscribed in the accounts of school science—'within the limits of experimental error'—need closer specification. The positive economists' version of this is 'other things being equal'. The crucial role of this condition has worrying implications for economic theory even when it is applied on its home ground, although as I shall later show, these are of even greater concern when economic explanations play, as it were, away from home.

As Hollis and Nell, to whom this critique is indebted, put it, prediction is never of 'what would happen', but of 'what would happen if . . .' Economic theory is never refuted by the failure of its predictions, for the predictions always predict what will happen under certain rather idealized circumstances, standardly perfect knowledge, costless entry to the market, no transactions costs, no collusion, etc. The cumulative effect of these *ceteris paribus* conditions, is to turn what often sounds like an empirical prediction, e.g.: 'If Jaguar UK produce where marginal costs equal marginal revenue, they will maximize their profits', into an analytic statement. For given the definitions of marginal costs, marginal revenue and profits, if the market is perfect and the cost curves conventionally shaped near the relevant areas of production, and *ceteris* are *paribus*, the statement is a tautology. How could one falsify marginal analysis? For believers in the theory, negative results simply reveal the imperfections of the market; but even for those willing to suspend their faith, it is impossible to distinguish the failure of theory from the failure of the circumstances in which it is applied to conform to the requisite conditions.

Or (to descend from the heights of marginal theory to the application of economic theory to individuals), if the axioms of rational egoism are not viewed as the psychological properties of individuals but tautologies, then once again, almost anything can be fitted into the account— altruism, sack cloth and ashes, self-mortification, you name it. As Von Mises acknowledged, the theory

> is indifferent to the ultimate goals of action . . . It applies the term happiness in a purely formal sense . . . The proposition: man's unique aim is to attain happiness, is tautological. It does not imply any statement about the state of affairs from which a man expects happiness.[10]

What does this reveal about the wider application of economic theories? Well, to parallel our example about the firm, predictions about individuals' or groups' actions will be purely analytical until we can fit the individual up with some *ceteris paribus* clauses, like wishing to maximize money holdings, or wishing to maximize security, or leisure, or equality or sociability, or any number of other aims, ideals or values individuals might have. These can be filled in on an *ad hoc* basis or on the basis of some cultural knowledge, discovered independently of the theory, about what it is that agents believe, value or take pleasure in, until the theory produces the right predictions. In a society in which economic considerations *narrowly construed* form a cultural norm, such as modern commercial societies, the assumption of a pervasive economic rationality may operate inexplicitly to provide the theory with content, and thus predictive, and explanatory power. The presence of such motivation may, however, be a logical prerequisite for the adequate deployment of such explanations. Even so, we may note that such 'explanations', although not technically falsified, can be brought into question by historians drawing attention to different aspects of the situation which render different facts important, or even, as in the examples below, suggest that it is something different that needs explaining.

The implications of these assumptions are just as serious, if less obvious, for retrospective, explanatory uses of the theory in history, as they are for predictive uses of them in contemporary economics. If 'economic' predictions are formal and indeterminate without the specification of the desires and beliefs of actors, similarly structured retrospective explanations must also be formal and indeterminate. The failure of the theory is more likely to be *revealed* where it is applied predictively, for it can, and often in fact does, fail to predict, although it is invariably rescued by pointing to the absence of appropriate *ceteris paribus* conditions. In the case of its retrospective use as explanation, no obvious 'failure' occurs because the outcomes, being historical facts, are known, and are already fitted into the explanation. But convincing though the explanation may on the surface appear, if I have correctly characterized its logical structure, its claim to have explained will be logically dependent on our retrospective knowledge of the aims and beliefs of the actors, whether or not these are actually specified or merely imputed from the observed actions of actors. Let us now turn to an example of economic explanation in history.

A much praised and influential book, representative of the 'new economic history' exemplified in our collection by Professor Jones, is *Structure and Change in Economic History* by Douglas C. North. In it he constructs an economic model of the first socio-economic revolution, the transition from a hunter-gatherer to a predominantly agrarian economy.[11] The purpose of the model is, he writes, 'to derive the conditions under which the scarce labour resource of the band would shift from its traditional occupation of hunting / gathering to agriculture'. He assumes that reallocation of resources will be determined by 'the maximization of the labour resource and, therefore, the economic welfare of the group'. Although there is no formal market for game or agricultural produce he assumes 'the band's preferences will establish these relative valuations', and he assumes those preferences will be stable over time. The conclusion he derives is that those stable preferences determined by the maximization of welfare will lead to the substitution of agriculture for hunting as either population growth, or competition, or exogenous decline in game takes place. Not only that, he predicts, from a tragedy-of-the-commons type argument, that the same processes will lead to a substitution of exclusive for common property rights. Now he is on fairly safe ground in deriving these conclusions, for we know, more or less, that this is what in fact happened. But the 'group welfare maximization' model itself only *entails* that result if certain assumptions are made. These are assumptions which, to archaeologists and anthropologists, are unjustifiable.

The model assumes population growth. Yet we know that many so-called primitive peoples have limited their populations, either through marriage practices, contraception or infanticide. So—in the absence of knowledge about cultural practices—the *assumption* of population pressure, an assumption made generally explicit in Professor Jones' paper, cannot be sustained.[12] North's model assumes, and I quote, an incentive to exploit the resource 'to the point where the value of the last animal killed is equal to the [search] costs of killing it'. But we know, (and so, he reveals, does North) that hunting peoples have highly respectful, even reverential attitudes towards their quarry, and elaborate, ecologically conservative taboos about depleting that resource. However, we are assured, these taboos will be overcome by competition between culturally distinct bands, since 'in a competitive situation no band has any incentive to conserve the resource, since the animals left to reproduce would be taken by its rivals.'[13] The explanation is elegant, and more complex than this sketch can convey. But we need to notice several things about it.

Firstly, notice that in the overcoming of ecologically conservative taboos, North assigns a crucial role to *cultural* differentiation. Secondly, the assumption of rational egoistic calculation is now operating as a psychological motive ('an incentive', 'would have no incentive to') rather than as a way of generating testable conclusions. Earlier North had adopted the Hayekian line by denying 'that the assumption that pre-historic man, when confronted with two alternatives would choose the one that made him better off' accurately *described* their behaviour. Rather he pursued a Darwinian, survival-of-the-fittest line: 'the bands that select the correct alternative, whether consciously or by chance will be favoured by a process of natural selection.'[14] But why is it in any case 'correct' for bands competitively to hunt game to extinction rather than co-operate in exploiting it at a sustainable level? If decisions are being arrived at randomly, there would seem to be as much likelihood of the one as the other. Indeed there is considerable rational choice literature which argues that, even assuming psychologically egoistic motives, anarchic solutions to fish stocks and tragic commons are possible.[15] Indeed the existence of intra-band limitations on over-exploitation seem to confirm the plausibility of this story. Why does the rational actor hypothesis lead us to assume that individuals accept band-level limitations on over-exploitation, but lead at the above-band level to disastrous competition? What is it *within the theory* that decides which way the evolution pans out, apart from our knowledge of how in fact it did?

There is a final curiosity to note. Hunting peoples, as Marshall Sahlins has noted, are amongst the most leisured in the world.[16] The high nutritional quality of their food and the relative ease with which each calorie is acquired leave them with plenty of time on their hands. Why should they not have employed their leisure by cultivating their gardens? Indeed, in the New World there is plenty of evidence that they did, the cultivation of squashes and peppers there seemingly dating back as far as archaeological evidence for that kind of thing could reasonably go. But such polyculture would be dependent on the chance existence of suitable wild plants, which were not available in Eurasia. (Just as the chance lack of existence of a suitable draught animal in America seems to have had important implications for their social and economic development). In the absence of such established alternative food sources, and given cultural conservatism, once the path to decline had been taken by a hunting band, one could imagine more and more time being spent, and greater and greater areas having to be covered to supply food needs from hunting. This would surely make it more and more difficult to find the time to effect the transition to agriculture or substitution of it for hunting, as the factors which North suggests push the band in that direction become more salient.

It is true that North's story can be tied in to reality, by filling in the specifications of the assumptions of the model with known facts about prehistory, or where these are unknown, plausible dummy variables. Once these are fully specified the particular explanation is complete and the model of explanation supposedly vindicated. But notice what this means. *A full specification of the circumstances turns out to include knowledge of the actual choices people made*, their 'revealed preferences', or, where formal markets exist, the prices at which goods are actually exchanged. The economic explanation thus relies crucially on a knowledge of the outcomes which enables us to work back to supposititiously derived statements about the rates or fact of substitutability of game and agricultural produce, or, in other circumstances, prices—which it might be thought it was the task of the theory to explain. What is the status of substitution rates or prices in this account? Are they explanations or descriptions (or indeed *a*scriptions of behaviour or choices)? If they are explanations, what are they explanations *of*? For on one view, the 'price story' about the agricultural revolution is simply a redescription of one aspect of it. We *know* that neolithic peoples had substituted agriculture for hunting. Does saying that this was because marginal returns to hunting decreased relative to those from agriculture tell us anything more? (Absent all the *reasons* why it might have decreased—reasons which might, and indeed have been elicited by researchers asking the answer to the original question without recasting it in terms of price theory) The explanation is radically under-determined, and quite consistent with other histories.[17] Notice what it means if prices and marginal rates of substitution are not specifiable separately from the circumstances they purport to explain: they fail to fulfill the first of our very modest criteria for explanation, and, if not quite falling into Hobbes' category of 'insignificant speech', can at best claim to be (admittedly sometimes elegant) redescriptions.

One answer to the question of what it is that rates of substitution and prices are an explanation *of*, was, as we have seen, that they are explanations of the preferences of the peoples who do the substituting, buying, and selling. Yet surprisingly this turns out to be an extremely tendentious claim, one which the gurus of economic theory have, as we have seen, almost universally rejected, although with troubling consequences for the grip of their theories on reality. But *if*, nevertheless, the description of individuals as something like rational utility maximizers is correct, and *if* outcomes can be fitted into a story leading to the correct conclusions, we might indeed seem to be explaining or at least modelling the social consequences of individuals' preferences and motivations. But there are two unknowns in the above story, not one: the rational utility maximizing hypothesis on the one hand and the preferences and motivations of individuals on the other. And we are only justified in presuming to have explained the second on the assumption that the truth of the first can be independently sustained, otherwise the 'truth' of the explanation may in fact be a property of the falsity of the hypothesis. If A+B=C, and A+B is the case, then C must be the case. But if we mistakenly *believe* A to be the case when it is not, then the fact that B is the case and that C is the case actually seriously undermines the A+B=C proposition. It is thus crucial that the truth of the rational utility maximizer hypothesis be demonstrable in isolation from its application to particular choices made by individuals. I shall now argue that it cannot.

Perhaps the most hard-nosed way of tightening up formulation of the rationality hypothesis is decision theory. Ironically this seems to demonstrate the impossibility of deciding the conceptual status of social choice theory. In decision theory an attempt is made to formalize the notion of rationality. There are two steps this, the first specifies under what conditions an individual's order of preferences could be said to be rational. A set of preferences are said to be rational if they are transitive (i.e., if A is preferred to B and B to C, A must be preferred to C), asymmetric (i.e., there is a rank discernible amongst preferences), connected (there are no gaps in the pairings over the range), independent (the independence of irrelevant alternatives) and if the preferences involving risk correlate coherently with the subjective values of the outcomes. The second part of the theory relates actions to preferences by asserting that a person with a rational pattern of preferences will chose from amongst those available the (or a) preference with the highest value.

This formulation may seem overly demanding, but it is really no more than an attempt to render precise the notion of consistent and unambiguous ordering, and this is surely about the minimum content that could be given to the notion of rationality. It may also appear to be one that is highly unlikely to be fulfilled, but that is, in a way, beside the point I want to make, which has to do with the way it reveals in general the difficulty of separating *any* formal criterion of rationality from the particular set of preferences of the individuals to whom the theory is applied.

Can the above account, *or anything like it*, be shown, to be true about human choice-making? Empirical investigations have invariably seemed to suggest not, and on the face of it this seems to imply that individuals are not rational. However, reflection on the results by theorists in this field has revealed to them the deeper problem of the indeterminacy of any such test.

The standard experiment in this field required individuals to make pair-wise choices within a small range of alternatives. The same alternatives were offered in subsequent sessions, but suitably masked in order to conceal the fact. There were no payoffs to individuals, and so no normal conditioning. Choice sets were then examined for inconsistencies. Individuals had become steadily more consistent over time. But how was this to be interpreted? As learning? As changes in preference? As falsification of the rationality hypothesis? Investigators acknowledge that it was *experimentally* impossible to distinguish between these alternatives. The problem does not seem to derive from the particular way in which rationality is formulated, although I am not sure how this could be proved. Rather it seems to derive from the fact that *any conceivable experiment necessarily tests simultaneously the hypothetical properties of the agent's preferences* and *their reasoning processes, and as a result it is not possible unequivocally to attribute wayward results to one or the other.*

However, another experimental example may suggest at least one irreducible element of this indeterminacy. In a classic experiment Amos Tversky asked a series of subjects to choose between:

1. A: a 50/50 chance of winning $1,000 or nothing, and
   B: a 100 per cent chance of winning $400

   and

2. C: a 1/10 chance of winning $1,000, and
   D: a 1/5 chance of winning $400.

Almost all subjects, naive or educated, chose B over A and C over D. This seems inconsistent with formal decision theory since the expected value of A is $1,000×1/2= $500, whilst the expected value of B is only $400, thus indicating a negative preference schedule for dollars, whilst preferring C over D is preferring an expected outcome of $100 over $80, indicating a positive preference schedule for dollars. Formally C and D each represent gambles with a 1/5 chance of the same outcomes as A and B, yet the opposite cell is chosen in each pair, violating the principle that equal value outcomes should be substitutable in the preference schedule. But, Tversky pointed out, the lack of *any* risk in choice B may in itself have had a value, so the results demonstrated risk aversion. However 'risk propensity' as another imputed psychological factor at work, only compounds the range of imputed unknowns we are trying to isolate and identify experimentally.

Moreover, it is worse than this, for Tversky then presented his subjects with the same choices, only with negative values:

1. A: a 50/50 chance of losing $1,000 or nothing, and
   B: a 100 per cent chance of losing $400

   and

2. C: a 1/10 chance of losing $1,000, and
   D: a 1/5 chance of losing $400.

This time A was preferred to B and D to C, once again demonstrating both negative and positive preference schedules for dollars, and violating the substitution constraint, but this time demonstrating risk-seeking. When negative outcomes were involved subjects violated their other preferences to seek a gamble for the same integer outcomes for which they had violated their other preferences to seek certainty when faced with positive outcomes.

To claim that this falsifies decision theory as a descriptive psychological theory seems to depend crucially on whether the subjects of the experiment shared the experimenter's characterization of the choices before them. The researcher wanted the individual to restrict their consideration to the relevant monetary values of the cells. But the negative outcome in A in the first table could be construed, *in the context of the other choices*, as 'missing out on getting $400', rather than an actuarial '$500'. Is this irrational? Only, it seems, by stipulation. Whether utility theory holds or not depends on how we allow individuals to construe the choices facing them. Tversky, Davidson, Hansson and others in the field conclude that there is 'no non-arbitrary way of deciding this within utility theory'.[18]

But if even the most rigorous attempts to specify what a rational economic actor is, turn out to produce indeterminate outcomes which *can only be rationalized by understanding how individuals construe the world facing them*, then surely, and as we have seen, any less rigorous formulations of the model must do so too. Rendering economic explanations determinate is then logically parasitic on an understanding of agents' knowledge. Accounts which offer explanations of past events without specifying agents' knowledge may appear successful, but they will always be under-determined without it.

Let me isolate the bones of the argument so far. Good explanation theories distinguish between what is to be explained and the terms used in the explanation. They also allow us to identify the conditions for the application of the theory independently from the formal part of the theory itself. Certain formulations of economic explanations, especially those of neo-classical economics as applied contemporarily, have serious trouble meeting the second criterion. They seem to meet the first criterion well enough since predicted prices seem distinct from the preferences they are supposed to model, indeed, distinct enough that their predictions sometimes fail.

When deployed retrospectively however, both of these problems are masked, for the historical data usually enables the circumstances in which the theory is being applied to be filled out, thus converting what might have been exposed as *ceteris paribus* assumptions into mere historical background fact. Secondly, the results of people's choices—whether substitutions of one activity for another, or price changes, are in fact known, and the imputation that these reveal preferences or values seems innocuous enough. However a rigorous analysis of the presuppositions behind the economic model of explanations seems to demonstrate that one or other of the criteria for a good explanation is breached. For if prices or actions are simply *identified* with revealed preferences then the one is not specifiable independently of the other (breaching the first condition), and it is furthermore then unclear what else it is they explain; and on the other hand if the attempt *is* made to articulate the relationship between preferences and action, the conditions for the application of the theory do not seem to be specifiable independently of the theory itself.

Actor's reasons explanations

So far the argument has proceeded by looking at attempts to generate explanatory relationships between actors and their behaviour through a reconstruction of the agent's desires, beliefs and procedures. However there is another way of gaining access to this information, and that is by the devastatingly simple expedient of listening to or reading what actors aver in speech or writing about these matters. If this seems a common-sensical, even banal approach, it is not without its pitfalls. However, I hope to show that it is superior to the one we have been considering.

On this view the explanation of the action is the reason the agent gives or would give for his or her doing it. It may be objected that I have shifted the ground by specifying my interests in 'actions' rather than events, processes etc. But I take it that in historical and social research events and processes comprise the (sometimes numerous) actions of individuals, and that there is no conceptual discontinuity between the two. There are some events—such as natural ones, e.g. the Lisbon earthquake—which of course do impinge on history (and they way they do so may well be seriously mediated by human action) but the event itself is not an action. Wars, famines, persecutions, enlightenments, revolutions (economic and otherwise) however are accumulations of, or constituted by, human actions. I take it we would rightly feel unhappy about the assertion of a social phenomenon that could not be unpacked in terms of individuals' actions, which is not of course to claim that the collective social result is always congruent with those acts or intentions. It is often claimed that genuine sociological explanations of the kinds essayed here in Bob Witkin's and Steven Mennell's essays must operate at a level of generality, and relate to social and structural phenomena which are simply not available at the individual level. To take the most famous example of this—Durkheim's explanations of suicide rates—it is clear that neither suicide *rates*, nor the social *anomie* which forms his explanation for one form of suicide, are properties of an individual. But a suicide is the *act* of an individual, and *anomie* is shorthand for a range of phenomena which are experienced by individuals in an every-day kind of way—frequent, or unexpected geographical relocation, absence of close relatives or supportive friends, uncertainty about how to evaluate social experiences and so on. To require that these explanations can always be *unpacked* in terms of actors' perceptions, is not to insist that they must always or continually be so, merely that we should be extremely sceptical about a social phenomenon which could not be.

The claim that reasons are explanations of actions may either seem uncontroversial to the point of banality, or so trivial as not to count as an explanation at all. Let us therefore, explore it further in the hope of anticipating each of these objections.

One way of bringing out the distinctive nature of this explanation is to contrast it with a third kind of explanation commonly claimed to typify those found in the natural sciences, often referred to as the covering law model of explanation. On this view instances are explained by showing that they fall under a suitable pre-established generalization. Thus the bursting of my daughter's balloon when placed near the fire can be explained as an instance of Boyle's Law, which is a generalization concerning the expansion of gasses exposed to heat, together with the finite elasticity of balloon rubber.

There are strong reasons for rejecting the applicability of this model to social phenomena, reasons well canvassed by J.S. Mill in his *A System of Logic*. In chapter 7 of Book VI of that work Mill refers the reader back to his discussion of the 'Chemical Method' in Book III chapter 10, where he had pointed out that deducing causes from observed effects can only operate where, as in the case of chemical phenomena, we can be reasonably sure that constant and simple causal relations obtain. This enables the 'method of difference' to be deployed. By looking at the different behaviour of compounds with and without, say, potassium, we can infer back from that behaviour certain properties of potassium without ever having to isolate it and analyse it individually. But where effects are the result of complex causes, and capable of being brought about by different causes, this 'method of difference' cannot be deployed. As an example Mill takes the issue—central to our concerns—of economic growth. We might expect that:

> If two nations can be found which are alike in all natural advantages and disadvantages; whose people resemble each other in every quality, physical and moral, spontaneous and acquired; whose habits, usages, opinions, laws and institutions are all the

same in all respects, except that one of them has a more protective tariff, or in other respects interferes more with freedom of industry; if one of these nations is found to be rich and the other poor, or one richer than the other, this will be found to be an *experimentum crucis*—a real proof by experience which of the two systems is most favourable to national riches.[19]

We might expect this to be the acid test, but it would not, and could not be. Firstly, the possibility of two countries being alike in all these respects is extremely remote. But even if we were to find such a case, says Mill, the existence of these similarities at an institutional and societal level 'are the effects of pre-existing causes' which may be many and interrelated in a variety of different ways, and quite incapable of being isolated by ticking off the similarities and leaving the differences:

> Why must the prosperous nation have prospered from one cause exclusively? National prosperity is always the collective result of a number of favourable circumstances, and of these the restrictive nation may unite a greater number than either of the others, although it may have all of those circumstances in common with either one or the other of them.[20]

The objections to this method apply whether we are trying to explain growth, assuming stagnation to be the norm, or, as Eric Jones does, explain non-growth, having assumed growth to be the norm. Several of the arguments reviewed in his paper seem to deploy this 'method of difference'.

However there is a further objection to this natural science model which, as promised, highlights the difference between explanations in terms of natural science generalizations and explanations in terms of cultural meaning or 'actor's reasons'. The classic exposition of this is Alasdair MacIntyre's discussion of Weber's attempt to establish an explanatory link between Protestantism and capitalism. Weber's method is Mill's method of difference.

> He shows that in China and in India all the preconditions of capitalism evident in Europe were present, except for Protestantism. But capitalism did not arise. Hence we have good reason to suppose that Protestantism is the cause of capitalism.[21]

Now MacIntyre is sympathetic to the idea that there is a link between Protestantism and capitalism. What he resists, and what I suggest he is

right in resisting, is that the link can be established either through
the measure of residues, or indeed through *any* assumption that the
relationships between belief and action can be characterized in terms of
scientific generalizations. Because the links claimed to be established by
scientific generalizations are contingent, they *could* link any belief and
any action. But if we reflect for a moment, this is not usually the import
of explanations in terms of beliefs. If I claim to be concerned about my
garden, and believe that drought will ruin it, and yet in the absence of
water restrictions and with opportunity to do so, fail to water it, this must
cast doubt on the belief. But it does not do so because it discomfits the
generalization that 'concern about gardens is highly correlated with
watering activity in droughts'. Indeed there need be no such generalization, indeed, no other gardens or gardeners but this one. The expectation that the gardener will water is established by the intentionality
implicit in his statement of his concerns and the actions necessary
to attend to them. In other words it is not by trying to construct
generalizations in which capitalism and Protestantism figure (or fail to
figure) that the link is established, but by looking at what a Protestant
believer claims to believe and what actions such beliefs seem likely to
result in. In fact, Weber does articulate such a connection between belief
and action, and this, in both MacIntyre's view, and my own, renders at
the least unnecessary, and at worst quite misleading the use of scientific-
type, generalizations:

> Weber in fact presents us with capitalist actions as the conclusion
> of a practical syllogism which has Protestant premises. To discern
> this logical relationship between belief and action was an
> enormous achievement. And because the achievement was this,
> the use of Mill's methods is entirely out of place; we do not need
> to juggle with causal alternatives. India and China did not
> strengthen and could not weaken his case about Europe. For it is
> not a question of whether there is a purely contingent relationship
> between isolable phenomena. And so constant conjunction is
> neither here nor there.[22]

Explanations based on actor's reasons (or beliefs) are then quite distinct
from explanations of the covering law kind. For actor's reasons *are*, as
we have seen, tied to their actions by more than constant conjunction.
The relationship between intention and act is in fact far more intimate
than that. So intimate that even though the intentions are present,
and realized in practice, if the action does not instantiate the intention

then the action is not sufficiently explained by it. Consider an admittedly extreme case:

> Oedipus hating his father, and bent on killing him, finds his way blocked by an old man.
> Enraged at being impeded, Oedipus killed the old man in his rage to get past.
> Unknown to Oedipus, the old man *was* his father.

Although Oedipus intended to kill his father, indeed, although he *did* kill his father, and even although it was his desire to kill his father that caused him to kill the old man that was his father, we cannot quite fully explain his killing his father in terms of his intention to do so. And the reason is that his desire and intentions were not effectively linked to the act in the right way. That is to say his act did not instantiate his intention in such a way as to render the intention a (sufficient) explanation of the act. The recourse to such nice philosophical distinctions as these is often ridiculed by social scientists, and held up as an example of the banality of theory. Yet in explanation, no less than in assessing guilt, blame and responsibility, the identification of intention and the kind of link that exists between intentions and their outcomes is clearly crucial.

If actor's perceptions and intentions *are* intimately related, are they, perhaps *too* closely related? It is sometimes said in explaining why intentions do not relate to actions in the way that causes and effects relate to each other under the covering law model, that they relate to each other 'logically'. This, I think, is misleading, for the relationship is certainly not an analytic one—it makes sense to assert the existence of intention and deny the existence of action, indeed, in the Oedipus case both are present, but not properly connected. The sad fate of poor Oedipus' father illustrates a perhaps surprising feature of actor's reasons explanations. That is that in them intention and action are logically independent, thus fulfilling the first criterion of all good explanations. For although intentions *do* explain actions, intentions can be present without the action (although not vice versa). There is a sense in which the meaningfulness of the action is intimately related to the meaningfulness of the intention, and in such a way, as we have seen, that any failure to sustain that symmetry breaks the explanatory link. This notion is generally true but it begins to bear a lot of weight as we move away from particular individual actions to classes of actions which bear a lot of conventional content. Thus my action in running into no-man's land carrying a white flag, *can* be explained by my desire to surrender, because of the conventional meaning attached not only to 'showing a white flag', but also to the action of 'surrendering'. My reasons for surrendering, must, of course, also be exposed.

Actor's reasons seems to provide what the economic model lacked—a way into the specific values, aims, repertoire of tasks, conceptions of action and agency which might specify what an actor might have in mind in making choices. They are therefore capable of providing the economic model with what, if I am right, it cannot do without in order to provide an explanation, namely an understanding of the specific perceptions and values which inform agents' decision-making processes.

However, there is, or seems to be, a serious objection. Although actors reasons are logically specifiable independently of their actions and so stand in the right relationship to each other, it might still be asked: how do we empirically identify intentions? For if we cannot specify how an intention can be empirically identified independently of the actions they purport to explain then we are going to fail the second test of a good explanation, that of being able to specify the conditions for its application.

It is true of course that 'intentions' construed as the private mental antecedents of action are not directly recoverable, indeed, according to some philosophers, it is not even clear that it makes sense to talk of such events or actions. It is worth, nevertheless, making the not entirely polemical point that even this view of intentions makes them no more and no less mysterious and metaphysical than utilities or preference schedules proved to be in the economic story. But, despite what might appear from the discussion of the explanation of individual actions, this is not in any case what is meant by 'intention' or 'reason' by anyone who asserts this method. The construal of intention is an attempt to explicate an irreducibly public and not an inscrutably private meaning.

On one strong view, deriving from Wittgenstein, the irreducibly public character of intention and belief are entailed by two propositions. Firstly the impossibility of a private language, and secondly by the meaning-bearing content of action as opposed to mere behaviour. If actions are essentially meaningful, and if action, as I would argue, constitutes most of what social scientists and historians are interested in, those meanings must be publicly available. For only language, or language analogues, can bear meaning, and to do so they must be public. Meaningfulness is public.

The injunction to discover the intentions of agents, is therefore based on the belief that the possible kinds of activity, aims, and beliefs available to human agents in any historical circumstance must be drawn from a kind of public repertoire which is presented to them in their culture (not necessarily of course, 'high' culture either). Consequently what it could occur to someone to want to do at any particular time and place must be shaped and limited by that individual's cultural forms. To play a game of football, the game must exist. To be able to surrender the conception and conventions of surrender must exist. To write a satire, the genre must exist. How genres are invented and repertoires extended is an interesting, but not insuperable problem which involves demonstrating the unintended emergent properties of cultural performances, the kind of demonstration at which social thinkers, following Mandeville, became increasingly adept in the eighteenth century. Thus 'intentions' are not private, but short for 'the socially available repertoire of meaningful actions'.

Agents' beliefs about what is the case, beliefs about the possible consequences of their actions, are, then, in principle recoverable. In any given case the amount of information needed to establish this may or may not be available, but this is an empirical question. Such information must be gathered where it can. The Rev. Ian Paisley provided a most revealing insight into the nature of Protestant fundamentalism, and therefore into the whole Northern Ireland imbroglio when, on *Desert Island Disks*, he nominated as his one book to go with the Bible and Shakespeare, Foxe's *Book of Martyrs*. Unless we can reconstruct the pattern of beliefs that go with such choices, (and the accompanying conviction that the Pope is Antichrist) we will fail to understand an important part of the situation there. Such understanding is not entering actors' minds, or rethinking their thoughts or any one of a number of such fanciful, but impossible, enterprises often attributed to those espousing this kind of cultural explanation; nor has it anything to do with the project of intuitive empathy which caused so much trouble in the recent debate about history teaching in schools. Recovering agents' intentions involves hard and painstaking work, reading what they read, seeking out the connections they might have made between apparently isolated or contradictory beliefs.

An example that catches what I am talking about, is given in Stephen Mennell's recounting of the story of the French General, his troops and the eclipse. The explanation of their different responses to the eclipse cannot even be articulated without reference to the intentions and meanings of the actors—by which I refer not to anything irrecoverably private, but to their shared and socially given sense of reality and their relationship to it.

It is important to be clear about what is being included and what is being excluded in the notion of 'actor's reasons'. I am including in 'actor's reasons explanations' an identification of their intentions in terms of their beliefs, their aims and ideals, and their conceptions of reality and available actions. I am dubious about the status of motives, and I am excluding roles or anything to do with them. Roles can be reasons for (a rather inauthentic kind of) action, but they cannot be reasons for belief. Or more specifically, the occupation of a role cannot be the actor's own reason for belief. Although people *say* things like 'having gas shares, I believe privatisation is good for the country', they never mean by that to justify the proposition supposedly believed: they never mean 'Because of the fact that I have gas shares, privatisation is good for the country.'[23]

It is of course possible that actors may have economic reasons for acting and that these can then constitute explanations for such action. But these would still be actor's reasons explanations, rather than the kind of economic explanations criticized in the earlier part of this paper. This is potentially confusing, and an example may help.[24]

In a major work, Robinson and Gallagher set out to challenge economic interpretations of imperialism in the particular case of the British occupation of Egypt in 1882.[25] Studying the justifications provided by the political actors involved, they concluded that the reasons explaining the occupation were (as given) mainly political. In a celebrated and critical discussion of the Gallagher and Robinson thesis, Hopkins has reasserted a kind of 'economic' explanation. But his clinching evidence is not the circumstantial one of the scale of British economic involvement in Egypt, but the discovery that other actors involved, businessmen and officials in Egypt, convinced of the danger to their economic assets, deliberately lobbied Dilke at the Foreign Office and Lord Hartington the India Secretary with exaggerated reports of the *political* danger. He concludes:

> the evidence collated in this essay has indicated that intervention did not spring from any danger to the Canal, from the spread of anarchy, or from French ambitions, but from the conscious and sustained defence of Britain's expanding economic interests in Egypt.[26]

This is emphatically *not* the triumph of 'economic explanation' over 'actor's reasons' explanations', rather it is the substitution of one set of actor's reasons for another, which we have reason to believe, in this particular case, to be those that operated. Being committed to actor's reasons explanations does not commit us to anything quite so naive as always believing what actors *tell* us are their reasons: people do of course, dissemble.[27] But even when they do it is not invariably the case that the concealed reasons are 'economic'.

Explanation can often only render the unfamiliar familiar, once it has succeeded in first refamiliarizing us with a sometimes very strange background. Stephen Mennell suggests, following Elias, that belief in animism and witchcraft can be explained through a supportive inter-action between individuals' 'extreme insecurity and hazard to life' and their concentration on emotional responses needed to deal with that. As a result 'their knowledge remains innocently egocentric and emotionally involved.' This may fit the credulous peasant but it does not explain why obviously sophisticated and intelligent writers like Bodin believed there were witches in league with the devil—with, needless to say, important consequences for many old and lonely women. To do this it is vital to understand the status of the Bible in Bodin's world in order to create the context within which witchcraft belief can be rendered explicable as part of a whole, and highly developed, culture. Once we do this, paradoxically it is the (for us) perfectly comprehensible rejection of witchcraft by Thomas Hobbes that needs explaining, not Bodin's credulity.[28] Focussing on actors' reasons is necessary even to re-establish correctly the agenda of what it is that requires explaining.

The ambivalence of economic explanation insidiously undermines the possibility of realizing this. For inasmuch as economic explanations function as *covert ascriptions* of motives to historical actors, they block off attempts to discover actors' true perceptions and intentions. In doing this they render the unfamiliar, familiar, by making other and earlier cultures *appear* to be motivated in the same way as our own. But this, however comforting it may be, is to falsify and impoverish history (or indeed other perceptions of contemporary reality) as well as to blind us to the culturally specific nature of our own motivational self-description, which, as Dario Castiglione's essay reminds us, is itself a cultural product, and a highly ambiguous one at that.

Conclusion

Actor's reasons explanations, unlike economic explanations, I hold, fulfill the minimal good explanation criteria laid down at the start of the paper. The explanation (actors' beliefs, intentions, conceptions of action etc.) are logically distinct from what is to be explained: what they did. Secondly the conditions for the application of the explanation: the particular circum-stances of the agent and their particular interpretation of the theory's categories are independently specifiable—it is possible to frame an account of Oedipus intending to commit patricide (and even actually killing his father in the process), yet distinguish the intention from the act. Actor's reasons explanations explain by locating a unique act within a potentially ever-increasing network of beliefs and perceptions on the part of the actor which are mutually supportive and validating. The more we learn of these, the more we understand the action, the more we can explain it.

Notes

1. I should like to express thanks for critical comment to the participants in the symposium, but in particular to Eric Jones whose original paper initiated this riposte and to the two editors for their stimulating objections. Thanks are also due to Martin Hollis who commented with typical generosity and encouragement on an early draft and to Bill Jordan for years of discussions on these matters. The usual disclaimers apply.
2. A characteristically witty and accessible discussion of these issues is Martin Hollis, *The Cunning of Reason* (Cambridge, 1987).
3. Thomas Hobbes, *Leviathan* (1651), part IV, ch. 46, pp. 374–5. The identification of a vacuum did historically involve severe difficulties. See Steven Shapin and Simon Schaffer *Leviathan and the Air Pump*, (Princeton, 1985).
4. M. Hollis and E. Nell, *Rational Economic Man* (Cambridge, 1975), pp. 25–6.
5. For a good introduction see the relevant sections of Brian Barry, *Economists, Sociologists and Democracy* (1970) or Michael Laver, *The Politics of Private Desires* (Harmondsworth, 1981) or (more critically) Anthony Heath, *Rational Choice and Social Exchange* (Cambridge, 1976). The literature has become extraordinarily sophisticated, for an accessible presentation see Russell Hardin, *Collective Action* (Baltimore, 1982).
6. Hollis, *Cunning of Reason*, p.17.
7. Milton Friedman, *Essays in Positive Economics* (Cambridge, Mass., 1953), pp. 14–15.
8. P. Samuelson, 'Comment on E. Nagel's "Assumptions in Economic Theory"', in *The Collected Scientific Papers of Paul A. Samuelson* (Cambridge, Mass., 1966), vol. II, p. 1175.
9. Paul Oppenheim, *Essays in Honour of Carl G. Hempel* (Dordrecht, 1969), p. 3.
10. L. Von Mises, *Human Action: A treatise on economics* (1949), p. 15.
11. Douglas C. North, *Structure and Change in Economic History* (New York, 1981), pp. 74 ff.

12. As North admits, ibid., p. 85.

13. Ibid., p. 81.

14. Ibid., pp. 80–1, 79.

15. Most influentially Robert Axelrod, *The Evolution of Cooperation* (New York, 1984); M. Taylor, *Anarchy and Cooperation* (New York, 1976); id., *The Possibility of Cooperation* (Cambridge, 1987).

16. Marshall Sahlins, *Stone Age Economics* (1974), ch. I ('The Original Affluent Society').

17. On under-determination in inductively based explanations see W.V. Quine, 'On empirically equivalent systems of the world', *Erkenntnis* 9 (1975), pp. 313–28. I am not aware that this has been argued to be also a property of economic explanations.

18. Amos Tversky, 'A Critique of Expected Utility Theory: Descriptive and normative considerations', *Erkenntnis* 9 (1975), pp. 163–73. See also Bengt Hansson, 'The Appropriateness of the expected utility model', ibid., pp. 175–93 and Donald Davidson, P. Suppes and P. Seigel, *Decision-Making: An experimental approach* (Stanford, 1957). Davidson gave up his career as an experimental psychologist as a result of this work and became a philosopher: the resulting work is in *Essays on Actions and Events* (Oxford, 1980).

19. J.S. Mill, *A System of Logic* (1967) Book VI, vii, p. 575.

20. Ibid., p. 576.

21. Alasdair MacIntyre, 'A Mistake about Causality in Social Science', in Peter Laslett and W.G. Runciman (eds), *Politics, Philosophy and Society*, vol. II (Oxford, 1962), p. 49.

22. Ibid.. p. 55.

23. Gerry Cohen, 'Beliefs and Roles' *Proceedings of the Aristotelian Society* 41 (1966–7), pp. 17–34 and Jonathan Glover (ed.), *Philosophy of Mind* (Oxford, 1976).

24. I am most grateful to Michael Havinden who originally introduced this example into the discussion.

25. R. Robinson and G. Gallagher, *Africa and the Victorians. The official mind of imperialism* (2nd edn., 1981).

26. A.G. Hopkins, 'The Victorians and Africa: A reconsideration of the occupation of Egypt, 1882', *Journal of African History*, 27 (1986), p. 385.

27. It is quite possible to sophisticate the account so as to deal with deception. See, e.g., Quentin Skinner, 'The Principles and Practice of Opposition: The case of Bolingbroke versus Walpole', in N. McKendrick (ed.), *Historical Perspectives: Essays in honour of J.H. Plumb* (1974).

28. The example is discussed by Quentin Skinner, 'A Reply to my Critics', in James Tully (ed.), *Meaning and Context: Quentin Skinner and his critics* (Oxford, 1988), pp. 236–8.

Part II
Production and Culture

Culture, Environment and the Historical Lag in Asia's Industrialization

E.L. Jones

Cultural explanation

The industrialization of much of East Asia, especially Japan, raises fundamental questions about the sources of economic growth. It also challenges the common assumption that growth is essentially or necessarily Western in origin. Two major issues which need to be discussed concern the propositions, firstly, that its culture denied Japan (or East Asia) the prize of industrializing spontaneously, while mysteriously enhancing its prospects of eventual imitative growth, and second that its natural environment created an economic structure incapable of industrializing on its own.

Influential circles in contemporary Japan believe that its culture is formative of economic life, not to mention inherently superior. In 1988 the Japanese Ministry of Education's Commission for UNESCO compiled for reprinting in English a series of 'Classics on Modern Japanese Thought and Culture'. This comprises ten volumes, originally published in Japanese, one in 1911, the remainder between 1921 and 1947. Titles include *Japanese Spirituality* (1945), *The Ways of Thinking of Eastern Peoples* (1947), *Studies in Shinto Thought* (1934), and of special note for present purposes, *Climate and Culture—A Philosophical Study* (1935) by Tetsuro Watsuji. An advertisement in *The Times Literary Supplement* (April 28–May 4, 1989) proclaims that, 'the republication of this series will be of great benefit for foreign people, in the context of growing cultural and economic exchange between their countries and Japan.'

Thus some Japanese think that 'foreign people' can be helped to understand the people of the Japanese Miracle by a series of books on culture, almost all of them published in the unfortunate period between 1934 and 1947. At least one of these works, Watsuji's, sees a nexus between the natural environment and Japanese attitudes or behaviour. A bestseller in the original, it portrays Japanese culture as specially forged in a special setting.

What, then, is this power of both culture and the environment to produce, shape or even check impulses towards industrialization and economic growth? With respect to culture, the question seems almost redundant. Commonly-accepted elements of 'culture' are plain to see; national 'cultures' are discussed to the point of stereotype; and in the literature of history and social science there are many assertions to the effect that 'culture', broad though the term is, constitutes a major explanatory variable. Furthermore there is a tendency to claim that culture is primary and economics secondary or 'socially embedded'.[1] Yet this distinction is at best a Little Ender, Big Ender one. It has to be demonstrated, not casually asserted, that culture influences the economy more than the economy influences culture, just as evolutionary biologists need to show, not merely assume, that culture adapts to biological imperatives.[2]

Culture is patently observable, even though it is a complex array of institutions and values with poorly defined boundaries. That Japanese or Chinese culture, say, differs from Western culture is not in real doubt, subject to specifying the elements included. This reality of culture may, however, be a crust on the surface, what Braudel might have called the 'factual history'. It needs to be explicitly ascertained whether the content inside the cultural labelling genuinely stays the same, whoever the ruler, whatever the regime, whatever the material or demographic circumstances, so that it is culture that mainly holds the sway and is itself largely unswayed.

Much discussion of the topic is rather uncritical. Only occasionally do we find an author who truly spells out his methodological position. One who does is Simon. In writing about demography he concludes that, 'in the context of *long-run* analysis [historically the crucial and distinctive aspect, ELJ], culture and values do *not* have independent lives . . . Rather, values and culture serve as intermediate variables between economic conditions and fertility, serving only to transmit the effect of income onto fertility behaviour . . .'[3] He sees values as neutral in the long run, though capable of cushioning the effects of changes in income or other variables in the short run, before the values themselves respond to economic change. He even hazards that the lag is about 25 or 50 years.

For the historian, the interest lies in these lags. Whatever the extent to which cultural variables adapt to changing prices, or ecological circumstances, they clearly do not do so instantaneously. Thus cultural history acquires a temporary autonomy as a result of the conservatism of human institutions. In a similar fashion, institutions and 'history' itself (prior experience) act to change the attitudes of others and in this fashion may have some life beyond the period and circumstances that created them. This does not however guarantee them complete exemption from current as well as past formative economic influences. Disentangling these reciprocal effects is clearly difficult. I do not want to pretend to resolve such a deep issue in a few words but merely to point out that many historians tend to resolve it only by assuming the independent force of culture without acknowledging either the possibility of deeper economic causation or the probable nature of lags and consequent transience of 'factual history'.

Where strong cultural traditions persist there may be little economic growth: but is it the traditions which determine this, or does the absence of economic change mean that no adjustment of values and practices has been brought about? Which drives or how do they interact? It is very hard to get a purchase on the topic in many historical writings, since these are seldom as clearly thought out as Simon's about the relationship between economic and cultural change. The entire area needs more attention. Nevertheless, my working hypothesis is that Simon is close to the mark. Note that the long history of characteristic differences between, for example, Western and Eastern culture does not invalidate this: all it need say is that there may have been no abiding reason for cultural phenomena to alter or merge. It is hardly surprising that societies persist with familiar practices in the absence of fresh and compelling circumstances or significant competition. For most of history the great traditions were not in the same market for ideas, they were effectively isolated. In isolation their distinctive features were not called on to change.

We can certainly perceive that since the nineteenth century there has been economic change in Japan and other East Asian countries: they have adopted and even improved on Western technology. At the economic level the 'factual history' has thus been amended, involving a massive accommodation in ways of life. There seems no reason to suppose in this case that the economic change was other than independently produced, with culture adapting to it.

This malleability of culture has to be noted, because the notions of fixity so common in historical writing cannot explain cultural origins or cope with the occurrence of change, for example change in one region but not another within the same culture area. One means whereby cultural values adjust is through cognitive dissonance. Rather than values being perpetual and determining, on occasions when conditions oblige the individual to change his or her actual behaviour a dissonance is set up in the mind, leading to a change in expressed values—a rationalization of what has been done and must now be lived with.[4] Similarly, where there is no apparent alteration in historical price or wage series, often taken to mean a primacy of 'non-economic' culture, in reality other economic properties may have varied—as with the 'coca-cola fallacy' in which the quantity or quality of a traded commodity shifts while leaving the customary price unchanged: a bottle of coke long remained at a dime but the size of the bottle decreased in stages.

What this amounts to is an affirmation that whatever our culture we are all brothers and sisters under the skin, and all subject to economic inducements. Culture is vital to our social identity at any one time but not necessarily to our long-term biological or economic selves. It is when we study societies cross-sectionally that culture looms so large: Islamic and other fundamentalisms are prominent phenomena, but they may be frictional or 'over-labelled' ones. They may not have the same 'content' as fifty years ago or in fifty years' time, especially if they come to be affected by rapid economic growth. Certainly they have force in the here and now, but the present may be viewed as a perpetual lag period, always adjusting towards but never actually catching up with underlying economic changes.

If we now start to approach the topic of East Asian industrialization, the commonest explanation of the region's apparent failure to industrialize first or independently is indeed a cultural one and derives from Weberianism. The thesis, put crudely, is that Confucianism was incapable of generating fundamental change because it lacked the values of the Protestant Ethic, notably thrift and hard work.[5] But this type of hypothesis cannot explain the different economic fortunes of regions which shared Confucian philosophy or the divergent economic performance of Confucian societies at different periods of history.[6] The result is that we have no reason to suppose that it can explain the differences between West and East. A related argument that East Asia, or at any rate China (gently Buddhist on this occasion?), lacked the manipulative drive for 'Faustian Mastery' which permitted the Western world to transmute natural resources into economic growth and simultaneously foul its habitat is an equally unsuccessful one.[7] When it comes to explaining long-run economic change, culturist arguments are arbitrary, one-sided, and fail a number of tests. They do not eliminate other possibilities. They pretend to an operational significance that culture is not shown to possess and cannot account for the variety of observed experience. Do arguments based on differences in the natural environment fare any better?

Oshima's environmental model

An appropriate model which interprets the history of East Asian industrialization in environmental terms appears in an article and book by Harry T. Oshima.[8] This will be taken as representative of the *genre* and dissected here. His primary concern is to explain the divergent growth performances of the various regions of monsoon Asia since 1945. He divides the region as Caesar did Gaul, examining the spectacular growth of parts of East Asia, the stirrings of a similar achievement in parts of Southeast Asia, and the absence so far of comparable growth in South Asia.

The different performances between the extreme modern cases are of course well known and often illustrated. T.N. Srinivasan has noted that whereas in 1965 India exported eight times, and the Republic of China ten times, the value of the manufactured goods exported by South Korea, the tables were so turned by 1986 that South Korea was exporting 4.5 times the value of India's manufactured exports and 1.5 times the value of China's.[9] There is clearly something for the development economist to explain.

However, Oshima notes that unlike Europe or North America the whole of monsoon Asia was poor until 1945. As we shall see this can be a little misleading but it is generally correct and the problem is thus not merely the recent divergence among Asian regions. The weaker examples of post-1945 growth would have been remarkable at most earlier periods; the general fact of transition to significant rates of growth in Asia has therefore to be explained. Moreover the pre-1945 condition itself needs to be explained unless we are to go on thinking of poverty as a state of nature: not only growth needs attention but non-growth too, especially once we realize that economic growth has had a fluctuating rather than a single stop-start history. There is evidently work for the economic historian as well as the development economist.

Instead of taking the customary approach of mentioning earlier poverty and afterwards ignoring it, Oshima investigates at some length what he perceives to have been the original equilibrium state. He thus starts by giving a background history of Asia and goes on to construct a model whereby its long poverty is to be understood. The model depends on the reported inability of complex, seasonal wet-rice agriculture to release labour to industry. This is the heart of the thesis—the ecological rigidity of monsoon farming with respect to the release of labour. The significance of this aspect of monsoon agriculture is pointed up, virtually justified, by contrasting it with a version of European economic history in which agricultural change did supposedly release labour and make possible rural domestic industries and the early factories.

The present paper will mention some positive aspects of Oshima's methodology but go on to criticize the following features:

(1) some elements of the methodology as it is applied to the particular case.
(2) the version offered of Asian (or Chinese) agricultural history.
(3) the contrasting version of European (or English) agricultural history.
(4) the formulation of the problem as one where the Asian 'lag' is to be explained by the absence of processes thought to be crucial because they seem to have occurred in the course of European economic growth.

Finally a more general explanation is put forward as to why Asia and other non-European areas remained poor (or non-industrial) until later than Europe. This alternative explanation shifts the responsibility from Asia's farming environment to its institutions, notably in the political sphere. It rejects the virtual technological determinism which makes the imperatives of wet rice cultivation the centrepiece and certainly does not depend on supposed differences between 'Western' and 'Eastern' cultures.[10]

There is a long historiography of environmental and technological determinism in many countries, of which the work of Karl Wittfogel on Chinese 'hydraulic agriculture' is the best known. The supposed ability of wet-rice cultivation to over-power its creators appears and reappears in the literature until the present day. In Japan, Watsuji's *Climate and Culture* was of this type. It contained a section on 'The Distinctive Nature of Monsoon Climate' and despite the fact that this includes many unsupported assertions about cause and effect, whereas Oshima provides a tighter model connecting monsoonal ecology and economic activity, the latter's work may perpetuate the tradition exemplified by Watsuji's book and the like.

An integrated account of the relationship between institutional and environmental factors would of course require a total economic history of Asia. For the moment it seems worthwhile to establish that the monsoon model is insufficiently general, and that, if we consider more realistic versions of agricultural history both East and West, ecological considerations appear instead to have been dominated by institutional ones.

Faced with a litany of corrections, it may seem that Oshima's work is being rejected out of hand but this is not the case. The cogency and importance of his work are precisely what make it worth debating. Indeed, Oshima begins with a methodological statement that is particularly appealing to the economist-economic historian. Since, as he observes, growth and development theories abstract from so much, Oshima urges the broadest study: he wants to 'catch as many fish as possible'. He thinks that economists know better than other social scientists what are the proximate, strictly economic, factors in growth and development. As a result they are the ones who ought to set the agenda. It is also their place to identify the ultimate forces acting on the economy, deep forces that other social scientists may then probe. In Asia, he declares, history deserves special attention; there, the long gestation period of the basic forces means that the seeds of growth lay in a distant past which the modern student must try to understand.

Application

When he turns to explaining the long poverty of Monsoon Asia, Oshima begins by quoting extracts on China from the major specialists, such as Joseph Needham, John Fairbank and Edwin Reischauer, who expatiate on what he calls 'stability'. Fairbank and Reischauer state that:

> The political, social and intellectual systems were basically so viable and so well balanced that not until this balance was destroyed by massive external blows in the nineteenth century was Chinese society again set in rapid motion . . . It was during this period that they fell behind the West in many aspects of material culture and technology as well as certain forms of economic and political organizations . . .[11]

while Needham proclaims that:

> There is no special mystery about the relatively 'steady state' of Chinese society . . . China was a coherent agrarian land-mass, a

unified empire since the third century BC with an administrative
tradition unmatched elsewhere till modern times . . . cemented
into one by an infrangible system of ideographic script . . . The
greater population of China was self-sufficient . . . the Chinese,
wise before their time, worked out an organic theory of the
Universe . . .[12]

These specialists however offer no compelling explanation of supposed
economic stasis and describe continued slow change even while talking as
though some ceiling had been reached.

The remainder of the Asian continent was, Oshima notes, 'turning
inwards'. This remark often appears in writings about Asia during what
was in European terms late medieval or early modern times.[13] A withdrawal from active overseas involvements certainly does seem to have
taken place. To the extent that this is to be blamed for 'backwardness',
the explanation is internalist. It is therefore radically different from the
fashionable neo-Marxist theories which, by exaggerating the scale and
likely consequences of Western influence at this early period, find the
cause of under-development to have been 'unfair' European trade.

'Turning inward' is a mysterious-sounding phenomenon. Why should a
number of separate Asian polities have been retreating from an involvement with the outer world, or even one another, in the century or so
before the Western intrusion? We may speculate that their individual
political cycles, as described for the countries of Southeast Asia by
Lieberman, happened to fall into negative phase.[14] These cycles were
versions of the dynastic cycle. In addition, it is at least open to argument
that there may have been a degree of substitution of religious concerns
for material ones, as a result of the approximately contemporaneous
missionizing by the major religions: Islam, Buddhism, Confucianism and
finally Christianity.[15] 'Turning inward' at least has the merit compared
with most arguments about cultural values or the environment that it
would be possible to make it historically specific.

Oshima asks why, if China 'fell behind', she did not borrow from
Europe as Europe had previously borrowed from her. The point to note is
that both 'turning inward' and 'failing to borrow' suggest time-specific
repressants on growth prospects. They suggest that there was a retreat
from the overseas market and from the prospect of vigorous technological
borrowing, both as a result of some potentially identifiable set of decisions.
This is a quite different explanatory mode from that of Oshima's actual
model, which is couched in terms of an environmental constant.

With respect to the environmental model, an assumption which may be queried concerns the necessity for the Chinese (monsoon Asians?) to labour intensively and exclusively at growing wet rice. The implication is that monsoon Asia was caught in a vicious circle in which the population had to increase in order to grow more rice for the growing population. Elsewhere in *Economic Growth in Monsoon Asia* Oshima explicitly refers to birthrates as a function of labour demand.[16] This notion of a demographic merry-go-round driven by the ecological peculiarities of the rice crop leaves unexplored the possibility of social choice, channelled by political, legal or customary institutions.

A further assumption is that wet-rice agriculture necessarily sustained a particular political structure, while those in power were effectively constrained by the limitations of the production system. Yet non-monsoon agricultures in the pre-modern world also sustained dynasty after dynasty of rulers and achieved equally little in the way of growth. The exploitative type of regime was more general than *monsoon* agriculture.

It is noteworthy that the historical literature cited by Oshima, and much of his discussion, tends to refer to China rather than to the whole of monsoon Asia. He defends this by observing that China's centralized bureaucracy left archives which do not exist in other lands. However, it is by no means certain that China is an acceptable proxy for monsoon Asia in its entirety or that the wet-rice river basins of China can stand even for the whole of China.

The matter becomes significant because Oshima intermittently shifts his ground between China and Asia on the one hand and England (which similarly dominates the Western literature) and Europe on the other. This use of proxies is not necessarily to be condemned. Nevertheless it complicates a reading of the thesis not only to have to consider the acceptability of the Asian proxies but to keep adjusting for the fact that English practice is a poor guide to practice in continental Europe. England and Europe are not agriculturally synonymous and 'lumping' needs to be done with care. All in all, building a comparative historical model of Asian and European economic development begins to seem a more intricate task than it may have done at first.

The Asian (Chinese) model

There was no choice in monsoon Asia, Oshima asserts, but to grow rice because under the reigning conditions of temperature and moisture rice produces the highest output per unit of land.[17] Oshima details the intensive activity of transplanting and harvesting rice and the complex operations involved in growing it under conditions of irrigation. He urges that the costs of monitoring labour under such a system would have been too high to move from small peasant family farms to the supposedly 'capitalistic' agriculture of Europe employing cheap hired hands.

Reportedly, the operations in monsoon agriculture were strictly seasonal. Farming was possible for only half the year but during that half there was so much work that labour was needed desperately. None could be spared for manufacturing work. (The assumption is that if little or no labour were released into rural industries this was because monsoon agriculture was incapable of releasing it, not that there were too few incentives to do so). The arable land was required to support the dense human population and very little could be spared to provide feed for horses or oxen. This reduced the available power for traction and haulage.

Transport and communications were so poor that handicraft workers supposedly could not travel to the cities even in the off-season. Workshops in the large, clustered villages supplied local markets for handicraft manufactures but dense regional concentrations of rural industry could not emerge, not only because they would have interrupted the supply of labour during the monsoon season but seemingly because the transport of goods would have been too difficult. As to the transition to full-scale industry, productivity was so low in the early, steam-powered factories that industrial wages were insufficient to draw labour off the farm. This argument seems quite distinct from the argument about inflexible agricultural work schedules, which ought to have made a case of this kind unnecessary.

By a further, also almost over-determined, argument the growth of manufacturing industry in China is said to have been impeded by the guilds. In Western Europe, on the other hand, non-mechanized but 'capitalistic' manufactures displaced the guilds. This particular explanation of Chinese experience in terms of the absence of a European process turns out to be triply inappropriate—firstly because the guilds in China never possessed the autonomy from the state exercised by European, especially English, guilds.[18] Their role was weaker, their dissolution was not crucial, and a different English word from 'guild' ought to be found for the Chinese institutions. Second, European guilds slowly faded away or adjusted to growth when it came and it is not made clear why the Chinese 'guilds' could not have done so. Third, it remains necessary to explain how the Chinese 'guilds' were eventually displaced. It is unsatisfactory to portray them as capable of blocking industrial growth in one period and simply vanishing by another. In China the 'guilds' did finally melt away when economic change intruded and the state found better and cheaper means of overseeing industrial producers. These so-called 'guilds' were the creatures of politics and economics, not their masters. Causation may have run in the opposite direction from the one indicated, from eventual growth to institutional change, not from institutional blockage to no growth. It ought also to be considered in this respect, too, how far the Chinese experience really did represent that of all monsoon Asia.

Oshima's model seems to ignore the rural concentrations of domestic and workshop industry that did arise in Qing China and Tokugawa Japan. In the latter there was a high degree of inter-regional trade, much of it coastal and using a specially-designed cargo vessel (like the Dutch *fluit*), the *bezaisen* or *sengokubune*.[19] This vessel was cheap to operate, with a large cargo capacity relative to its size, able to carry 100 tons of rice. It went a long way to solving any problem of transport. Japanese peasant industries were enabled to match the scale and skill of rural domestic industrial districts in Europe. As Bronfenbrenner has pointed out, industrializing Japan possessed a large reservoir of skilled labour, rural and (already in the Tokugawa period) urban.[20]

Given this history, the difficulties of rural-urban labour mobility and traffic in goods in Japan and indeed in much of Asia seem over-drawn. City industry managed well enough in Russia by employing seasonal workers from the countryside and could have done so in Asia: by Oshima's own account, work in the export-crop plantations of Indonesia was alternated with the production of food crops in the villages.[21] Away from the coasts or rivers of Asia there may have been high costs involved in shifting commodities, but given the limited output anywhere in the early stages of industrialization, the equivalent of Yankee pedlars could surely have managed to hawk goods around. Had there been sufficient economic activity and incentives these problems could have been overcome. Asia's environment may have shaped the nature of its economic growth but it is implausible to believe that historically the environment actually precluded growth any more than it has done since.

The European (English) case

The Asian model is set against the superior ability of European (or English) agriculture to release labour for rural domestic industry and subsequently for factory work. This contrast depends on stylized facts concerning Western agricultural history which tend to mislead in a number of ways. Not the least of these arises from permitting English experience to stand for that of the whole of Europe, a common enough trap into which English-language writers may be even more likely to fall.

The implication that there was no seasonal shortage of farm labour in Europe is a misapprehension. The demand for labour to take the harvest was the critical shortage between 1800–80, as the area and then the yield of the small grain crops swelled. Estimates for Britain, France and Germany reveal the falling supply of harvest labour and expanding crop demand over that period.[22] A large-scale introduction of the scythe was the first response, the reaping machine came later. This is not to say that the scythe was in all respects preferred to the sickle; its greater propensity to shatter the ears and spill the grain was well known and its use had long failed to spread from grass mowing to the grain crops. It might have been resisted still had the upward trend of yields and alternative employment for labour during the nineteenth century not been more than strong enough to offset the spillage and loss of food.

The impression given that European farm workers were unskilled field hands is likewise misleading. There were elements of robot-like drudgery in reaping, hoeing gangs and the like but not evidently more than in planting and transplanting rice. The range and intricacy of tasks in the agricultures which were founded in Europe's immense variety of soils and topography, besides the tasks associated with its especially numerous livestock, were remarkable. Lack of skill should not be read from parts of the system to the whole; from the rustic manners of farm workers or peasants; or from Marx's taunt about the idiocy of rural life. In respect to labour availability, seasonal demand, and skill the distinction between Europe and Asia can easily be overdrawn.

The mechanism by which agricultural change in Europe is supposed to have generated industry is through the development of mixed farming, though Oshima does not use the term. When arable farmers found that they could combine crop growing with livestock production they were able to abandon domestic industry and specialize in husbandry. This separation was reputedly impossible in Asia. Mixed farming certainly developed in light-soiled districts of England and in them cottage industry tended to wither away. On heavier soils the thickening of rural domestic industry combined with livestock grazing came to compensate. This was not an overall separation of agriculture and industry but a slow, involved recombination of one branch of farming with handicraft manufacturing. The intensification of rural domestic industry in any case pre-dated the development of mixed farming rotations based on the sowing of turnips and clover as field crops.

Older notions of the form and timing of an agricultural revolution are not helpful and do not apply to the whole of Europe. The crux is whether rural domestic industrialization led directly to industrialization in its powered, factory form. It certainly led in that direction, through its effects on capital accumulation, transport links and the conditioning of labour to non-farm routines. Yet those of us who used to urge a link have to take account of the finding that in major industrial districts the factory system had independent origins.[23] If the protoindustrial-industrial link was indirect, the role of agricultural change in creating European industrialization is diminished.

Formulation

The European template thus does not have the shape that is supposed. If the postulated relationships were not evident in Europe, the fact that they were missing in monsoon Asia can lend no support to the idea that their absence was the key, or rather the lock, there. In any event, the original scale of factory industry was so small that recruiting a workforce was not an insuperable problem either in Europe or Asia, especially given conditions of faster population growth.

Despite these conclusions, the procedure of comparing the economic history of Europe and Asia is still likely to strike the student as justified. If agricultural differences are rejected, it may be thought that we should simply turn to looking harder at Europe for some other positive change, a different propellant; and we should then turn back to find in its inevitable absence from Asia the true source of backwardness.

This is as if every other case of growth must be a follower of the British or European industrial revolution. Earlier Asian experience, notably under the Song, had shown such an hypothesis to be false. What is more likely is that growth was the result of common human impulses and was a recurrent phenomenon in a number of societies. Analyzing the means by which it was usually suppressed, and then the way whereby on rare occasions the suppressants were removed, is more instructive than delving into the archives of Europe for some other novelty to which the vital change may be attributed if only all other variables are held constant.[24]

A more general explanation

The enquiry is in any case mildly ambiguous, asking both why monsoon Asia was poor (which is a question about growth or rather non-growth) and why it was overtaken by European industrialization. The procedure juxtaposes versions of English/European and Chinese/Asian history. But do we really need, as the substantivist school of economic anthropology used to tell us, a different explanation for each society, each place and period? If so, since any subdivision into places and periods is a matter of scholarly choice, how are we to define the parts? By the standard divisions of history? the conventions of area studies? These problems will fade away if we can find a source of under-development common to Europe and Asia.

The fact that since 1945 most of monsoon Asia has achieved real economic growth shows that rice growing does not constitute a permanent obstacle. Rice growing has not been abandoned, something else in the economic environment has shifted. Moreover, we cannot attribute the earlier economic growth and industrialization in Europe wholly to technical changes in (English) agriculture. Neither continent's growth equation is to be fully solved by referring to the ecological or technical potentialities of its farming system.

We need to look elsewhere for an explanation, away from the natural environment as well as away from culture. In my view the resolution lies in perceiving that the nearly universal rent-seeking propensity of pre-modern politics was what mainly suppressed growth. This shifts the task to explaining how rent-seeking behaviour came to be curtailed at specific times in different countries. A neurotic compulsion for rent-seeking was common to pre-modern rulers and elites. It led to confis-cations, high and arbitrary taxes, and at a miserly best to entrepreneurial uncertainty. It led to the establishment of, or indolent connivance at, institutions unfitted to give rise to vigorous economic change. Together with the very real material difficulties of starting from a low income base (certain environmental costs would no doubt have figured among them), rent-seeking and its secondary effects on social behaviour and institutions seem sufficient to have damped down growth.

What needs to be acknowledged about 'pre-industrial' Asia is the paradoxical fact of prolonged economic expansion, that is expansion in total GNP. Even if one believes, unhistorically, that Asia witnessed no technical or institutional changes of substance until the very recent past, its prolonged population growth guaranteed that fresh investment decisions had constantly to be made. But the bridge any society had to cross in order to convert expansion into sustained growth in per capita GNP was usually barred by some Asian Horatio or other. Nevertheless, on a few privileged occasions the negative political factors were defeated long enough for a crossing. There were at least two major Asian occurrences, under the Song and the Tokugawa.[25] At other times the difficulties came crowding back, producing depressing secondary effects like 'turning inwards'.

My underlying assumptions are that an impulse for fruitful economic activity is ever-present in human society, but is typically stifled, and that in the broadest sense, once disincentives are removed, humanity is creative enough gradually to overhaul or bypass cultural, technical and ecological difficulties. In this formulation what we observe is a different political experience in East and West, though the basic experience insofar as it affected economic life was surprisingly similar in Japan and western Europe.

Realistically, not all societies can have been equally likely to have achieved growth even in the absence of major political impediments. This point may be conceded even though we do not know enough about the internal workings of myriad societies to rank their political 'potential for growth'. For the moment, equal potential is the parsimonious assumption. The ancient creativity of Asian societies certifies that Asia was quite capable of surmounting the barriers.

The problem was not the monsoon. Monsoons (like specific cultures) were not universal even in Asia. Nor is the problem to be avoided by referring to the history of Europe as inimitable. Different, yes, but not uniquely exempt from the forces affecting all large societies. A general thesis in terms of incentives and investment decisions, politically frustrated or fostered, links the fate of both, indeed of all, societies. Europe's particular political history eroded rent-seeking in a more sustained way than in China, for all the brilliance of the Song, and earlier than in Japan. Thus it was Europe that first permanently derailed the slow, majestic course of expansion without growth which had characterized *very* long-run human history.

Explaining Asia in terms of Europe is perpetually tempting. But by that token we might have to ask in reverse why Europe (and everywhere else) fell behind the China of the tenth through the thirteenth centuries. Europe had no eternal privilege, merely one at a given period, the result of a fortunately early and persistent political release of economic energies. The more interesting question is not why one of these regions 'fell behind' the other, but why China did not repeat its own earlier growth success and develop that into industrialism.[26] The answer cannot lie in virtually ahistorical features like culture or the monsoon.

Notes

1. For a major statement see Clifford Geertz, 'Culture and Social Change: The Indonesian case', *Man* n.s. 19 (1984), pp. 511–32.
2. Vernon Reynolds, 'The Biology of Religion Revisited' (paper read to the Third Workshop on 'Demography, Economics, and Organised Religion', at Magdalen College, Oxford, 9–10 November 1990), does seek to demonstrate that culture in the shape of religious precepts largely adapts to demographic behaviour, itself ultimately determined by the riskiness of the environment. See also Vernon Reynolds and Ralph Tanner, *The Biology of Religion* (1983).
3. Julian L. Simon, *The Effects of Income on Fertility* (Chapel Hill, N.C., 1974), p. 105.
4. On these matters, see Kaushik Basu, Eric Jones and Ekkehart Schlicht, 'The Growth and Decay of Custom: The role of the new institutional economics in economic history', *Explorations in Economic History* 24 (1987), pp. 1–21.
5. This argument has now been turned on its head with respect to the economically-positive values of post-Confucianism. Either way the primacy of values is being assumed.
6. Mark Elvin, 'Why China Failed to Create an Endogenous Industrial Capitalism', *Theory and Society* 13 (1984), pp. 379–91; E.L. Jones, *Growth Recurring: Economic change in world history* (Oxford, 1988), pp. 99–101.
7. See E.L. Jones, 'The History of Resource Exploitation in the Western World', *Research in Economic History* Supplement 6 (1990), pp. 235–52, and sources cited therein.
8. Harry T. Oshima, 'Why Monsoon Asia Fell Behind the West Since the Sixteenth Century: Conjectures', *Philippine Review of Economics and Business* 20 (1983), pp. 163–203; *Economic Growth in Monsoon Asia: A Comparative Study* (Tokyo, 1987). Professor Oshima's thesis is sometimes more emphatically stated in his article than in the book. Following scholarly convention, specific allusions here are to the latter as the more recent of the two.
9. *IMF Survey*, 5 February 1990, pp. 45–6.
10. This should not be read as a dismissal of all environmental explanation. See in particular J.L. Anderson and E.L. Jones, 'Natural Disasters and the Historical Response', *Australian Economic History Review* 28 (1988), pp. 3–20, for a discussion. As to cultural differ-

ences, it may be noted that a recent book by Jack Goody, *The Oriental, the Ancient and the Primitive* (Cambridge, 1990), suggests that unlike Africa, kinship practice in Asia has much in common with that in parts of pre-industrial Europe, thus de-emphasizing the East-West divide in this respect.

11. John K. Fairbank and Edwin O. Reischauer, quoted by Oshima, *Economic Growth in Monsoon Asia*, p. 34.
12. Joseph Needham, quoted in ibid., p. 34.
13. See E.L. Jones, *The European Miracle* (2nd edn., Cambridge, 1987), pp. 170–1.
14. Victor B. Lieberman, *Burmese Administrative Cycles: Anarchy and conquest c.1580–1760* (Princeton, 1984).
15. Anthony Reid, *Southeast Asia in the Age of Commerce 1450–1680*, vol. 1, *The Lands below the Winds* (New Haven, 1988).
16. Oshima, *Economic Growth in Monsoon Asia*, p.45.
17. However while rice produces 4 per cent more calories per unit weight than wheat, it supplies only 60 per cent of the protein and less of many minerals and vitamins. (Sucy Thomas and Margaret Corden, *Tables of Composition of Australian Foods* (Canberra, 1970), p. 12, table III. Their evaluation may not strictly apply to the average of earlier varieties). An advantage of rice is that it is easier to prepare, which may have been significant where fuel wood was scarce. Despite this, the crucial differences among crops may relate to the productivity of labour rather than of land.
18. Cf. Jones, *Growth Recurring*, pp. 125–6.
19. Katherine Plummer, *The Shogun's Reluctant Ambassadors: Sea drifters* (Tokyo, 1984), p. 33.
20. Martin Bronfenbrenner, 'The Japanese "Howdunnit"', *Trans-action* 6 (1969), p. 33.
21. J.D. Clarkson, *A History of Russia from the Ninth Century* (1962), pp. 321–7; Oshima, *Economic Growth in Monsoon Asia*, p. 40.
22. E.J.T. Collins, 'Labour Supply and Demand in European Agriculture 1800–1880', in E.L. Jones and S.J. Woolf (eds), *Agrarian Change in Economic Development: The historical problems* (1969), pp. 64–5.
23. Pat Hudson, *The Genesis of Industrial Capital: A study of the West Riding wool textile industry c.1750–1850* (Cambridge, 1986).
24. Cf. Jones, *Growth Recurring*.
25. Ibid.
26. Cf. id., 'The Real Question About China: Why was the Song economic achievement not repeated?', *Australian Economic History Review* 30 (1990), pp. 5–22.

Cultural Values and Entrepreneurial Action: The Case of the Irish Republic

Paul Keating

I

As the title to this paper suggests its concern will be to examine the relation between cultural values and entrepreneurial activity in Ireland. More precisely, it will try to determine whether and to what extent the cultural values to which Irish entrepreneurs relate their material interests determine the limited and irregular commitment to productive activity exhibited in their economic behaviour. Let me say here and now what this paper is not about: it is not an historical study of Ireland's failure to develop economically, and it is not claiming that the behaviour it tries to analyse is the sole cause of that failure. As a late developer Ireland faces obstacles which those who industrialized before her did not have to face. It would also be idle to pretend that a small, peripheral economy can be developed by waving a magic wand. Nevertheless, the auguries are not all bad; Ireland is not short of capital; she has developable natural resources, not least in her land; she has access to markets; she has a well developed infrastructure, a well educated workforce, and a stable liberal-democratic government which is very friendly to private enterprise and which has provided an environment which is very hospitable to it, not least with reference to grant incentives and corporate taxation policy—corporation tax on manufacturing is ten per cent, and export profits are tax exempt. This is the background against which the behaviour of Irish entrepreneurs must be examined and assessed.

It is, of course, true that the Irish economy developed significantly in the years following the publication of the *First Programme for Economic Expansion* in 1958. What is also true, however, is that most of the growth resulted from state activity and Foreign Direct Investment into the country. The contribution of Irish entrepreneurs has been restricted by virtue of their limited and irregular commitment to business activity. It is time to see how this limited and irregular commitment shows itself in the contemporary Irish context.

II

The judgement about limited commitment is not difficult to sustain. It is well exhibited in the corporate behaviour of large Irish companies; their investment in research and development and in new products is low by international standards and when set against the development needs of the economy;[1] their failure to take advantage of the opportunities offered by grant and tax incentives and by access to new markets has been cited as 'a major factor inhibiting Irish industrialization'.[2]

Smaller Irish companies also follow a limited pattern; they set their sights below their full potential; they are not vigorous enough in analysing markets or the competition; they are not effective enough in overcoming production and marketing problems which cost them profitable opportunities for growth.[3] The Irish Industrial Development Authority confirms this; notwithstanding an impressive package of grant and tax incentives only one-third of I.D.A. supported small companies employed more than ten people, a fact which 'points to the absence of an international outlook . . . characterized particularly by a lack of investment in developing new products for export markets'.[4]

Evidence like this suggests that much Irish industry is undynamic and content with what, when it is considered against the needs of a developing economy, must be considered an unsatisfactory status quo. It is no wonder, therefore, that an erstwhile director of the Irish Management Institute was provoked into the comment that, 'while some Irish management teams are second to none . . . the other end of the scale is *appalling*' because far too many retain the attitude that 'the home market will do well enough' (emphasis added).[5] Growth-oriented Irish entrepreneurs are also critical of the many who are content to make 'a nice, neat little profit . . . without much growth'.[6] They also point to an ignorance of world standards, a lack of commitment to hard work and low levels of honesty and reliability, which they see as all too prevalent in Ireland.[7] Thus a textile entrepreneur admitted to Fogarty that unreliability had left a 'trail of disaster' behind it in an export market,[8] while an agricultural processor complained:

> We still have to live down the total dishonesty of those who sold
> meat in England . . . the bad quality . . . heifers sold, bought and
> delivered genuinely for three weeks, and then the cows . . . and
> . . . any trick of the loop work.[9]

The Industrial Development Authority confirmed the '*consistently poor
trading practice*' of Irish agri-business companies (emphasis added)[10],
while investigators discovered the 'variable quality', 'lack of consistency'
and 'unreliability of supply' of Irish products.[11] That quality continues to
be a problem is not difficult to demonstrate; surveys carried out in 1986
and 1988 indicated that Irish lamb had a poor reputation for quality in its
principal export market;[12] 70 per cent of food firms and manufacturing
companies who applied for the Irish Quality Association's Quality Mark
failed to meet the required standards;[13] in the tourist trade Irishness was
recently said to be 'the antithesis of quality';[14] while industry generally was
said to be losing £500 million a year through inadequate quality control.[15]

The evidence presented so far suggests that entrepreneurial commitment to business activity is limited. This is bound to hinder the country's
development achievement which requires, as Parsons puts it, that entrepreneurs 'serve the goals of *Production* beyond the levels previously
treated as normal, desirable or necessary in [a] society' (emphasis in the
original).[16] There are, of course, a minority who want to try. For these,
however, life can be a frustrating business. As one of their number
expresses it:

> Anyone with drive, with a truly innovative or entrepreneurial
> spirit cannot fail to be dragged down by the sheer torpor that
> characterizes our society . . . All of [which] reminds me of the
> Spaniard who asked the Celtic scholar if the concept of *manana*
> existed in Irish and was told: 'we have nothing with quite the
> same sense of urgency.'[17]

III

If the commitment of Irish entrepreneurs is limited, their business conduct
is also often irregular in the sense that there is a widespread propensity to
engage in unethical and unscrupulous activities. This is well attested to by
an entrepreneur who gained his early business experience in Britain:

> I have been rather horrified in fact, since I came back to Ireland,
> at the low moral values. I am not speaking of sexual matters, I
> mean generally. People will make appointments which they do not

keep, they make them glibly with no intention of keeping them. Business people will make promises which they can't keep, and they seem to think that they are doing you a favour by making the promises, that this is as far as they are expected to go. What I would call the Protestant work ethic is badly needed here . . . I wonder if it is based on religion, or on the education they have got which is so religious here. That is why Ireland needs the North like a sore needs an antiseptic.[18]

This entrepreneur's view is by no means idiosyncratic, as the following comments of Professor Michael Fogarty, who interviewed a number of Irish entrepreneurs, show well enough:

> One of the most disturbing features of these interviews was *how often* informants came back to the thesis that what families, schools, the Church, the social system and the business system itself have failed to produce in Ireland *is people with the basic virtues of honesty, integrity and hard and purposeful work* (emphasis added).[19]

We have already seen some evidence of unscrupulousness with reference to agri-business. And there is yet more. For example, the farmers have been warned that they are in danger of destroying their £2,000 million a year beef industry by injecting up to seventy per cent of cattle slaughtered with illegal hormones, growth promoters and antibiotics.[20] These substances are provided by black market racketeers; there is a massive black market for them, evidently encouraged by the meat plants who use the 'green Ireland image' when exporting.[21] Slaughterhouses have also constituted a problem:

> For years the existence of *a significant number* of local abbatoirs who neither respect hygiene or veterinary regulations nor pay associated levies, undermined the efforts of licensed slaughterhouses to compete effectively on home and export markets (emphasis added).[22]

Another example of the damage done by illegal activities is provided by the bakery industry. Here illegal bakeries who ignore planning, tax and health laws have captured twenty per cent of the Irish confectionery market. As a result forty-four legitimate bakeries went out of business between 1985 and 1987, and more were expected to follow.[23] The general impact of illegal activity was summed up by a Parliamentary committee which reported that 'Businesses which have tried to observe the law have been decimated . . . by the activity of unscrupulous competitors . . . who do not officially exist . . . who operate . . . without incorporating their businesses, registering for VAT [and] operating [tax and social insurance] provisions for their employees'.[24] Between 1979 and 1983 the Special Enquiry Branch of the Irish Revenue Commissioners discovered some 23,000 illegal businesses—a feat performed by a unit employing only twenty people, and one which prompted the Parliamentary Committee to wonder how many more illegal operations might have been discovered if greater resources had been devoted to rooting them out.[25]

Generally speaking only 33.5 per cent of Irish employees meet their PAYE liabilities on time, and only 24 per cent of traders are punctual with their VAT payments—the comparable British figures are 95 and 61 per cent respectively.[26] When one discovers that 31 per cent of employers and 36 per cent of traders have still left their liabilities unmet after six months, it becomes obvious that business people use the revenue authorities as a source of working capital; these authorities have been made, in effect, into a bank making interest free loans to unscrupulous business people— although interest is formally charged on arrears hardly any of it is actually paid.[27]

Tax evasion in Ireland has reached massive proportions; it has reached the point where 'only mugs pay their taxes' and where tax officials suspect that the government's failure to confront the problem is conditioned by the fact that many of the culprits are leading supporters of the political parties.[28] Unscrupulousness here is by no means confined to the corporate sector; individual tax morality among the farmers and the self-employed is also very low. In fact the Irish have been described as 'a nation of tax dodgers'.[29] In 1986, for example, the total assessed as outstanding from all sources amounted to £3,883 million, of which £1,578 million was accounted for by income tax and £97 million by social insurance charges. In all, it was estimated that only £664 million of these outstanding charges would be collected, including only £205 million of the income tax and £41 million of the social insurance charges outstanding. Even allowing for excesses in the estimates, this represents evasion on a massive scale—the total income tax yield for 1987 was £2,721.7 million.[30]

IV

To repeat, I am not claiming that the conduct I have described constitutes the sole reason for Ireland's failure to develop economically. What I am claiming, however, is that the conduct is socially problematic in the development context because the limited and irregular commitment disclosed in it must have a negative impact on the prospects of development achievement. In the first place it is hard to see how entrepreneurs who are not committed enough to drive the production threshold beyond the levels 'previously treated as normal, desirable or necessary' can generate the growth which development needs. Secondly, the unscrupulousness has damaged Ireland's reputation and has put legitimate business under unfair competitive pressure and thus hindered its prospects of surviving and thriving. Finally, the unscrupulousness has, with reference to the tax question, deprived the state of much needed revenue and has thus hindered its capacity to aid development by funding incentives and infrastructural investment. So, how is this conduct to be explained?

In answering this question it might be tempting to suggest that the patterns of commitment exhibited by Irish entrepreneurs have nothing to do with the cultural values to which they relate their material interests. In other words, it might be claimed that the limited and irregular patterns of commitment which they display are a function of a limited and irregular supply of means and opportunities, and that Irish entrepreneurs are as committed and regular as they could be in the circumstances that confront them. It is, however, impossible to sustain this view in the face of the evidence. Ireland is not short of capital. Nor is the country short of useful natural resources; it has plenty of good agricultural land and the best tree growing conditions in Europe, ideal conditions for the development of high value-added food and wood processing industries, for the products of which markets existed and exist. Yet Ireland's record on both fronts is a very poor one; the food processing industry is very undeveloped and a wood processing industry hardly exists. When we remember that the successful Danish and Finnish electronics industries were founded on the specialized mechanical needs of their respective food and wood processing industries, we can see something of the possibilities that were open, and left unrealized, in the Irish case.

The fact that hypotheses about the lack of means and opportunities will not stand up to examination is demonstrated by the view of the Irish themselves. The authorities I cited in Section II were chosen with some care; they are people who are involved in Irish business life and who know the situation they confront. Accordingly they include a banker (Carroll), economists (Kennedy, Giblin and McHugh), a management education specialist (Patterson), representatives of the Irish Industrial Development Authority (White, McKeon), the chief executive of the Irish

Quality Control Association (Murphy), the chief executive of a leading co-operative (Brosnan), a selection of entrepreneurs, and finally, the current minister for industry and commerce in the Irish Government (O'Malley). These men are not complaining about a lack of means and opportunities; they are complaining about the lack of what they take to be adequate levels of commitment and the resultant waste of opportunities.

In any case arguments about a lack of means and opportunities could not explain the propensity to engage in unscrupulous conduct. The farmers who are in danger of destroying their industry are not short of opportunities—they have £2,000 million a year's worth of opportunities —and neither are those who are losing £500 million a year through inadequate quality control. On the basis of the evidence it is impossible to take seriously the idea that the conduct described in this paper can be explained by reference to a limited and irregular supply of means and opportunities. To what extent might cultural values help us to explain it?

V

In what remains of this paper I want to try to show how a reference to the cultural values to which the Irish relate can help to explain the patterns of commitment to economic activity which I have described. Since these patterns accord closely with the salients of Max Weber's ideas about economic traditionalism, I shall take my point of departure from his thinking.

Weber saw that the people who created the modern capitalist economy were marked by distinctive character traits; they oriented to their economic activity as an ultimate value, and were committed to the endless expansion of their enterprises by regular, disciplined work, effective management and honest dealing.[31] The type of entrepreneurship involved rested in a character that was distinctive by reference to the following traits: (i) a refusal to subordinate economic activity to any other value; (ii) a hard, competitive individualism that refused to be satisfied with the *status quo* and so pursued expansion as a matter of duty in a 'calling'; (iii) an ethical outlook which, in the interests of disciplined work, rational management and honest dealing, suppressed the spontaneous, impulsive and ethically irregular sides of human character. Weber considered this type of human character to be unnatural; in the state of nature people were easy-going and spontaneous; they were not given to either rigorous discipline or to an unlimited commitment to economic activity. Far from it, the commitment to economic activity was limited by tradition, an interest in leisure and consumption and by the values of anti-materialist religions.

The traditionalistic type of character can, therefore, be defined by reference to: (i) a tendency to subordinate economic activity to values which limit commitment to it; (ii) an ethos which is anti-individualistic, anti-innovative and rooted in satisfaction with traditional patterns of action; and (iii) a tendency to spontaneity and impulsiveness which finds outlets in leisure, festivity and irregular and unethical dealing.[32] Weber coined the term traditionalism to characterize the resultant orientation to economic life: a sleepy, undynamic attitude marked by low levels of commitment, which, being ethically unregulated, was compatible with irregular outbursts of unscrupulous energy in the pursuit of gain.[33]

I am not concerned here with the correctness or otherwise of Weber's account of the character transforming process that emerged in seventeenth century Europe—the infamous Protestant ethic thesis. What is more to the point here is Weber's observation that once a modern capitalist economic system is established it becomes a self-sustaining *milieu*; it is a competitive, individualistic, innovative environment and those who do not measure up do not survive. Values in committed entrepreneurship are, therefore, 'policed' by pressures residing in the social structures of developed capitalist societies.

Values in individualistic, innovative and dynamic commitment will not, however, find support in the structures of pre-capitalist societies. For example, in small-scale, rural communities bound together by strong kinship and communal ties, in which economic security is seen to depend on ties of solidarity and reciprocity, the individualistic innovator is likely to be viewed with hostility. Here values are likely to emphasize conformism and moderation of commitment to economic activity, more so if the traditional patterns accord importance to leisure and communal festivity and are supported by anti-materialist religious ethics. This is the kind of society in which economic traditionalism flourishes. For the less well off the absence of a dynamic commitment fosters security because it carries an assurance that traditional patterns will not be disrupted. For the better off, the absence of values in commitment enable them to enjoy a comfortable prosperity without the need to feel obliged to invest too much energy in developing the resources on which their prosperity is based.

Historically Ireland was a society of small rural communities, the economic security of whose members depended on ties of solidarity, reciprocity and mutual aid. The people who inhabited these communities were renowned for their wit, warmth, vivacity, cheerfulness, friendliness and for their love of conversation, music and dancing. As Hutchinson observes, these attributes

> could be mainly cultivated only during hours of leisure. They are the products of leisure, [just] as the dourness of the lowland Scot and the north-county Englishman is the product of Puritanism and the mystique that grew with the industrial revolution.[34]

Hutchinson is, of course, referring here to the factors considered salient by Max Weber; an ascetic religion which accommodated itself to materialism and thus put value premiums on the suppression of impulse and spontaneity in the interests of establishing a vocational commitment to innovative dynamism in economic life, and the support it received from the developing structural pressures associated with the emerging capitalist cosmos. The mass of the Irish oriented towards Roman Catholicism, a religion which was less accommodating towards materialism, and which confined its asceticism to the monasteries, leaving, as Max Weber[35] points out, the naturally spontaneous character of life in the world untouched. The poet Keats hated Scottish Calvinism; it had deprived the people of their traditional holidays and spread a dismal gloom over the land. Yet he recognized that the Scottish ministers had formed their people into 'regular phalanges of savers and gainers', into 'a thrifty army [that could not fail] to enrich their country and give it a greater appearance of comfort than that of their poor rash neighbourhood'.[36] The neighbourhood in question is Ireland.

Keats is no doubt being ethnocentric in these implicit references to the laziness and indolence of the Irish. Yet we should not fall into the same trap in defending the Irish. As Hutchinson points out, the Puritan-industrial virtues

> were irrelevant to societies, such as the Irish and many others, organized on the basis of quite different assumptions: and the use of such terms as 'laziness' or 'indolence' in discussing them [is] an unjustified extension to them of concepts developed in circumstances and according to beliefs, that were entirely different. Such ethnocentricity has not yet disappeared from the arguments of all liberal historians, some of whom believed either that the Irish were not 'lazy' but worked very hard; or, if they were admittedly lazy, were justifiably so because of the economic and political

situations in which they found themselves. The possibility that, for the Irish themselves, such categories had no meaning is not considered.[37]

The reasons for this lack of salience are not far to seek; in the small, relatively poor rural communities orienting towards communal solidarity, mutual aid and anti-materialist religious ethics, the committed, individualistic innovator would not be an acceptable character. If nothing else, such innovators would threaten the community solidarity in which people's sense of economic security resided. As a result people's material interests would orient them towards the anti-individualistic, anti-innovative and anti-materialist ethics embodied in the traditional values and in Roman Catholicism. The result, given that Catholicism left the naturally spontaneous character of extra-monastic life untouched, was a value system that put no positive premiums on high levels of entrepreneurial commitment and ethical regularity.

This situation also suited the interests of the materially more prosperous classes; it enabled them to enjoy a comfortable prosperity oriented towards status concerns and consumption, without imposing any obligation towards the development of the resources on which their prosperity was based. As the historian J.J. Lee[38] points out, there was no shortage of capital in nineteenth-century Ireland. However, the farmers and business people used it for dowries, gave it to their sons for a professional education and used it to gain respectability by cultivating the life-styles of the Protestant upper class; they were not interested in developing trade. The small urban middle class also 'aped the gentry'; they oriented to canons of reputability rooted in leisure and consumption.[39]

Irish nationalism was restorationist in character; those who elaborated its values wanted political change, i.e., independence from Britain, but not change in what they took to be the true Irish identity. This was seen to lie in rural society. Gaelic civilization was rural civilization, and this had to be preserved as the true basis of an unchanging Irish identity and as the only basis on which a happy, healthy, virtuous life was possible.[40] Preserving this identity entailed protecting Ireland from the stains of urbanism, materialism, cosmopolitanism, industrialism and commercialism, all or any of which seemed calculated to undermine the cherished identity, values and modes of living. Thus the writer Sean O'Casey equated Ireland with 'Language, Literature, Earth, Tree, Happy People', while Britain, by contrast, was characterized in terms of 'Textiles, Glass, Blast-furnaces, Commercialization, Industry, Mammon, Old Age

Pensions, Social Security, Meals for Needy People', and, presumably, a great deal of human misery.[41] Inevitably the same writer went on to declare that Ireland 'never was, never will be . . . furnace burned . . . Commercialization is far from her shores.'[42]

The values of Irish nationalism were not an ideological reflection of the material interests of any section of the Irish people; the poets, artists, writers and revolutionaries who elaborated them were drawn from all segments of Irish society, not excluding the Anglo-Irish aristocracy and the urban working class. In consequence the values came to constitute the canon of Irish identity and the basis for individuals' evaluations of themselves and others in terms of the quality of their Irishness. The assessment base provided was preservative, not *innovatory*; to qualify as a good Irishman or Irishwoman one had to uphold the traditional order, *not to change it*. When Irish people related their material interests to the values of nationalism, therefore, they received a clear signal: *no change*; the inhibiting culture and structures described above received a massive validation.

Roman Catholicism underwrote the nationalist vision; the Church saw the rural environment as the one in which its flock could best work out its spiritual destinies free from the materialistic distractions associated with too much commitment to the things of the world. Catholicism, therefore, validated traditionalist nationalism. And traditionalist nationalism returned the favour by making Catholicism part of the canon of Irishness. Given its anti-materialist ethos, Irish people who relate their material interests to the values of Catholicism will find that these dictate a limitation of commitment to economic activity in the interest of believers' spiritual welfare. Irish business people are quite happy to admit this.

> Managerial people [in Dublin] *quite commonly* acknowledge *that their more relaxed attitude towards business activity stems from their religious outlook on life*. In the words of one husband: 'I think we Irish are quite different from the English and Americans: the ones I've met seem to be wrapped up in the almighty pound and dollar. I've dealt with many Englishmen and my impression is that money and what it brings are their God. But we cannot get as concerned as they over business and material things. *We are less active in these matters because always in the background of our minds we are concerned with a more fundamental philosophy* (emphases added).[43]

The values of Catholicism and nationalism took root in Irish society because they found an echo in the material interests of the generality of the Irish people. They could appeal to the materially less well-off because they invested their rural lives with a health, a dignity and a spirituality which had long been lost in the materialistic rat races of the urban, industrialized world. They appealed also to the comfortably-off professionals, traders, producers and farmers because they invested the *status quo* with an aura of sanctity and demanded no changes in the traditional patterns of action and social structure. Thus they lent an aura of dignity to lives of comfortable prosperity, and did so, moreover, without giving rise to the feeling that it had to be paid for by undue exertion and extension of commitment to the development of the economic resources on which the prosperity was based. Reputability here was defined in terms of consumption and life-style, not production. And the development of production has suffered as a result:

> The prospect of developing a large food processing industry was hampered by, among other things, the unwillingness of farmers who controlled the processing co-operatives to forego any short-term advantage on the price of their products with the result that the co-operatives were starved of development funds.[44]

This statement must be considered against the background for the boom conditions enjoyed by Irish agriculture in the years following the country's entry into the European Community: farm incomes rose by 400 per cent; land prices rose from £100 per acre in the mid-fifties to £4,600 per acre in the mid-seventies—this was higher than the price of land in The Netherlands with its vastly more productive agriculture.[45] The farmers who starved the co-operatives were not themselves starved of funds. As Coogan reminds us, however, these were often consumed: 'Costly home improvements were effected. The eating out habit spread and overdrafts mushroomed.'[46] Above all, however, the old habits and business methods persisted and militated against the development of a high value added food industry:

> The simplest thing to produce on a farm, and the most lucrative, was a bullock. All a farmer had to do was to glance at the beasts every day, take a few elementary precautions such as dosing and ensuring provision of fodder, and he made money. Why bother with the uncertain exhausting business of planting vegetables? If he did bother he often held that ingrained rural prejudice that contracts and fixed prices are dangerous snares set by the purchaser to trap the poor producer. If someone offered a better

price for his crop, he blithely sold at the eleventh hour, thereby
disappointing either a wholesaler or a vegetable processor who
might go bankrupt or at least go elsewhere next year. This would
leave the farmer with the following year's crop on his hands, and
create boom/glut situations in which farmers washed their hands
of vegetable production altogether. As a result a steady tide of
Israeli, Cypriot, Dutch, Portuguese, Polish and even Canadian and
American vegetables, including potatoes, found their way into
Irish supermarkets. Since the end of the 1970s shoppers have been
able to rifle through countless packages of West German and
Dutch chips and frozen vegetables in the freezer compartments of
Dublin supermarkets without finding any Irish brands.[47]

The consequences of the limited and ethically irregular commitment to
entrepreneurial activity could not be better expressed.

VI

In this paper I have tried to show that a traditionalistic orientation to
economic life is widespread in Ireland as demonstrated by the evidence
touching on the limited and ethically irregular patterns of commitment
presented in it. I then suggested that these patterns of commitment could
not be explained by reference to some supposed entrepreneurial adaption
to an environment in which the supplies of means and opportunities were
themselves limited and irregular. Finally, I tried to show how a complex
of values derived, in parts, from interests in mutual aid and reciprocity,
from interests in consumption and status and from an anti-materialist
religious ethic, emerged and was consolidated by the ideal of a restorationist nationalism. As a result Irish economic actors came to relate
their material interests to values which were anti-individualistic, anti-
innovative and which indicated, and *sanctioned*, patterns of commitment
which were limited and irregular. This has created a situation in which
economic life becomes meaningful in orientation towards security and/or
comfortable prosperity based on satisfaction with traditional markets,
techniques, products and modes of action—some of which are ethically
irregular—without any felt obligation to increase economic effort at the
cost of leisure, consumption and status considerations. The failure of Irish
nationalism to repudiate traditionalism and to put positive premiums on
high levels of ethically regulated commitment to economic activity is
substantially responsible for this situation.

Nothing in these pages should be held to be a negative value judgement on Irish culture; the author is an Irishman, and all the sources and comments cited are Irish in origin. The fact that a value complex seems ill-adapted to a purpose, i.e., economic development, is not a criticism of that complex when the people who carry and transmit the complex feel indifferent to, or uneasy about, development because it is seen as either irrelevant, or even threatening, to their security and preferred modes of living. The trouble is that from the 1950s increasing numbers of Irish eyes have turned towards development as the only way to end the emigration, poverty and stagnation which were long established features of the Irish social and economic scene. As the comments cited in the text illustrate, these people are becoming frustrated at what they take to be the failure of their own people to adjust their attitudes and to behave in ways that are more appropriate to the achievement of development.

If there is a critical tone in this paper, therefore—and there is—it is a critique that is generated within Ireland; the paper reports that critique and does not generate it. The critique arises from a manifest disjunction between ends and means. In so far as Irish governmental and public opinion have come to favour development as an end, they have come to will the end. Until they come to develop higher and more regulated levels of economic commitment, however, they are clearly not willing the means. The evidence supportive of the latter point is clear enough; the 'sheer torpor' that characterizes Irish society; the fact that for too many Irish entrepreneurs the home market will do well enough; the £500 million a year lost through inadequate quality control; the fact that businesses that have tried to observe the law have been decimated; the fact that the schools, Church, family and business system have failed to inculcate the virtues of honesty, integrity and hard and purposeful work. All of these point to the fact that a limited and irregular commitment is widespread. The fact that it is widespread, tolerated and unbroken, suggests that the cultural values through which the Irish render their life situations meaningful are permissive of it. All I have tried to do here is to show how and why this is the case. Given that the Irish have opted for a private enterprise route to development—a route that requires dynamic, innovative entrepreneurship if it is to be travelled successfully—the message from this piece is obvious: unless or until the Irish value orientation changes, they may continue to travel hopefully but are most unlikely to arrive!

If this paper has theoretical implications—and in a modest way I think it has—then they must point in the direction of qualifying the view that a value disposition towards economic activity that is appropriate to the achievement of economic development emerges as a reflex of economic conditions that are appropriate to achievement of development, i.e. that development prospects are to be reckoned in terms of the availability, or lack of, capital, resources, opportunities etc. and do not primarily have to do with the cultural values carried by actors. While favourable economic conditions are vital prerequisites, i.e. a necessary condition, they are not, the evidence from this paper would suggest, always a sufficient condition for the achievement of economic development. Actors must, after all, interpret and give meanings to their social activities, including their economic activities. Once this is admitted it seems perfectly reasonable to suggest that their subjective meanings are constructed out of the cultural values to which they orientate. By values here I mean the standards which people invoke in making judgements about what is good or bad, right or wrong, ugly or beautiful etc.; they are the standards employed in making judgements as to what constitutes the good life for the individual. While values appropriate to success in a developed capitalist economy and society may arise as a reflex of the economic conditions prevailing in such a society, there is no reason a priori to assume that they will emerge in traditional societies which are attempting the transformation to modern capitalist production. Values in these societies may be reflexes of pre-capitalist economic bases and/or be reflective of non-economic pre-occupations issuing from a culture in which individualistic innovation, work and accumulation have not become dominant preoccupations to the detriment of leisure, festivity, the ties of community and/or religious or national aspirations. Actors orienting to values of this type may come to define their idea of the good life in non-capitalistic terms and thus render their economic lives meaningful in ways that do not move them in the directions of seeing lives devoted to endless work, tradition-breaking innovation and materialistic business expansion and wealth accumulation, which disrupt traditional patterns and prejudice leisure, religious and other non-economic interests, as either sensible or desirable. Resultant definitions of the good life will not sanctify economic activity as a life-dominating preoccupation to which high levels of economic commitment are required, but will leave it rather as a 'thing indifferent', to be pursued, as expedience dictates, in conditions in which it is subordinated to non-economic ends. The result will be a moderate and irregular commitment to economic activity which will act as a brake on economic development even when objective economic conditions are not unfavourable to it. That, at any rate, is what the evidence suggests happened in Ireland. And, unless Ireland is unique, this suggests that cultural values must be reckoned, along with economic conditions, as salients in the business of theorizing about development.

Notes

1. P. White and J. McKeon, both in *Irish Press*, Dublin, 22 March 1987.
2. K.Kennedy, D. Giblin, and D. McHugh, *The Economic Development of Ireland in the Twentieth Century* (1988), p. 214.
3. N. Carroll, *Irish Press*, Dublin, 6 April 1989.
4. Industrial Development Authority, *Annual Report* (Dublin, 1986), p. 14.
5. B. Patterson, *Business and Finance*, Dublin, 11 June 1987.
6. Cited in M. Fogarty, *Irish Entrepreneurs Speak for Themselves* (Dublin, 1972), p. 67.
7. Ibid., pp. 81, 89–91, 97–100; L. Gorman, and E. Molloy, *People, Jobs and Organisations* (Dublin, 1972), p. 90; P. O'Farrell, *Entrepreneurship and Industrial Change* (Dublin, 1986), p. 160.
8. Fogarty, *Irish Entrepreneurs*, p. 80.
9. Cited in ibid., p. 90.
10. Industrial Development Authority, *Annual Report* (Dublin, 1970), p. 70.
11. Industrial Development Authority, *Development Study of the Irish Beef Packaging and Processing Industry* (Dublin, 1977), p. 115; McKinsey & Co. Inc., *A Marketing Opportunity for Agricultural Products—Beyond the Farm* (1977), p. 33.
12. P. Kelly, *Irish Press*, Dublin, 19 July 1988.
13. J. Murphy, *Irish Independent*, Dublin, 16 July 1987.
14. D. Brosnan, *Irish Press*, Dublin, 28 November 1986.
15. D. O'Malley, *Irish Independent*, Dublin, 28 April 1990.
16. T. Parsons, *Structure and Process in Modern Societies* (Glencoe, Illinois, 1960), p. 140.
17. J. Quinn, *Irish Independent*, Dublin, 17 August 1986.
18. Cited in Fogarty, *Irish Enrepreneurs*, p. 97.
19. Ibid., pp. 96–7.
20. Irish Veterinary Union, *Irish Independent*, Dublin, 7 December 1987.
21. P. Lane, *Irish Press*, Dublin, 29 March 1988.
22. P. Jordan, 'Food industry needs action in '88', *Industry and Commerce* March 1988.
23. P. Howick, *Irish Times*, Dublin, 8 January 1987
24. Oireachtas Eareann, *Report of the Committee on Small Businesses* (Dublin, 1984), p. 16.
25. Ibid., p. 17.

26. Irish Tax Officials Union, *The Sick Tax System: Proposals for a Cost Effective Cure* (Dublin, 1987).
27. Ibid.
28. Ibid.; D. McAlease, 'The Black Economy', *Business and Finance*, Dublin, 27 October 1987.
29. B. Halligan, *Evening Herald*, Dublin, 15 November 1986.
30. Irish Tax Officials Union, *Sick Tax System*.
31. M.Weber, *The Protestant Ethic and the Spirit of Capitalism* (1930), pp. 48–53.
32. Ibid., pp. 56–70.
33. Ibid., p. 57.
34. B. Hutchinson, 'On the Study of Non-Economic Factors in Irish Economic Development', *Economic and Social Review* 1 (1970), p. 517.
35. Weber, *The Protestant Ethic*, pp. 118–19, 154.
36. H.B. Forman (ed.), *The Poetical Works and Other Writings of John Keats* (1883), vol. 3, p. 171.
37. Hutchinson, 'On the Study of Non-Economic Factors', p. 517.
38. 'Capital in the Irish Economy', in L. Cullen (ed.) *The Foundation of the Irish Economy* (Cork, 1969), pp. 56–7, 61; see also, id., *The Modernisation of Irish Society* (Dublin, 1973), pp. 16–18.
39. Hutchinson, 'On the Study of Non-Economic Factors', p. 515.
40. T.Brown, *Ireland: A Social and Cultural History 1922–1985* (1985), p. 59; M. Goldring, *Faith of Our Fathers: A Study of Irish Nationalism* (Dublin, 1987), p. 59; E. De Valera radio broadcast in 1943 cited in Brown, *Ireland*.
41. Cited in Goldring, *Faith of our Fathers*, p. 56.
42. Cited in ibid., p. 55.
43. S. Humphries, *The New Dubliners* (1966), p. 219.
44. Kennedy, Giblin and McHugh, *Economic Development of Ireland*, p. 261.
45. T.P. Coogan, *Disillusioned Decades: Ireland 1966–87* (Dublin, 1987), pp. 142–4.
46. Ibid., p. 144.
47. Ibid., pp. 144–5.

Employers, Workplace Culture and Workers' Politics: British Industry and Workers' Welfare Programmes, 1870–1920

Joseph Melling

Introduction

Recent research on work relations and industrial attitudes has emphasized the contribution of 'workplace culture' to the effective management of output and labour. Sociological studies of current management practices in Europe, Japan and North America have documented the extent to which business consultants are promoting 'corporate cultures' as a means of engaging the workforce in the goals of the enterprise.[1] Employers in Sweden, for example, have designed 'new cultural programmes' to foster a concern for quality control on the shop floor and an identification with the satisfaction of the customer.[2] The purposes of such business policies as cultural programmes and profit-sharing are a subject of current debate, though most commentators recognize that such initiatives have been framed within the political conditions of the 1980s.[3] Historical research on the industrial workplace has been dominated by discussions of the wider political loyalties of wage labour and the place of working-class institutions within the capitalist order. Edward Thompson's massive study of industrial change and working-class culture has inspired an enormous literature on popular protest, as well as more detailed studies of capitalist industry.[4]

The ways in which workplace relations contribute to social change and political stability remain a central focus of research in social history.[5] Much of the literature on industrial skills and workplace attitudes in nineteenth-century Britain, for example, has been concerned with the contribution of the division of labour to the maintenance of employers' hegemony and the capitalist order.[6] Marxist accounts of class stabilization range from the descriptions of the labour aristocracy in Victorian Britain, to explanations of technological subordination and deskilling which occurred (it is argued) in different forms during the first and second waves of industrialization.[7] These historians have sought to explain shifts in the politics of labour by reference to the changing division of labour and the structure of the working class.[8]

These explanations of workplace and class relations have been subjected to vigorous criticism in recent years, as further research has discovered the complex progress of technology and skill in different sectors of the industrial economy.[9] Such research reveals that industrial workers did not experience a single decisive loss of control over their working lives in the decades before 1850. There was no coherent process of technological change which could induce a massive trauma of alienation and class action as workers experienced the new factory regimes. The decisive transition in manufacturing from handicraft production and individual contracts to the 'real subordination of labour' driven by automatic machines is no longer accepted as an accurate description of industrialization even in Lancashire textiles.[10] Such a recognition weakens the whole foundations of the factory culture and class-stabilization thesis on which works such as Joyce's study of paternalism are based.[11] Labour contracts and authority relations in the industrial workplace were enveloped in various forms of internal contracting and piecework throughout the nineteenth century.

Similar conclusions can be drawn from recent research on technological change and systematic management at the end of the nineteenth century, where the evidence suggests a more complex picture of regrading and gender subordination than the earlier model of deskilling and craft radicalism found in 'new left' history.[12] The decades before 1914 emerge as a period of growing (if uneven) systematic management rather than the triumph of Taylorism. Employers resisted the full rigours of scientific management not only because of the enormous costs of a rigid surveillance of the workforce, but also as they realized that the flexibility of skill and piecework systems gave them the capacity to exploit intelligent human beings at a competitive advantage over fixed technologies.[13] The costs of such a minimalist approach to industrial innovation were to become more apparent in the interwar years, but the reliance on existing product ranges and manufacturing techniques was widespread in British industry.[14]

This research has eroded the base of evidence which many earlier historians relied upon to sustain their explanation of the politics of industrial workers in the nineteenth and early twentieth centuries. An alternative explanation for the political stability of industrial Britain was provided by Joyce in his influential study of employer paternalism in industrial Lancashire.[15] Joyce suggests that the technological progress of cotton spinning and the family relations of the textile mills provided the employers with a model for control of factory labour, which was reinforced by the 'culture of the factory' and the paternalist practices of the cotton firms.[16] This industrial paternalism laid the basis for the political supremacy of the industrial masters in Victorian Lancashire, as workers expressed their deference in support for their particular employers in the textile towns of the area. It was only the decline of the family-owned firm and the spread of industrial conflict at the end of the nineteenth century which explains the spread of socialist politics in Britain. Even then it was regions such as the West Riding with a rather different industrial and social structure and more fragmented trade unionism which were prominent in the new politics of Labour rather than Lancashire.[17] Throughout, Joyce emphasizes the extent to which workplace culture (and in particular the culture of the textile factories) influenced the social and political loyalties of industrial labour.

Although Joyce's analysis of class politics in industrial Britain has been subjected to various criticisms, there has been only a limited discussion of the broad chronology of paternalism suggested in his work.[18] Recently there has been a substantial amount of research on family labour in industrial production, including the findings of Whipp and Dupree, which raise important questions about the interdependence of capitalist development and the institution of the family.[19] Other recent contributions to the literature on workplace relations have provided sharp criticisms of both Marxist analyses of shop floor conflict and the kind of cultural explanations of industrial behaviour offered by Joyce, replacing these with an emphasis on the key role of bargaining and political institutions in shaping the relations between employers and workers.[20] This revisionist view of labour politics argues for a detailed examination of the internal life of institutions and the relations which develop between leading actors in the trade unions, employers' organizations and the state. Union politics are dominated by rival factions, led by political entrepreneurs bidding for the support of members whilst seeking an accommodation with powerful coalitions beyond the ranks of labour.[21] Such a neo-institutionalist critique may be a valuable corrective to the heroic view of class struggle in the workplace and the exaggerated emphasis on factory culture, though the affect of this approach is to minimize the role of cultural values in determining industrial or political behaviour, in favour of institutions which possess their own evolutionary logic.

This essay will suggest that the values of employers and workers *have had* a significant influence on industrial behaviour. Rather than drawing on the notion of paternalism to characterize employers' attitudes and behaviour, however, this essay suggests that a concept of *compliance*, which has both political and cultural elements to it, is a better basis for understanding the relations between employers and workers and the eventual emergence of new politics. Far from the practices of paternalism declining with the emergence of new business structures, it is argued that the most comprehensive schemes of business welfare were more commonly associated with advanced companies than small or moderate family concerns. This is not to deny the significant impact of welfarist pioneers and ethical businessmen on the thinking of contemporary employers, but to suggest that most welfare schemes were devised by employers with a rational concern for efficiency and profitability in the enterprise rather than being the result of spontaneous and altruistic gestures.

This point can be sustained when examining the behaviour of leading firms in the field of welfare before 1914. The pursuit of rationality and profitability within the firm has also to be seen in the context of the mounting industrial unrest of the late nineteenth century and the anxieties amongst firms about the spread of political sentiment amongst the workforce. Industrial welfare programmes were framed against a background of intense public debate over the citizenship of labour and the scope for state action in the labour market. The limited success of employers' schemes (and other voluntary efforts) was to provide a vital context for the growth of state action in the field of workers' welfare before 1914. Even the most rational strategy of business was framed in a cultural and political context. We can perceive this context more clearly by examining the nature of citizenship in industrial society and the discursive struggles in which workers engaged to extend their rights in capitalist production and society. Many such struggles were concerned with the legal rights of employees and further limited the scope for the employer's extra-legal dominance of workers both on the shop floor and in the provision of social benefits. The contest over workers' rights and business welfare formed an important reference point for the actions of state policy-makers before 1914.

The following section discusses some of the literature on workplace relations and outlines an argument on the significance of social power and authority relations at the workplace and in the making of workplace culture. The cultural values of employers and workers are seen as *resources* which influence their capacity to determine the outcome of conflicts. This argument is elaborated in a discussion of the welfare policies of industrial employers and an examination of the growth of socialist politics amongst manufacturing workers in the years before 1914. It is suggested that the changing relationship between industrial capitalism and the state did not result in a radical shift of power in either the workplace or British society.

The politics of production

The argument that Lancashire employers adopted the practices of paternalism in the decades after 1850 has been challenged by historians who provide evidence of interest conflict in the textile districts during the mid-nineteenth century.[22] Other writers have questioned the extent to which the policy of paternalism can be found in other districts of industrial Britain.[23] There are also some difficulties with the concept of 'paternalism' itself, which should be recognized. It is frequently argued that paternalist practices derive from the pre-industrial and even pre-capitalist values of landed society, though scholars have made very wide and varied usage of the term to describe political as well as social practices in urban as well as rural society.[24] In the specific context of industrial Lancashire, as depicted by Joyce, public celebrations of 'paternalist' loyalties appear to have been associated with Tory Anglicanism, whilst at other moments the bonds of loyalty seem to have extended to nonconformist dynasties. The connections between economic dependence and political deference, which are critical to the 'paternalist' argument, are frequently assumed to exist rather than clearly demonstrated.

The weakness of such arguments is that they derive attitudes (such as deference) from the evidence of behaviour which is open to various interpretations. For paternalism in one sense implies that there is a willing and positive reciprocity between masters and workers as to the rightful place of each in the social order. There is little doubt that many firms arranged events in the workplace and local areas which would serve as 'rites of intensification' and encourage employees to identify with the life of the enterprise, though the success of these initiatives was always contingent rather than assured. Secondly, paternalism implies (as the concept of 'patriarchy' does not), a benign regard of capitalists for the well-being of their workforce. This assumes a mutual agreement on the real interests of employees and the promotion of schemes to maintain a close connection between millowners and workers. Thirdly, the concept as used by writers such as Joyce suggests a *dominance* of workers' culture by the values of the employer and a subordination of labour to the political as well as the economic regime of the industrialist. Relations in the workplace are reduced to a formal hierarchy of command in which overlookers are able to regiment male workers and their families, whilst female labour is pinned down by the family economy in the factory and the home.

Not only are such arguments weakened by the clear evidence that technology did not subordinate workers in production, but there must be doubts that the outlook and values of a social class can be so decisively dominated by the employer. The evidence from Britain and other countries is that manufacturing employers sought to *appropriate* the skills, customs and understanding of the workers in meeting the demands of both specialist and mass production markets. This acknowledge-ment of the employer's reliance on the practical culture of the manual workforce was confirmed by the acceptance of autonomous benefit schemes within the enterprise, which were sponsored by the firm but largely controlled by the workforce. Even in these circumstances the term 'paternalism' hardly reflects the complexity of the reciprocal under-standing which exists. More generally, it can be argued that the relations between capitalists and workers must always have some element of strategic calculation as well as normative evaluation, and that employers and labour will constantly appraise the behaviour of the other in the light of perceived interests and moral sense. Even with their formidable economic and social resources in industrial society, manufacturers could rarely achieve the level of dominance in Britain (or other European societies) which the paternalist model implies.

The limits to employer dominance and workers' deference can be understood more clearly if we begin the analysis of relations in the labour market rather than examining subordination in the technical and social structure of industry. In his discussion of production, Marx placed the analysis of the wage contract before the examination of the labour process, emphasizing the employer's difficulty of assessing the precise amount of work which could be extracted for a set wage.[25] The problem of 'implicit contracts' is generally recognized as a problem for employers seeking to bind labour to provide a satisfactory level of output without incurring significant transaction and legal costs or restricting flexibility. Bowles and Gintis have argued that the capitalist's inability to rely on the labour market to provide a precise amount of worker output reflects the 'contested exchange' between employers and workers, as each party seeks to avoid conceding more than the minimum.[26] Here lies the root, they argue, of the exogenous system of labour controls and the characteristic power relations of capitalism, as employers impose sanctions against the non-producers.[27]

This analysis is helpful in explaining the nature of the effort bargain which firms make with their workers, though it ignores the evidence we can find in Joyce and many other sources that workers actively collaborate with management inside the workplace. Workers appear to draw on a wide range of values in deciding on their work effort, rather than making a strategic calculation of their individual interests. This view is supported by Akerlof's work on the importance of sentiment in the labour contract and the benefits to both employers and workers of reciprocal tolerance, which enables each side to exchange 'gifts' of indulgency and responsible behaviour.[28] Burawoy has developed this concept of reciprocal relations within the enterprise in his studies of the workplace, suggesting that the labour process and payment systems can provide workers with material and psychological rewards when they play the output game in production.[29]

For all his theoretical sophistication, Burawoy relies on a fairly simple model of evolutionary development to explain employers' labour management strategies. For he argues that there was a broad shift in the form of control used by employers from the paternalist (and patriarchal) regimes of early factory life to the more subtle hegemonic and consensual order of modern industry.[30] The coercion implicit in market and workplace despotism was replaced by the more complex and subtle strategies of 'manufacturing consent' as employers learned from historical experience. The heavy hand of paternalism was replaced by a subtle game of consensus. Other writers have suggested that an important form of labour control was provided in the creation of segmented labour markets as firms sought to retain a core of skilled labour and exploit the cheaper unskilled and female workers for less secure work.[31] This essay suggests that such a chronological model of labour management is unsatisfactory and that elements of accommodation and friction can be found in both the nineteenth- and the twentieth-century workplace. Moreover, the substance of hegemony and consent lay in the cultural values and shared understanding of the actors involved rather than the assumed outcome of a particular strategy.

Arguments about the employer's despotism or dominance at the workplace, which are reproduced in some accounts of factory paternalism, should therefore be treated with scepticism. The success of skilled males in increasing their bargaining position and political autonomy during the mid-nineteenth century suggests that such claims are misleading. Even within the factory and workshop the limits to the legal and market power of the employer left him heavily dependent on supervisors and technical grades who enjoyed a remarkable autonomy from the direct control of their masters well into the twentieth century. It was such groups of senior employees who exercised the prerogatives of capital on an everyday basis and who were responsible for maintaining the legitimate authority of the owner in the production process. It was also through the practical hands of the supervisors and other intermediate employees that the 'gifts' of tolerance and reciprocity were exchanged between the firm and its workers. The requirement on the employer to secure an acceptable level of effort, which is merely implicit in the labour contract, means that the compliance of labour has to be secured by a political regime within the workplace in which managers and supervisors are the key figures.

The findings of Akerlof, Burawoy and others demonstrate that normative values as well as the delegation of authority play a powerful part in the relations of production. It is arguable that the hegemony of employers depends not only on the ties of control and reciprocity described by Burawoy, but on a complex infrastructure of political relations and cultural values beyond the factory. Such a view differs from that of writers who, following Marx, have contrasted the rights of citizenship in civil society with the despotism of the employer in the workplace.[32] Rather than accepting this view of absolutism in production, it is more realistic to acknowledge that the economic power of the capitalist usually depends, to an important degree, on the legal and political rights prescribed by the state. Therefore the authority relations of capitalism are defined by a specific *political constitution* as well as the institutions of production.[33] Even the conflicts between 'economic classes' of employers and workers implied a cultural definition and political mobilization of their distinct interests: classes do not exist in a discrete economic sphere, away from the world of political representation.[34] Such a definition always occurred within a particular historical context. The terms on which industrial authority is established and sustained will be determined by struggles over the limits of citizenship in the workplace, as well as the specific contests over skill, work-load or family relations. The issue of citizenship in production was vividly exposed in the conflicts over state munitions production during both World Wars.[35]

The different sources of social power and autonomy suggest that the capitalist employer rarely enjoyed unlimited authority in securing the compliance of his workforce and that different forms of reciprocity were required, particularly when industrialists used large amounts of skilled and technically autonomous labour as did British manufacturers in the nineteenth and twentieth centuries. To govern production efficiently, firms had to possess authoritative resources (to use Giddens' terms) as well as the allocation of capital.[36] These resources effectively belonged to those who could command legitimacy. Since the practical work culture of the labour force was invariably saturated with the customs and habits of inherited tradition, their collective knowledge could be a formidable obstacle to the employers' capacity to dominate labour.[37] The strength of the workers lay not only in their collective understanding of how things were produced or carried (which Frederick Taylor emphasized), but in the customary recognition of what different work practices meant to the workers themselves.

If the employer's material resources were usually unrivalled, the cultural resources of the workforce could be decisive. The constitution of authority in production depended not only on the allocation of property, or the peculiar political constitution of capitalism in each society, but also the capacity of the different actors to assemble the cultural resources to sustain their objectives. The limits and costs of industrial coercion were apparent in countries such as Britain during the nineteenth century. The scope for dominating the institutions of labour was also fairly restricted. Most firms adopted labour policies which are reasonably well described by Margaret Levi's phrase, 'quasi-voluntary compliance'.[38] Such a regime was the creation not only of a particular political settlement between industrial capitalism and the state, but also the practical and cultural struggles of employers and workers to define terms of compliance. The political constitution of British capitalism was less secure at the end of the nineteenth century, as masters and workers contested the limits of authority and liberty, drawing on the contemporary discourse of positive rights and property defence to define their prerogatives.

To elaborate this argument the following section examines the changing labour policies of British employers in the later nineteenth and early twentieth century. It is argued that we can understand the continued use of welfare policies by manufacturers as a response to a particular kind of crisis of authority in production, and to a changing political context for the relations between capital and the state. Out of these struggles emerge new kinds of workplace cultures and a fresh conception of citizenship which contributed to the remaking of workers' politics at the beginning of the twentieth century.

Employers' welfare and workplace culture in Britain

It is the welfare regimes created by industrial employers in the mid-nineteenth century which have attracted most attention from historians interested in the making of British class society. The evidence of employers' benefits in the nineteenth and early twentieth centuries reveals that the chronology and impact of industrial paternalism outlined by Joyce is (at best) problematic. It is more satisfactory to locate the provision of social benefits in the employers' continuing search for compliance in the workplace and the locality. For the welfare innovations of industrial firms were *usually* designed to meet some specific local need of the enterprise, though the terms on which benefits could be introduced were directly determined by the legal and political framework within which capitalists operated. In the later nineteenth-century workplace welfare became one of the areas where the struggle for an enlarged citizenship for working people was closely fought. To understand the full implications of welfare provision it is necessary to examine the labour needs of the enterprise and the contractual expectations of capital and labour. These expectations will determine whether welfare provision will become a source of voluntary compliance or a focus for a contested exchange (or even conflict) between employers and workers.

There are various possible explanations of these business welfare strategies. The first set of explanations cover the rational needs of the firm, including the need to attract scarce labour skills, retaining valuable human capital once workers are trained, providing the employer with greater control over the 'social wage' of the employee and rewarding effort or loyalty through incentives such as profit-sharing. In addition to these schemes to regulate the labour supply, a second group of incentives can be found in the employer's need to control and discipline the work-force. This is why, some writers suggest, the firm's interest in welfare expenditure grows with the increase of labour unrest. Employers pursue a 'cycle of control' through the welfare programmes in their industry.[39] Thirdly, some employers pursue non-market goals of power, status and personal reputation. Welfare schemes are devised to enhance the prospects of the capitalist gaining public office or social honour, including gaining the support of his workers in electoral contests. It is difficult to separate the personal rewards of the employer from the needs of the enterprise, since model welfare programmes may benefit the firm by raising the public awareness of its products and function as a form of advertising, as well as celebrating the achievements of its owners. The prominence of some consumer-goods firms in both early brand advertising and welfare management indicates the complex blend of costs and benefits involved in the schemes of soap manufacturers or confectionery makers.

Each kind of explanation suggests that there was a strategic rationality in the promotion of workers' welfare, though the role of philanthropy and altruism is not excluded from such models of welfare motivation. The 'paternalism' model offered by Joyce emphasizes the complexity of employers' actions, though there is a strong suggestion that the wider social and political concerns of the Lancashire textile employers persuaded them of the need to offer welfare as part of an exercise in public leadership during the mid-century decades. Certainly, the economistic explanations of company welfare outlined above offer only a partial account of the origins and timing of such social benefits and profit sharing.[40] The picture of dominant benevolence given in many accounts of business welfare is also misleading. Where studies such as Joyce's are helpful is in drawing attention to the *political* character of welfare provision: industrialists are concerned not only to sustain their prerogatives in the workplace but also to strengthen their political presence in industrial society. The political settlement of the mid-nineteenth century (1846–67), which defined the content of citizenship in Victorian Britain, gave employers a powerful voice in local government but also emphasized the virtues of workers' voluntary efforts and their freedom to organize.

This helps to explain the controversy over industrial welfare. Throughout the nineteenth century the ability of employers to *impose* different 'benefits' on their employees remained a contested issue. Many firms extended their industrial credit schemes to bind the mobile workforce to their particular factory or district. The abuse of 'truck' was still the subject of legislation in Britain during the 1890s. In particular, the compensation of workers for accidents remained a source of intense controversy until the Workmen's Compensation legislation of 1897–1906 stipulated that employers could not induce their workers to opt out of state protection unless they offered benefits which were at least comparable to those available under the law.[41] Only large and powerful employers such as the railway companies could insert compulsory membership of the enterprise scheme in private legislation, thereby excluding their employees from the ban on compulsion under truck and accident legislation. The campaigns to restrict the power of the employer to compel their staff to contribute to schemes were joined by the early 'Lib-Lab' Members in Parliament, as the representatives of the coalmining districts sought legislation to restrain mining companies from deducting subscriptions to accident and other 'mutuals' at the pithead.

These struggles reached a peak before 1880 when the first Employers' Liability Act was passed and another wave of complaints culminated in the Compensation Act of 1897. In contrast to the impression given by Joyce, many of the welfare schemes of the industrialists were bitterly resisted by trade union members and even those schemes jointly managed between employers and workers' representatives went into decline during the mid-1870s and later 1880s as the unions gained in strength. Without the power to compel their workers to participate in accident insurance and medical benefit arrangements, employers found these arrangements less attractive. For the 1880 legislation enabled firms to contract out of the provisions of the Act and to offer their own liability insurance. As workers increasingly refused to subscribe to such measures and the legislation of 1897–1906 offered legal remedy in the courts for injured workers, industrialists turned to commercial and business mutual insurance as a means of dealing with the financial risks of accidents at work.

It is often noted that 'paternalist' employers were responsible for engineering new industrial communities in different regions of Britain during the mid-nineteenth century.[42] The evidence suggests that such projects always had a powerful economic imperative and were usually confined to major firms in periods of great prosperity. The construction of model industrial communities obviously went beyond the strict requirements of the enterprise, but the strategic needs of the firm has to be acknowledged even in the most expansive projects. Moreover, the ability of the employer to dominate the lives of the workforce was limited even in these sculptured settlements. It was in industries employing large numbers of female workers and lesser skilled males that some of the more celebrated experiments in community-building occurred. There were also examples of impressive housing schemes in the expanding coalfields, though the bulk of the colliery dwellings were of such poor standard that they became a serious point of contention by the end of the nineteenth century.[43]

The main difficulties facing employers who sought to use non-wage benefits to secure control of the workforce were the investment costs and growing resistance from the better organized (and more skilled) sections of the workforce. Throughout the middle and later decades of the nineteenth century the voluntary associations of industrial workers struggled for their autonomy from the patronage of their social superiors. Even where the relations between dominant firms and local workers remained reasonably good, there are signs that mutual benefit societies were breaking the bonds of dependence which existed in some districts. This does not imply that welfare services were ruptured in all industries. New and expanding sectors of production were the sites of major schemes after 1880. Even the centres of heavy industry saw new provisions introduced in the 1890s. What was different was the purpose and function of many such projects. They were often designed to weaken the hold of trade unionism, as employers accused the union leaders of exploiting their own friendly benefit funds for strike campaigns. In particular, metalworking firms used the new confederations of employers to develop collective (non-contributory) welfare schemes to prise away the supervisory and technical staff from the grip of the manual trades. In the protected markets of the gas industry, pioneering firms devised profit sharing and copartnership schemes in response to the disturbing spread of new unionism at the London works in the 1880s–90s.

Such evidence suggests that the practices of industrial welfare did not pass away after the mid-nineteenth century. Nor were such practices dramatically successful in imposing a new culture of business loyalty and workplace cooperation on industrial workers. The strongest bonds which held powerful groups of industrial workers together in this period were provided by the *occupational cultures* which distinguished the peculiarities of a specific trade from the customs and rules of other workers. Not only the craft fraternities but also the operatives of the textile factories developed occupational identities which embodied the particularisms of the district or locality as well as the peculiarities of the production process. Such occupational loyalties were sustained by the institutions of trade unionism, organized on the basis of trade or task rather than the membership of an industry. In the skilled occupations the rules and rituals of apprenticeship maintained the discipline of the craft with its folklore and sanctions well into the twentieth century. Most employers recognized and utilized these occupational loyalties and had little inclination to spend their scarce resources on ambitious welfare projects to weaken the trades —at least until the conflicts of the late nineteenth century.

More important for the maintenance of reciprocity between employers and workers was their subscription to a common *industrial* culture of practical knowledge and traditional customs. The most important element in this shared culture was the emphasis on practical experience and learning-by-doing rather than abstract or theoretical knowledge. Foremen and managers were promoted on the basis of shop floor experience, which bound them to the workers in a common intellectual culture which was well-established in the middle decades of the nineteenth century. McClelland has shown the extent to which masters and skilled workmen accepted their shared interest in the maintenance of 'the trade', with the employer's possession of capital matched by the craftsman's property rights over his skill.[44] This acknowledgement of the employer's prerogatives was qualified by an assertion of the masculine freedom in the use of non-work time, whether drinking in the pub or labouring in the allotment.[45] There were areas of shared understanding with the employer and some elements of an industrial culture in which both participated, but there were necessary tensions over reciprocal rights and the limits of authority inside and outside the gates of work.

The institutions which secured the claims of capital and labour were formed in the economic and political struggles of the mid-nineteenth century (particularly the 1850s and 1870s). Here again employers and workers joined in creating voluntary organizations outside the direct supervision of the British state. From their formative experiences these associations developed a vigorous scepticism about the benefits of government control of their affairs. Even the legal system, where some of the most important battles over workers' welfare occurred in the later nineteenth century, was not welcomed as a model for resolving industrial disputes. This emphasis on voluntary bargaining and financial autonomy helps to explain the compliance of industrial workers in the later nineteenth century. The position of senior males in the workplace meant that it was male associations which validated the claims of workers to the property of skill and seniority. Such conceptions of rights and freedoms were not relics of a lost world of artisanal culture but were embodied and reaffirmed in the practical struggles of the skilled unions to gain public acceptance and legal status during the 1870s. The triumph of voluntary efforts gave practical meaning to working-class citizenship in the period and explains the ambiguous welcome which such associations gave to the demand for state solutions to social problems. In the struggles for libertarian reform and legal immunity in the period 1832–75, labour associations advanced from the artisan politics of the early nineteenth century to the labour mentality of the late Victorian years, but the conception of citizenship was perceived as the birthright of independent males rather than the property of a class.

The industrial employers actually *shared* with these self-help associations a suspicion of government growth in the nineteenth century. The literature on industrial employers rarely acknowledges the extent to which manufacturing industry was entrenched in a world of provincial supply and institutions. After 1850 the balance between central and local government was maintained by the workings of the Poor Law and the municipal rates. Divided by competition and trade, it was religion and family connections as well as political loyalties which bound the leaderships of local business communities together. Such civic responsibilities appear to have been more important to the maintenance of urban power than the creation of 'paternalist' regimes within the factory, since they provided public-spirited businessmen (who included commercial and banking as well as industrial dynasties) with the means to erect monuments to their sense of duty without exhausting the enterprise. One important project which wealthy entrepreneurs *were* often willing to finance was the building of churches for the spiritual welfare of the urban community, including that of their own workers.

By the end of the nineteenth century many such initiatives had been exhausted. The limits of private and public benefaction were reached in cities such as Bradford, Liverpool and Bristol. The balance of reciprocity in the workplace was disturbed by conflicts over work-load and management reforms. Senior skilled males still dominated manufacturing production but new groups of male and female workers were organized in trade unions during the 1890s. The craft societies were themselves forced to shift from their 'primitive autonomy' in the workplace and local bargaining to more formalized procedures of central negotiation.[46] In the urban centres of production the older 'civic gospel' of the business community was being challenged by more radical programmes of municipal expenditure.[47] Women were involved in neighbourhood campaigns on housing and local services, as well as being employed in larger numbers in industry. The monopoly of male craftsmen over the public presentation of workers' claims to citizenship was being challenged as fresh groups were mobilized.

Between the 1890s and the 1920s it is possible to trace the emergence of fresh forms of workplace culture in Britain at a time when the citizenship of the worker under capitalism was being contested. The following section briefly considers the spread of socialist politics among

industrial workers and the responses of employers and the state to the
evidence of political action in the workplace.

Industrial workers and the growth of socialist politics

The contribution of workplace cultures to the growth of socialist
politics in Britain and other countries remains to be explored. Joyce has
suggested that the decline of paternalistic practices and of the distinctive
family structure of work in such sectors as cotton textiles, contributed
to the transformation of British politics at the end of the nineteenth
century.[48] In particular, the impact of new technologies on the skills and
status of the craft workforce has been seen as a major contribution to
the growth of workplace unrest and the spread of syndicalist ideas
amongst the industrial workforce before 1914. Marxist accounts of these
radical movements have often stressed the role of union bureaucracies in
defusing shop floor conflicts, containing rank and file militants and
marginalising the most exploited groups among the workforce.[49] Even
historians who have been highly critical of the 'rank and filist'
interpretation of working-class unrest provided by Marxist writers have
continued to emphasize the strategic importance of craft workers and
of bargaining institutions in determining the pattern of workplace
relations.[50] These 'revisionist' historians have argued that the outbreak of
industrial militancy before and during the First World War was an
expression of the entrenched craft conservatism and destructive sectionalism which actually inhibited the growth of stable socialist politics in
Britain, at least until the experience of state control persuaded the union
leaders of the scope for responsible management of the economy.[51]

   The growing consensus amongst historians that workplace action was
inherently sectionalist and politically sterile is open to debate. For such a
view disregards the diverse culture of industrial workers and their re-
evaluation of political possibilities in the early decades of the twentieth
century. By the end of the nineteenth century, the terms of compliance
which had been established in the mid-Victorian years were being
erased as women and the lesser skilled came to challenge the hegemonic
position of senior males in the production process.[52] As a new wave of
technological and organizational changes were introduced and struggles
between craft workers and employers intensified before 1914, the
authority relations of the workplace were reappraised and industrial
supervision became the subject of bitter controversy. Even the customary
respect for practical experience was eroded as employers introduced new

methods of work study and job pacing in the more advanced plants. As the customary respect for handicraft standards came under critical scrutiny from employers, frictions intensified and a number of firms resorted to business welfare as a means of re-asserting their authority and to foster a new culture of enterprise loyalty in the workplace. In this way a new moral basis for reciprocity and the exchange of sentiments could have been laid. Evidence suggests that the business welfare movement enjoyed limited success and the workplace unrest of the pre–1914 marked the decline of reciprocal customs in different sectors of industry. As the employers responded by insisting on formal rules and bureaucratic procedures to govern production or settle disputes, so their employees devised new arrangements to protect their autonomy on the shop floor and increase union discipline rather than relying on the 'primitive autonomy' of the craft group.[53]

In their drive to reduce unit labour costs in manufacturing industry, many firms were disrupting customary practices and controls as they increased the workloads on employees and introduced new techniques, payment systems and workplace organization where possible. Strategies to improve productivity included the crude use of female and youth labour, particularly apprentice labour, in branches of metalworking, printing and consumer goods to replace more expensive males. Supervisors and shop managers were placed under increasing pressure to police the piecework systems and enforce a tighter regime of control on new machinery.

The decay of customary values and the spread of new organizational forms can be seen in the contrasting regions of west Scotland and the West Riding of Yorkshire. It was in these areas that the ILP established itself as a significant political force at the end of the nineteenth century, challenging the Liberal Party's hegemony after the crisis over Irish liberation (in 1886) weakened the hold of the Gladstonians. The origins of socialist support can be traced to the different industrial experiences of both regions at this time. During the late 1880s and 1890s there were clear signs of increasing unionization—particularly the West Riding— including the effective organization of women and the lesser skilled. Although the dominance of senior males within the trade union movement was still overwhelming, the prominence of female and un-skilled workers was vividly demonstrated in the struggle which occurred at the Bradford mill of the Cunliffe-Lister family.[54] The fragmented geography of wool textile production in the West Riding and the absence of strong union organization gave the strikers little chance of success, but the struggle marked a turning point in labour relations during the 1890s and cleared the way for the foundation of the Independent Labour Party in 1892. After generations of compliance and the anxiety of local Liberal employers to present themselves as the true representatives of working people, customary loyalties declined and the ILP ran vociferous campaigns against the local industrialists who had dominated the public life of the wool towns since the passing of Chartism. This political challenge was largely contained by the Liberals before 1914 and the bargaining power of labour was limited until the First World War, but the leadership provided by Tom Maguire formed part of a fresh coalition of support for the values of independent Labour.[55] The concern with the wider social condition of labour and the enlargement of citizenship to enclose the concerns of women at work and in 'the community' can be traced in the early conferences of the ILP.

Whilst the West Riding faced the decline of some traditional trades (superseded by the new ready-made clothing factories as large employers), the west of Scotland was booming. Trade unionism was a weak growth until the 1880s when the distinct metalworking trades were rapidly assembled in the engineering and shipbuilding societies. The occupational cultures of Clydeside were a resource for defending the particular trades against the encroachments of their rivals *and* the employer.[56] There is no doubt that skilled males remained overwhelmingly dominant in the Clyde economy, as women were barely represented in the heavy industries which boomed before 1914. It is also apparent that employers and workers subscribed to an industrial culture of the practical working man, launching ships or locomotives with a limited amount of theoretical expertise and mechanical technology. An important element in this empiricist culture was the acknowledgement, by employers, of the autonomy of male craft workers who devised their own customs and practices to regulate the quality of output. The era of reciprocity based on customary regulation was gradually eroded by economic and institutional forces which changed the basis of compliance and consent in the workplace by 1914.

Evidence of a weakening in the ties of reciprocity can be found in the pattern of industrial conflict before 1914, as tradesmen faced the attempts of engineering and shipyard employers to tighten their control of the local labour market. The primitive autonomy which the craft trades had enjoyed gave way to a institutional procedures that required both official and unofficial policing by the unions. Occupational loyalties were reasserted in the defence of craft prerogatives, though skilled tradesmen also cooperated in forming local 'vigilance committees' at which unofficial stewards could discuss common strategies, corresponding with the district committees of the unions and the Trades Councils which played such a significant role in the early days of Scottish union organization. From these conflicts of skilled workers and employers emerged a complex 'culture of solidarity'.[57] To dismiss these attitudes as the expression of 'craft conservatism" or male sectionalism is to ignore the evidence of cooperation amongst trade groups and also with those possessing lesser skills, such as 'machinemen', at this time.[58] Compliance was still a contested issue in 1914, as the local trades struggled to retain their customary regulations. During the First World War the tensions between firms and workers were dramatically increased by government policies on dilution and conscription, though it was the ILP's campaigns on rents and housing which drew the industrial workforce into a successful challenge to the Liberals and the state.[59]

The social conditions of the industrial workforce was addressed by some prominent firms before the 1890s, particularly where large employers could dominate local government and *partially* regulate local labour markets by their influence over the Poor Law. Industrialists mainly supported the Liberal Party which dominated central Scotland in the nineteenth century, though the controversies over Home Rule, tariffs and social reform weakened its hold over the business community. By the 1890s local employers faced the growth of strong trade societies in the workplace and socialist agitation in the wards of many municipal burghs. The ILP campaigned strongly against the housing conditions found on the Lanarkshire coalfield, whilst ironworking trades supported the call for municipal rebuilding of slum areas. Local firms responded by introducing welfare programmes to contain the independence of the skilled workforce and retain the loyalties of key supervisory grades. These could not prevent workers abandoning the mutual accident schemes developed after 1880 in favour of union schemes. With the passing of new compensation legislation, increasing numbers of firms turned to commercial and mutual insurance schemes as a way of defending the interests of the company against the claims of injured workers. There were also serious limits on the amount of housing expenditure the employers could undertake.

The contribution which the politics of skill and workplace culture made to the growing influence on socialist parties on the Clyde is not easily summarized. The intellectual culture of skilled males was derived from a tradition of religious libertarianism which was characteristic of urban Protestantism in Scotland, as well as the occupational identities of the workforce.[60] This enabled autodidacts to draw on the commonsense assumptions of the theological and political life of west Scotland to construct a radical critique of capitalism and sustain support for the ILP in the area. Smith has argued that it was the outbreak of war which gave a minority of revolutionary Marxists the opportunity to use these cultural resources to orchestrate a direct challenge to the British state from the munitions plants.[61] Her analysis illustrates the importance of intellectual and political cultures in Scottish society, though it exaggerates the continuities between Victorian Liberalism and Labour socialism, as well as the contrast between shop floor unrest and struggles for constitutional campaigns for social citizenship in the early twentieth century. For the intellectual formation of the ILP owed a great deal to the workerist leadership of Tom Mann and others who argued that any *Labour* Party must draw on the practical historical experience of working people for its intellectual resources rather than defer to literary socialists on the Fabian or the revolutionary left. This vigorous prejudice was transplanted into the Parliamentary Labour Party, though self-educated Scottish luminaries were tolerated by trade unionists.

A second influence on the campaigning style of Labour was imprinted by the ILP's evangelical commitment to 'making socialists' by urban crusades and large public gatherings.[62] Even in west Scotland, Maxton and other brilliant orators devoted their energies to campaigns of conversion, whilst the less brilliant tacticians concentrated on building up the networks of support in local organizations which underpinned the success of the ILP in municipal elections. Health and housing issues rather than industrial questions were the main cause of the ILP's gradual electoral progress before 1914. It was the War itself which openly politicized workplace relations and forced the convergence of industrial and social grievances in the conflicts of 1915–19.[63] During the conflicts over wages, dilution and conscription, the legitimate authority of the employers was damaged if not shattered. Masculine craftsmen worked alongside female trainees and trade unionists saw their bargaining rights supplanted by state directives.

The result was a fragmentation of industrial culture and occupational loyalties. Many craftsmen insisted on a return to pre-War conditions whilst a significant body of unskilled workers were rapidly unionized in these years. During the period of the Reconstruction debate (1917–20), many workplace activists reached towards a politics which would enlarge social citizenship by providing for industrial democracy and radical welfare reforms. Although there were challenges to the doctrine of voluntary bargaining by free agents before 1914, it was the Wartime struggles which placed economic and political reform on agenda of both skilled and unskilled unions. Industrial democracy and active citizenship on the shop floor became a serious political question in the post-War era. Only the return of large scale unemployment and political disintegration in 1920–22 marked the clear retreat of workers to their customary defences of sectionalism and empirical pragmatism. The ILP appears to have accomplished a partial transformation of industrial workers' culture but largely failed to integrate workplace and community campaigns in a way which could disturb the political constitution of capitalism during the 1920s.

Conclusions

This essay suggests that the workplace is an area where different cultural resources are produced. For culture constitutes both a way of seeing the world *and* a resource for dealing with the relations of production and power in which actors are engaged. If the contract of labour and the prerogatives of the employer are the foundation of capital's power over labour, cultural values are an essential part of reciprocal relations in production. The need for the employer to enforce the implicit terms of the labour contract sets the scene for a contested exchange in the workplace. The costs of surveillance and coercion explain why firms seek to establish a basic level of reciprocity to sustain the legitimate authority of the management in production. The capacity of the employer to secure the cooperation of labour will depend on the extent to which reciprocity can be maintained when the close proximity and surveillance of workers is removed. The way in which workers behave depends on normative as well as strategic calculations. It was the employers' early recognition of the benefits for the firm of workers' autonomy which explains the appropriation by industrial capitalism of the traditional working techniques, family employment and payment systems rather than the crude subordination of labour to the despotism of the factory. The cost of such autonomy can be measured in the extent of craft restrictions, union membership and voluntary associations amongst workers in the nineteenth century. These were constrained within the formal hierarchy of authority until the growing conflict of the pre-1914 period forced employers to reassert their right to manage production. This offensive took place in a context where business was seeking to assimilate workers to a new era of welfare capitalism and where the British state was engaged in accommodating the demand for a reappraisal of social citizenship. It was ultimately the government which assumed responsibility for a welfare programme which formed part of the new political constitution for industrial capitalism.

From this perspective it has been suggested that the model of 'paternalism' does not provide an adequate analysis of employer-worker reciprocity: it is conceptually incapable of sustaining the explanation it seeks. Similarly, the reference to 'deference' in describing workers' politics is problematic: it assumes that because people do not rebel they accept and positively acknowledge the right to govern of their social superiors. Historically, the political regime of the workplace has been constituted by specific settlements between capitalism and the state rather than dictated by the logic of market relations or technology. In order to understand the compliance of industrial workers with the authority of industrial capitalism we have to understand the complex relations of reciprocity at work, including the *cultural* terms on which compliance is arranged. If the prerogatives of the management and the autonomy of the workers held the culture of the workplace in tension, there were also areas where the employers and the employed shared practical and moral values. It was on these that the reciprocity of the contracting parties depended. One of the most powerful themes in British industrial culture was the endorsement of the importance of empirical experience over theoretical understanding. This celebration of experience over rationality, itself a feature of the peculiar character of native empiricism, was assimilated into the political culture of Labour in a way which affirmed the validity of historical tradition but deprived Labour politics of the analytical capacity to interrogate capitalism and the state.[64]

These shared values helped to sustain the new political settlement of the early twentieth century, upon which the boundaries of citizenship were redrawn. At the end of the nineteenth century the implicit power relations of the workplace and the private regime of the employer became part of a political struggle to determine the boundaries of contest and consent. During these struggles, fresh forms of organization and distinctive 'cultures of solidarity', as Fantasia has described them, emerged amongst industrial workers.[65] Some sectors of industry were able to promote loyalty to the enterprise in this period by a combination of human relations management, profit-sharing ventures and the cultivation of garden communities in sight of the works, though in heavy manufacturing industry business welfare had very limited success. The failure of industrial welfare schemes to contain the new cultures of solidarity in the centres of greatest unrest forced the state to reconstitute the political framework for capitalism by an elaboration of public 'welfare' schemes, which incorporated both powerful commercial interests and voluntary schemes in a national programme of contributory insurance.

These reforms were not a simple functional response to the crisis of authority facing industrial employers at this period. The restructuring of the political constitution of capitalism was the expression not only of a contract between dominant institutions but also the outcome of struggles between actors with different material and cultural resources. Workers fought for an enlargement of their citizenship on the shop floor at a period when liberal reformers sought to confine positive liberties to the kind of welfare rights which T.H. Marshall depicted as a seminal advance in social evolution.[66] The result was that the Liberals defined workers' needs in terms of social improvements rather than industrial democracy. Whilst the limits of business welfare forced the state to reappraise the 'labour problem' in 1906–14 and again in 1917–20, the campaigns of workers for improved compensation and the right to work did not culminate in the public control of the capitalist economy—still less workers' control of production.

The limits of socialist politics in Britain can be attributed, in part, to the rigidity of workers' cultures as well as their resilience. The emphasis on historical experience, which E.P. Thompson celebrates as the great achievement of the English working class, could be a source of analytical and organizational weakness when the socialist parties sought to consolidate their programmes. The pragmatic and defensive quality of workers' empiricism was overcome at key moments of political advance. Practical struggles in the workplace seriously weakened the bonds of reciprocity between employers and workers between 1890 and 1920. The ILP was able, in some districts, to fuse workplace and urban campaigns in the crisis of the 1914–18 War. The years 1915–20 were a period of fluid political cultures when both workplace sectionalism and party sectarianism lost their edge, opening the prospect of an integrated culture of solidarity. Workplace democracy as well as trade privileges was on the agenda. It was only after the defeats of the early 1920s that workers retreated to the defences of workplace custom and occupational bargaining, as their practical experience exhausted the promise of political action. What remained was a resilient association of the older industrial districts with the politics of Labour. For Labour itself had become part of the historical experience of workers and of a working-class culture.

Notes

1. B. Turner (ed.), *Organizational Symbolism* (Berlin and New York, 1990). This essay has its origins in a contribution to a conference on European working-class culture, held at the Sorbonne in Spring 1988. I am grateful to the participants for their comments and particularly to Patrick Fridenson, Lars Magnusson, and Birgitta Skarin-Frykman for their advice and to Jonathan Barry for his excellent editorial suggestions.
2. P. Willis, *Soup from Nettles* (Swedish Institute of Social Policy, Vasteras, 1989), pp. 16–18.
3. P.D. Bougden, S.G. Ogden, and Q. Outram, 'Profit Sharing and the Cycle of Control', *Sociology* 22 (1988), 607–9.
3. G. Brulin and T. Nilsson, 'New Societal Forms of Managerial Corporatism: New forms of work organization as a transformations vehicle?' *Arbetsrapport* (ALC, Stockholm, 1990).
4. See E.P. Thompson, *The Making of the English Working Class* [1963] (Harmondsworth, 1968), pp. 297–317 for the tragic view of industrialization; R. Johnson, 'Three Problematics: Elements of a theory of working-class culture' in J. Clarke, C. Critcher and R. Johnson (eds), *Working-Class Culture. Studies in history and theory* (1979), pp. 215–17.
5. P. Joyce, 'The Historical Meanings of Work: An introduction', in id. (ed.), *The Historical Meanings of Work* (Cambridge, 1987).
6. R. Johnson, 'Culture and the historians' in Clarke *et al.* (eds), *Working-Class Culture.*
7. G. Stedman Jones, *Languages of Class: Studies in working-class history* (Cambridge, 1983); J. Foster, *Class Struggle in the Industrial Revolution* (1977); R. Price, *Labour in British Society. An interpretative history* (1982).
8. A.J. Reid, 'Economics and Politics in the Formation of the British Working Class', *Social History* 3 (1978), pp. 347–62; cf. Stedman Jones, *Languages of Class.*
9. W. Lazonick, 'Organization and Technology in Capitalist Development' in id., *Competitive Advantage on the Shop Floor* (Cambridge, Mass., 1990); M. Berg, 'Women's Work, Mechanisation and the Early Phases of Industrialisation in England' in Joyce (ed.), *Historical Meanings of Work*; H.F. Gospel, *The Management of Labour* (Cambridge, 1991).
10. W. Lazonick, 'Industrial Relations and Technical Change: The case of the self-acting mule', *Cambridge Journal of Economics* 3 (1979), pp. 231–62; id., 'Production Relations, Labor Productivity and the Choice of Technology: British and U.S. cotton spinning', *Journal of Economic History* 41 (1981), pp. 491–516.

11. Cf. G. Stedman Jones, 'Class Struggle and the Industrial Revolution', *New Left Review* 90 (1975), pp. 35–70.
12. A.J. Reid, *The Division of Labour in the Clydeside Shipbuilding Industry* (Cambridge, 1980); id., 'Dilution, Trade Unionism and the State in Britain during the First World War' in S. Tolliday and J. Zeitlin (eds), *Shop Floor Bargaining and the State* (Cambridge, 1985); J. Zeitlin, 'From Labour History to the History of Industrial Relations', *Economic History Review* 40 (1987), pp. 159–84; J. Melling, 'British Employers and the Development of Industrial Welfare, 1880–1920', University of Glasgow Ph.D. thesis (1980); id., 'Whatever Happened to Red Clydeside? Industrial conflict and the politics of skill in the First World War', *International Review of Social History* 30 (1990), pp. 3–32.
13. W. Lewchuk, *American Technology and the British Vehicle Industry* (Cambridge, 1987).
14. R. Whipp, *Patterns of Labour. Work and social change in the pottery industry* (1990), p. 210.
15. P. Joyce, *Work, Society and Politics: The culture of the factory in later Victorian England* (Brighton, 1980).
16. Ibid., pp. 152–73.
17. Ibid., pp. 331–42.
18. J. Dutton and D. King, 'The Limits of Paternalism: The cotton tyrants of North Lancashire 1836–54', *Social History* 7 (1982), pp. 59–74; M.W. Dupree, 'Firm, Family and Community in the Staffordshire Potteries: Wedgwood and Etruria in the mid-nineteenth century' (paper presented to the conference on 'Enterprise and Community', Glasgow, March 1991). I am grateful for permission to cite Dr. Dupree's paper.
19. Whipp, *Patterns of Labour*; Dupree, 'Firm, Family and Community'.
20. Reid, 'Dilution, Trade Unionism and the State'; Zeitlin, 'From Labour History', pp. 160–1, 167–8; id., '"Rank and Filism" and Labour History: A rejoinder to Price and Cronin', *International Review of Social History*, 34 (1989), pp. 100–1
21. Zeitlin, 'From Labour History', pp. 168, 178; id., '"Rank and Filism"', p. 94.
22. Dutton and King, 'Paternalism'.
23. Dupree, 'Firm, Family and Community'.
24. H. Newby, *The Deferential Worker* (1977); E.P. Thompson, 'The Moral Economy of the English Crowd in the Eighteenth Century', *Past and Present* 56 (1970), pp. 132–6; id., 'Patrician Society, Plebeian Culture', *Journal of Social History* 7 (1974), pp. 382–405.
25. K. Marx, *Capital* [1886] ed. Moore Aveling (1912), pp. 163–5.
26. S. Bowles and H. Gintis, 'Contested Exchange: New microfoundations for the political economy of capitalism', *Politics & Society* 18 (1990),

pp. 168, 178.

27. Ibid., p. 167; cf. M. Burawoy and E. Olin Wright, 'Coercion and Consent in Contested Exchange', *Politics & Society* 18 (1990), pp. 253–5.

28. G.A. Akerlof, 'Labor Contracts as Partial Gift Exchange', *Quarterly Journal of Economics* 97 (1982), pp. 544, 550; cf. A.W. Gouldner, *Patterns of Industrial Bureaucracy* (1955).

29. M. Burawoy, *Manufacturing Consent. Changes in the labour process under monopoly capitalism* (Chicago, 1979), pp. 85, 93; id. and Olin Wright, 'Coercion and Consent', pp. 256–7.

30. M. Burawoy, *The Politics of Production. Factory regimes under capitalism and socialism* (1985), pp. 95–9, 122–8.

31. W. Reich, D. Gordon and R. Edwards, *Segmented Work, Divided Workers* (New York, 1980); C. Craig *et al.*, *Labour Market Structure, Industrial Organisation and Low Pay* (Cambridge, 1982), pp. 8–9; M. Glucksmann, *Women Assemble. Women workers and the new industries in interwar Britain* (1990), pp. 10–17.

32. Cf. A. Giddens, *A Contemporary Critique of Historical Materialism. Power, property and the state* (1982), p. 205.

33. Cf. G.R. Cohen, *History, Labour and Freedom: Themes from Marx* (Oxford, 1988), pp. 5–13; Burawoy, *Politics of Production*, p. 11.

34. cf. P. Hirst, 'Economic Classes and Politics' in A. Hunt (ed.), *Class and Class Structure* (1977), pp. 130–1.

35. J. Hinton, 'The Citizen on the Shop Floor. Joint Production Committees in the British engineering industry during the Second World War' (unpublished paper, University of Warwick, 1990), pp. 2–3.

36. Giddens, *A Contemporary Critique*, pp. 4–5.

37. L. Magnusson, 'Custom as Inherited Tradition? Culture and work in Eskilstuna during the nineteenth and early twentieth century' (paper presented to the conference on working-class culture, Sorbonne, Paris, 1988).

38. M. Levi, *Of Rule and Revenue* (Berkeley, 1988), pp. 52–5.

39. H. Ramsay, 'Cycles of Control: Worker participation in sociological and historical perspective', *Sociology* 11 (1977), pp. 481–506; Bougden *et al.*, 'Profit sharing'.

40. Bougden *et al.*, 'Profit sharing', pp. 624–5.

41. Melling, 'British Employers'.

42. J. Reynolds, *The Great Paternalist. Titus Salt and the growth of nineteenth-century Bradford* (1983).

43. J. Melling, 'Scottish Industrialists and the Changing Character of Class Relations in the Clyde Region' in T. Dickson (ed.), *Capital and Class in Scotland* (Edinburgh, 1982).

44. McClelland, K. 'Time to Work, Time to Live: Some aspects of work

and the re-formation of class in Britain, 1850–1880' in Joyce (ed.), *Historical Meanings of Work*, pp. 189–91; Rule, 'The Property of Skill in the Period of Manufacture' in ibid., pp. 110–11; cf. Magnusson, 'Custom as Inherited Tradition?'.

45. McClelland, 'Time to Work, Time to Live', pp. 204–6 and *passim*; cf. H.F. Moorhouse, 'The "Work Ethic" and "Leisure" Activity: the hot rod in post-war America' in Joyce (ed.), *Historical Meanings of Work*, pp. 240–1, see also the essay by Philip Corrigan in this volume.
46. R. Price, *Masters, Unions and Men* (Cambridge, 1980); Melling, 'Whatever Happened to Red Clydeside?'.
47. D. Smith, 'Capital, Labour and the Civic Gospel: Industry and politics in Birmingham, 1830–1914' (paper presented to the conference on 'Enterprise and the Community', Glasgow, 1991).
48. Joyce, *Work, Society and Politics*.
49. J. Hinton, *The First Shop Stewards' Movement* (1973); K. Burgess, *The Challenge of Labour* (1980); Price, *Masters, Unions and Men*; id., *Labour in British Society*; M. Savage, *The Dynamics of Working-Class Politics* (Cambridge, 1987).
50. R. McKibbin, *Ideologies of Class* (Oxford, 1990); Reid, 'Dilution, Trade Unionism and the State'; Zeitlin, 'From Labour History'.
51. I. McLean, *The Legend of Red Clydeside* (Edinburgh, 1983); Reid, 'Dilution, Trade Unionism and the State'; G.R. Rubin, *War, Law and Labour* (Oxford, 1987).
52. Savage, *Dynamics of Working-Class Politics*.
53. Melling, 'Whatever Happened to Red Clydeside?'.
54. Id., 'British Employers'.
55. E.P. Thompson, 'Homage to Tom Maguire' in A. Briggs and J. Saville, *Essays in Labour History* (1960); Johnson, 'Culture and the Historians', p. 58.
56. Reid, *Division of Labour*.
57. R. Fantasia, *Cultures of Solidarity* (Berkeley, 1988), pp. 15–20.
58. Melling, 'Whatever Happened to Red Clydeside?'; Cf. McLean, *Legend of Red Clydeside*.
59. J. Melling, 'Clydeside Rent Struggles and the Making of Labour Politics in Scotland, 1900–1939' in R. Rodger (ed.), *Scottish Housing in the Twentieth Century* (Leicester, 1989).
60 J. Smith, 'Commonsense Thought and Working-Class Consciousness', University of Edinburgh Ph.D. thesis (1980); id., 'Labour Tradition in Glasgow and Liverpool', *History Workshop Journal* 17 (1984), pp. 32–56.
61. Id., 'Taking the Leadership of the Labour Movement: The ILP in Glasgow, 1906–1914' in A. McKinlay and R. Morris (eds), *The I.L.P. on Clydeside* (Manchester, 1991).

62. S. Yeo, 'A New Life: The religion of socialism in Britain, 1883–1896', *History Workshop Journal* 4 (1977), pp. 53–6.
63. McKinlay and Morris (eds), *The I.L.P. on Clydeside*.
64. cf. P. Anderson, 'The Figures of Descent', *New Left Review* 161 (1987), pp. 20–77.
65. Fantasia, *Cultures of Solidarity*, pp. 19–20.
66. B.S. Turner, 'Outline of a Theory of Citizenship', *Sociology* 24 (1990), pp. 189–91.

Cultural Influences on Economic Action

Sidney Pollard

I

The debate on entrepreneurship and culture has hitherto largely been conducted on two quite separate levels. One one level, what one might call the 'strong' version considers societies without any form of a capitalistic market economy, let alone modern industrialism. In these cases it is therefore possible for the whole gamut of cultural influences to be hostile to even the most primitive form of capitalistic enterprise as such. In some societies, any form of money-making may be considered wrong, inferior or sinful; in others, it is rather the exclusive or dominant concentration on private gains which is frowned upon. In extreme cases, neither income nor property in our sense are regarded as desirable objects to be maximized, and scales of value obtain which are as difficult for us to grasp, as capitalist values would be for the people in those societies. Whatever the details, the assumption is thus often made that it is the sum total of cultural influences in the widest sense which operate to inhibit the development of a progressive market economy in favour of conservative traditionalism.

Clearly, such societies are not found in modern Europe, and are rare elsewhere today. Much of the literature is therefore concerned with 'primitive' societies in exotic parts of the world, the province of the anthropologist,[1] rather than the economist, or it is developed largely imaginatively, or as part of a counterfactual argument, by sociologists.

The range of weapons which a culture can muster against the potential market-oriented entrepreneur is formidable. One powerful element of the defence of the status quo generally lies in the religion of a society or in its range of superstitions, inasfar as these can be distinguished from each other. This works on at least two levels. The aspects of selfishness, greed and materialism inherent in successful entrepreneurship can be represented as unethical, so that the innovator would feel himself morally corrupt as well as giving offence to his fellow men. It can also be represented as being displeasing to the divinity and therefore likely to lead to punishment in due course. Equally powerful weapons may be provided by moral or religious obligations laid on members of the society which conflict with entrepreneurial purposes, such as the obligation to hand all surplus over to the poor or to the monks or medicine men, or to spend a large part of the day in devotions, or limitations on contracts with infidels.[2]

More powerful still, perhaps, are the sanctions which society maintains to uphold its conventions of behaviour, if they are transmitted through the esteem or contempt of one's fellows. If we grant for the moment that money alone is only rarely a motivating force for entrepreneurial behaviour, and that esteem, status, political or social influence, etc., are also very strong, and in part are the objectives to be purchased with the material gains made in business, such cultural inhibitions can be destructive to the point of being fatal to business initiative. An interesting sidelight of the workings of this was provided by a report by a Nigerian colleague at an international conference. He described how, after years of hard work, a major inland city was at last linked up by telephone with the rest of the world, the shining new wires being a token of progress for the forward-looking members of the community. Some days later the lines went dead, and the poles stood empty once more. Within a week or so, beautifully formed figurines, made from new copper wire, appeared in the town's market. The point of the story was that, by and large, the population found this unremarkable, and certainly did not condemn the transfer of the wire to alternative uses. What incentive, then, for a telephone company, or for a merchant depending on it?

Even Nigeria is, of course, a highly developed and structured society compared with many of those studied by anthropologists which provide the most clear-cut examples of cultural differences from our own society that are so large that our whole system of values and motivations is foreign to them, as theirs are foreign to us. These are outside my expertise, though one notes with dismay, if other experts are to be believed, that even the most honest observers of primitive societies are not above re-interpreting what they see to conform to their pre-existing notions, quite apart from those, and some of the best among them, who observe wrongly or record falsely.

If we posit that all societies did in the past maintain barriers against what we would nowadays call the entrepreneur, there must have been occasions of very strong entrepreneurs, or very weak barriers, to allow the first breaches which could then be widened by lesser men. The early capitalists would then have to survive a severe struggle with their consciences, as successful Italian merchants certainly did in the days of Francesco Datini. At the same time, the heavy artillery led into the field against capitalistic activity, and in particular against usury, by the Roman Catholic Church, as indeed by most other major religions, points to the fact that there is something in the make-up of human beings and of their societies which would be drawn towards business activities if this promised material gain, in the absence of religious and social taboos. The churches were clearly conscious of battling against human nature when they brought their moral disapproval to bear on the successful money-making entrepreneur.

It is not in the least necessary to assume that the drive of these pioneer capitalists was simply money: the 'capitalist spirit' which so impressed Weber and Sombart—the latter unduly neglected in this country—consisted of far more than greed for riches, as Dario Castiglione reminds us so convincingly in his paper. There was, on the one hand, the drive to do a good job, to do things better than before, more rationally since superstition and prejudice had turned out to be worthless, and to take up opportunities that were lying fallow, and there were also the excitements of risk and innovation. But on the other hand, men were undoubtedly also driven by the hope of personal advancement and esteem, the recognition of fellow men and the membership of the social elite—sentiments not unfamiliar within the competitive and unscrupulous Roman Catholic hierarchy of the day which regularly thundered against 'usury'. All these we recognize as being 'human', as making us what we are.

At any rate, thus the barriers were broken.

II

This hasty and most inadequate survey is intended to be no more than a framework for the second, 'weak' version of the influence of culture on economic development, which is the version more appropriate to the contributions to this collection. Here we are dealing with organized, structured societies at a far later stage of development than the examples on which anthropology erects its notions on how society works. These economies have a complex division of social labour, a considerable surplus of output over sheer physical needs, a potential for economic growth and some success in the sense of past growth and technical progress, if only slowly and over a lengthy period. Nevertheless, they are societies which at some stage have hit a barrier which prevents them going forward to the technical breakthrough we call the industrial revolution, to the modernization of social structures associated with this development, and indeed to any recognizable form of market capitalism. Even though they may not be totally stagnant, from our modern point of view they appear to be backward and incapable of development. Can 'cultural' influences be made responsible for those examples of 'failure' to develop?

Eric Jones examines the most famous case of all, that of China. Leading Europe in every respect by the thirteenth and fourteenth centuries of our calendar, Chinese society had proved not only capable of creating and absorbing a whole range of technical innovations, but had proved itself also capable of generating and debating numerous innovative ideas, in philosophy, science, medicine and many other fields. Yet sometime around that era, progress stopped, economic growth and structural change ceased, and he would be a bold man who could guess how long it would have taken China to find her own way to a successful capitalist market economy (or something at least equally efficient) had the pressure from the West not intervened.

A cultural explanation would seem to be attractive,[3] but as Jones shows, those offered lack substance and proof. None of them can explain, not only the stagnation, but simultaneously also the preceding progress. Jones' own favoured explanation, an excessive preoccupation with rent-seeking on the part of the Chinese, is interesting in that, unlike cultural explanations, which are always specific to a particular cultural context, it can be of more general application. Like Mancur Olson's more far-reaching law of progressive ossification,[4] it is capable of explaining upward movement as well as stagnation, the completion of one cycle as well as the start of the next at a higher level. As another example, consider some of the less-developed Latin American countries today. Money-making, rapacity, and market orientation certainly exist, yet the obstacles to forming social structures which would favour development, such as fair taxation, the end of gangsterism by estate-owners, a judiciary, police force and army free from corruption, etc., are considerable. The rule by the army and/or the landed classes is, of course, a matter of power rather than culture. Does it make sense to blame their cultural prefer-ences for failing to use their undoubted potential to foster economic development, and what meaning could be attached to 'culture' in this context?

Against these may be set the example of Japan. In historical time and therefore more easily observable than in other comparable cases, the merchants occupied in Japanese traditional society the lowest place in the social order, below the warriors, the peasants and the craftsmen. Nevertheless, many had become rich by the time the Tokugawa period ended, and some of them slid very easily into leading 'capitalist' positions, together, of course, with members of the other classes.[5] It may be, and in fact it has been argued, that traditional Japanese culture which had survived two hundred years of total isolation from the rest of the world with very few internal changes, was, in the face of clear appearances to the contrary, really quite well tailored to form the seedbed of the most impressive economic 'miracle' of this century. But then the question remains how we distinguish between those influences which appear to be inhibiting and in fact were so and others which have the same appearance but turn out to have been harmless.

III

If therefore we reject the rather crude version of 'cultural influence', there is a more refined version of the 'weak' theory on the influence of culture on capitalist progress. This refers to societies which are undoubtedly capitalist; societies in which capitalism has in fact, existed for centuries in many, in most or indeed in all sectors of the economy. Employers are capital-owners who seek to make a profit, employees are propertyless wage and salary earners, though, as always, there are many mixed forms beside the pure forms of these social categories. Nevertheless, it is alleged, there may be powerful cultural influences in existence which inhibit the potential power of the economic agents from acting in such a way as to maximize economic progress or, to be more precise, to allow society to make the most of its economic opportunities.

One textbook example of this constellation, certainly the example with the largest literature, is the story of the relative decline of the British economy since around 1870. Much hard work, at the painstaking level of the story of individual firms and industries, and at the level of the economy as a whole, has gone into the debate as to whether there was a 'failure' of British entrepreneurship as early as the decades before World War I. But there has also been the work of cultural historians. Most influential among them has been Martin Wiener[6] who set out to prove that the cause of the economic malaise was a 'decline of the industrial spirit' in Great Britain. An equally powerful case, and one which is rather more easily squared with the facts, has been made for the half-century since the 1930s by Corelli Barnett.[7]

Despite the wide acclaim which he received at the hand of the public at large, Wiener has not had a very favourable reception by economic historians.[8] Apart from many matters of detail, there are at least four major reasons for this. The first, and possibly the most important, of these is that the evidence produced is largely of a cultural variety. It may well be true that the poets and possibly even the novelists declaimed against the Philistines, against the satanic mill towns, the greed for money and the calculating spirit, the restlessness and insecurity of the new industrialism. It may also be true that Englishmen hankered after rustic idylls enough to insist on little gardens for their town houses (or on country houses if they could afford them) and on parks for their towns, that the public schools inculcated aristocratic values and that other schools aped them to do the same, that everyone loved a lord and no one loved the Gradgrinds, and that industrialists, if they had made enough money, liked nothing better than to retire to the country and become JPs and, if possible, acquire a title.

But it does not follow in the least that this had any effect on the vigour with which industrialists pursued the expansion of their firms or the maximization of their incomes, however measured. For every business man of a wealthy family who distanced himself from his firm, another can be found who entered the market, innovated and pushed forward. Captains of industry might well wake up in the morning in a replica of an ancient country house, but then they drove or rode into town and proceeded to conduct their businesses as well as those who stayed in the suburbs. Nothing could be more nostalgic than Port Sunlight or Bournville, but there was nothing lacking in the industrial spirit of William Lever or of the Cadburys.

The connection between the 'culture', even if it was the prevailing one—a judgement which would be difficult to prove—and business performance has not been made by Wiener, and this is reinforced by a further two reasons which have made economic historians sceptical of the Wiener thesis. One is that exactly the same cultural influences were at work before 1850, which is the starting year for Wiener, and indeed right through the period of the Industrial Revolution, which surely cannot be accused of lacking a progressive industrial spirit. Those years were the high period of Romanticism and of the Lake poets, the period of much country mansion building by merchants, bankers and even industrialists like Arkwright, of evangelicalism and country house politics. Why did none of this inhibit industrial progress then?[9]

Thirdly, similar cultural influences were at work in contemporary societies in Europe at the time of the alleged British decline, in particular in the German economy, which is generally paraded as an example of success against British failure in the late nineteenth and early twentieth centuries. There, too, the literature romanticized the quiet rustic ideal and denigrated urban money making; there, too, aristocrats ruled and dominated 'Society' and every successful businessman tried to become a squire and acquire a title; there, too, the prestige schools and the universities concentrated on the classics and kept out the useful subjects like engineering. Yet these traditionalist cultural pressures did not inhibit successful, one might almost say miraculous, economic and industrial growth.[10]

Lastly, there is some doubt also over the alleged 'decline' of the British economy. Though it grew more slowly than it had done in some periods in the past, and slower than some contemporary catching-up economies, it kept well ahead of all other countries with the exception of the USA in absolute terms. In terms of industrial exports *per capita* it still led the world, and exports were growing fast right up to 1913. Though in some sectors the British economy was no longer in the lead, in others, such as coal, shipbuilding and cotton, it still dominated world markets; it led in banking, insurance, shipping, in innovations in retail distribution and the manufacture of many articles of mass consumption such as popular newspapers, chocolates and cigarettes. If the culture was hostile, how could so much progressive entrepreneurship have survived to develop so vigorously? If it could survive, how significant could the cultural influence have been?

The problems of the last fifty years highlighted by Corelli Barnett are of a different order. Here, too, the go-ahead enterprise of the City of London, the technical superiority of British farmers over those on the continent, and the relative success of some industrial sectors are not in doubt. But other major industrial sectors showed signs of decay, and there would certainly have been some identifiable causes for this. It would, however, be highly problematic, and going well beyond the scope of this paper, to link these with cultural influences in a direct way.

It should be noted that Wiener's and Barnett's notions of 'culture' are themselves rather limited, referring essentially only to those aspects which affect professional and business decisions, but leaving out a whole range of other constituents of what is normally included in it, from religious beliefs at one end of the spectrum to fine art and aesthetics at the other. It could even be argued that there is a continuum, from pure balance sheet accounting at one extreme to the contemplation of ethereal values at the other, with economics and what sociologists call relevant 'culture' as rather arbitrary divisions within it.

In his wide-ranging paper, Iain Hampsher-Monk tackles this problem from a different angle. 'Economic' decisions, including the decisions which determine growth and development, he contends, cannot be explained by purely economic motivation alone, such as the desire to buy cheap and sell dear. Objections to such simplistic assumptions of neo-classical economics are raised by him at two levels. At one level, many other motivations, such as friendship, sympathy, the desire to cut a dash, power-seeking, empire-building, etc., can be shown to enter into economic decisions beside the monetary or price factor. At a higher level of abstraction, he asserts that economists have failed to establish any form of satisfactory explanation for human action, being at most able to judge only from the actions themselves, from which motivations are then inferred by methods which are essentially faulty and unscientific. It is for this latter lacuna that Hampsher-Monk proposes research into actors' reasons explanations as the most promising approach.

The first of these two critical approaches generalizes the specific views of such as Wiener and Corelli Barnett, since the non-price elements in decision-making are to a considerable degree influenced by the cultural background of the acting individual. Economists have, of course, always been aware of the non-price and the counter-price elements in market decisions. Backward-sloping demand curves, labour supply curves of the oddest shapes, and interest structures which reflect very different estimates of future prospects are to be found in every textbook. Adam Smith preceded the writing of *The Wealth of Nations* with the publication of his *Theory of Moral Sentiments*, in which he pictures man as mainly seeking the approval of his fellow members of society, rather than maximizing money income. Much of the revision in modern economics in similar directions has been concerned with the behaviour of managerial personnel in the large corporations, presumably the main location of entrepreneurship and decision making in the modern economy. Here too, a wide range of 'satisficing' goals, from promotion within the organization, empire-building, scoring off others, and a quiet life, to milking the enterprise for one's own purposes has been discovered in an approach perhaps best formulated by Oliver Williamson.[11] Does this mean that the determination by price must now be discarded, and that economics has been barking up the wrong tree all along and should have concerned itself with 'cultural' matters?

Surely this would be going too far. In modern enterprise the non-price manoeuverings of executives are dependent, in the end, on a satisfactory performance according to the traditional criteria of stable or rising returns, or returns no worse than those of other comparable companies. If the company fails to achieve these basic goals, directors will ask questions and shareholders will rebel, and the company may even be taken over by another group disposing of surplus superior management skills. Redundancies of top executives, as well as of lesser ones, on such occasions, are not unknown. In other words, behind the flurry of all the internal chicanery there is the overriding imperative of showing adequate, even if not necessarily maximum profits, which in turn means hitting a target which no one can calculate beforehand, and which therefore has to have a safety margin. For that basic drive, the traditional economic thinking is a reasonable approach.

Curiously, even labour responds essentially to the imperative of an adequate or correct monetary reward, even though individual wage-earners are more likely still than high-powered executives to look to other satisfactions, or to minimize other dissatisfactions, at their place of work. Even in the rather extreme case of the well-known study of a factory where the workers' efforts are partly turned into competitive 'fun', a long way from neo-classical economic assumptions,

> if wages are sufficiently low, workers will feel unfairly treated. Such unfair treatment will take the fun out of playing a game whose results benefit the firm. This reduction in fun will have the immediate effect of less willingness by workers to make out . . . The day-to-day experience emerges out of the organization of work and defines the interests of the various agents of production once *their basic survival—which, as far as the workers are concerned is an acceptable wage—is assured* . . . In the case where workers have animosity towards their employer, higher wages will cause workers to feel less badly about relieving the boredom by playing a game which yields a surplus to the firm. Or, alternatively, if workers have loyalty to their employer, low wages will cause workers to feel less badly about playing a game which fails to benefit the firm.[12]

Similar complexities can be discerned in the behaviour of trade union leaders. In Britain in particular, they have to cultivate a macho image;

they must be seen to stand up to the boss, to be as fearlessly radical as other leaders, to take an active part in politics and to strengthen their members' loyalty to the union and its leadership. But in the end, they are judged primarily by their success in negotiating wage rates, hours and conditions, as the basis for all the other desirable ends.

The cash nexus, clearly, is not everything. Economic theorems based on price have to be refined by influences which may in the widest sense be called 'cultural', and/or which derive from alternative motivations of the individual. But it would be folly to neglect prices in the explanation of how the market economy functions. Like all sciences, economics started with some crude, and only broadly valid generalizations. Progress consists in refining these in the light of new evidence, rather than declaring them to be worthless.

This is not to excuse the crudities of some simplistic approaches. An interesting example is supplied by Tversky's experiments cited in Hampsher-Monk's paper. Were subjects irrational in preferring lower risks, even at some sacrifice in possible income, at one time and not at another? Risk aversion is a phenomenon well-known to economists, and the costs of riskiness, the sacrifice people are willing to make to reduce risks, can be measured in many particular markets. Yet we know that people who insure their houses and prefer low-yielding ·fixed-interest securities to high-yielding, but volatile shares, and who show therefore every possible sign of risk-aversion, bet on the football ·pools in their millions, take out lottery tickets and possibly even amuse themselves with one-armed bandits, though in each case it is well known that only a part of the stake will be returned to the players so that the odds are much less than 100 per cent as a whole, on top of the riskiness. Are they irrational? Or is risk aversion not the only element that enters into their action, but in addition there are the thrill and excitement of the game, or the challenge of pitting one's luck against the probabilities, as a form of diversion for which people are prepared to pay? In the same way the public will throng switchbacks and other (apparently) dangerous contraptions at fun fairs who would yet seek to drive as carefully as possible on safe roads. Risk aversion is not enough as an explanation—but neither can it be discarded. It would be idle to debate which is more important, the price nexus or the broadly cultural influences by which it is modified, just as it would be idle to argue whether the bone structure or the flesh is more 'important'. Good economists start with price as the calculable element, but take on board as much as they are able of what can be seen as non-price regularities.

The second, more fundamental, critique by Hampsher-Monk, that economists only study actions, and not the motivations behind them is, of course, valid. Economists have passed that self-denying ordinance,[13] for the very good reason that one cannot study everything at once and that a great deal still needed to be done in their own sphere before venturing into other specialisms. In any case, quite a different expertise would be needed to enquire into motivations. Moreover, as a social science, economics must be concerned with regularities and statistical probabilities in the mass in the face of the totally unpredictable action of the individual. Yet it is precisely the latter which informs the concept of actors' reasons explanations. Each individual has his or her own bundle of motivations, and it may even be that they turn out to be discoverable, but the interesting question for a social science is not the make-up of every individual bundle, but the grouping of all of them, and the question then becomes why some motivations are evidently more operative at some time rather than another, in some societies, and among some classes of people, rather than in others. Can we assume that these are purely stochastic bunchings, as the unpredictability of each individual might suggest? Or is there some explicable difference as to time, influence, market pressure, government fiat, or whatever else the humble economist or other social scientist has hitherto considered as his field, to explain the bunching of behaviour and to suggest, for example, why some societies are rich in entrepreneurship and others are desperately short of it?

Paul Keating's Irish economy also belongs to the second type of debate, Ireland being not totally out of the capitalist sphere culturally, but geared in such a way that successful economic growth fails to result. Irish businessmen, as depicted in his pages, clearly do not lack entrepreneurship; on the contrary they are extremely active in rent seeking, in cheating the tax authorities, the European authorities, and their trading partners precisely in order to make gains themselves. There has indeed never been any doubt that even in the most progressive economies, businessmen, managers, and workers will include illicit and immoral actions in their repertoire of maximizing their gains, if they think they can get away with them. 'Institutional' economics and economic history are based on this recognition, and have been concerned for many years with describing these methods of maximization as well as counting the costs of contract enforcements.

Keating's paper, however, the database of which cannot be questioned, goes further than this. In the Irish Republic, it appears, dishonesty and disinterest in economic productivity are so dominant that they have become an explanation for the slow growth of the Irish economy. One of the strongest arguments for a cultural explanation for this phenomenon is that the foreign enterprises have had no difficulty in using the available resources to increase output, so that there is no obvious material reason why native entrepreneurs could not do likewise.

There are three partly interlinked groups of causes which may be held responsible for the Irish malaise. One is the history of resistance to British domination, with an implicit tradition of moral satisfaction in thwarting the legal authority. The second is a tradition of longing for a rustic, contemplative, traditional life, which may be opposed to the modernizing efficiency of the British. The third is the peculiar influence of the Roman Catholic Church in Ireland. Of these, the first is much the most plausible, since some of the key points of the indictment of Irish business behaviour concern the inability of the government to enforce its rules. People do not pay taxes, and they do not carry out the terms of their contracts if it does not suit them. In both cases, a strong government would enforce obedience and thereby remove these very real obstacles to growth. There is here some similarity to conditions in the less developed Mediterranean countries, and above all to most of the Third World, where it is clear to many observers that business cannot flourish if taxation is arbitrary, if state organs are corrupt and if breaches of contract go unpunished. Yet Ireland is not a backward pre-capitalist society; the skills are there and the foreign firms, at any rate, flourish; and the steady emigration to Britain and other countries is witness to the fact that numerous people are willing to make enormous sacrifices in their personal lives in order to improve their economic position.

It is however, not entirely clear why resistance to British rule, which ended almost seventy years ago, should still affect business policies today, particularly since resistance to the British was sporadic at best and most people were as law-abiding in Ireland as in other parts of the United Kingdom most of the time. We have seen that in other societies determined entrepreneurs will overcome such obstructions to their advance: why then should Ireland be held up by the dead hand of two generations earlier?

Turning to the second cause, it is clear that poets and a certain type of political scribe will always yearn for a real or mythical past, for some alternative to the business world. Were Irish poets more potent, or their readers more malleable, then elsewhere to be affected by nostalgia for the days of yore? And lastly, the Church: next to the former Communist Party, the Roman Catholic Church must surely be the organization most successful in imposing a uniform shape and doctrine on its believers across all the frontiers. Catholic societies spawned early capitalism in Italy, and Roman Catholic Belgium was the first continental country to adopt the industrialization process successfully: why should the same Church in Ireland have quite a different influence? Could it be that it is not the Church which has influenced Irish society, but the other way round?

Single examples may always be subject to particular, unique or contingent causes and it is dangerous to generalize from them. There are undoubtedly numerous examples of entrepreneurial and business groups which have broken through barriers of culture, even of class power, to pursue their individual economic ends by increasing productive or marketing efficiency and thus driving their whole society forward, not merely to higher income per head, but also towards the more profound changes of social structure and social ethos that generally follow. It would seem, looking at those cases, that economics is more powerful than 'culture', the foundations more significant than the superstructure.

However, there are also innumerable examples of societies in the past and even in the present in which every effort made, by their own leaders as well as by international organizations, to drive them into economic modernity has so far failed, and in which there are no material reasons for the failure, only the dead weight of a hostile culture. Taking this term broadly enough, to include moral and religious traditions, the political culture, market (or rather non-market) behaviour and so on, their braking power seems plausible enough.

It would be a poor result to say that sometimes economic imperatives, driven by selfish individual interests, will break down any and all cultural barriers to economic growth, and at other times they do not. Can we go a little beyond such a trite conclusion? I believe that the debate built around the papers presented here has moved us at least two small steps forward. One would be to recognize that it is within the power of the Schumpeterian entrepreneur to defy his society and win through, but that, at an early stage, society may in fact prevent a Schumpeterian entrepreneur from emerging in the first place. Without at least a minimum number of interested individuals, the momentum and the direction of which Stephen Mennell speaks, which forms the framework within which individuals exercise their free will and decision-making power, may not be generated to begin with. Thus some societies resist capitalist economic growth most successfully, to their own loss of income and of welfare.

A second conclusion would be that an active economic population does not necessarily guarantee economic growth to the limit of the society's technical possibilities. Individuals may be competitive, ambitious, greedy for the largest possible incomes, and living in a society which allows them to pursue their ends with considerable freedom, yet they may be induced, possibly by prevailing cultural influences, but possibly also by the structure of the economy, by relative prices and resource availability, by misleading information or harmful economic policies on the part of the central government, to seek their own satisfaction in ways that will not help the economy forward. Numerous economies are so structured that they will encourage rent seeking; i.e., gaining at the expense of others, rather than by adding to the sum total of goods and services. It may be a moot point to decide whether a problem of this kind should be termed economic or cultural. Economists have taken some note of it in the past, and they will certainly have to take even more note of it in the future.

Notes

1. E.g. S.M. Greenfield *et al.* (eds), *Entrepreneurs in Cultural Context* (Albuquerque, 1979).
2. Joel Mokyr, *The Level of Riches. Technological creativity and economic progress* (Oxford, 1990), pp. 189, 200.
3. Joseph Needham, *Science and Civilization in China*, 6 vols (Cambridge, 1954–86); Mark Elvin, 'Why China Failed to Create an Endogenous Industrial Society', *Theory and Society* 13 (1984), pp. 319–91; id., 'China as a Counterfactual', in Jean Baechler *et al.* (eds), *Europe and the Rise of Capitalism* (Oxford, 1987); John A. Hall, 'States and Societies: The miracle in comparative perspective', in ibid.
4. Mancur Olson, *The Rise and Decline of Nations* (New Haven, 1982).
5. Johannes Hirschmeier, *The Origins of Entrepreneurship in Meiji Japan* (Cambridge, Mass., 1968).
6. Martin Wiener, *English Culture and the Decline of the Industrial Spirit 1850–1980* (Cambridge, 1981).
7. Corelli Barnett, *The Audit of War: The illusion and reality of Britain as a great nation* (1986).
8. C. Dellheim, 'Notes on Industrialisation and Culture in Nineteenth-Century Britain', *Notebooks in Cultural Analysis* 2 (1985), pp. 227–48; Bruce Collins and Keith Robbins (eds), *British Culture and Economic Decline* (1990).
9. Peter L. Payne, 'Industrial Entrepreneurship and Management in Great

Britain', *Cambridge Economic History of Europe*, vol. 7 (Cambridge, 1978).

10. N. Rainer Lepsius, 'Das Bildungsbürgertum als Ständische Vergesellschaftung', in id. (ed.), *Bildungsbürgertum im 19 Jahrhundert*, vol. 3 (Stuttgart, 1990), p. 15; Hans-Ulrich Wehler, 'Deutsches Bildungsbürgertum in Vergleichender Perspektive', in J. Kocka (ed.), *Bildungsburgertum im 19. Jahrhundert*, vol. 4 (Stuttgart, 1989), p. 223; S. Pollard, 'Reflections on Entrepreneurship and Culture in European Societies', *Transactions of the Royal Historical Society* 5th ser. 40 (1990), pp. 153–73.

11. Oliver E. Williamson, *The Economics of Discretionary Behaviour* (Chicago, 1967); id., *Economic Organisation* (Brighton, 1985); id. *et al.* (eds), *The Firm as a Nexus of Treaties* (1989).

12. George Akerlof, 'Gift Exchange and Efficiency Wage Theory: Four views', *American Economic Review, Papers and Proceedings* 74 (1984), pp. 81–2 (italics in original).

13. 'Economic analysis proceeds on the basis of preferences that are considered to be given (even though they may occasionally be changing) as a result of physiological needs and psychological and cultural propensities. Any number of quotations from economists and economic textbooks could be supplied to the effect that economics had no business delving into the reasons why preferences are what they are, and it is implicit in such denials that it is even less appropriate for economists to inquire how and why preferences might change.' Albert O. Hirschman, *Shifting Involvements: Private interest and public action* (Oxford, 1982), p. 9 (but see p. 10 for efforts to overcome this).

Part III
Consumption and Culture

Excess, Frugality and the Spirit of Capitalism: Readings of Mandeville on Commercial Society[1]

Dario Castiglione

Premise

It was Dr. Johnson's opinion that every young man had *The Fable of the Bees* on his shelves in the mistaken belief that it was a wicked book. Nowadays, social scientists have taken the place of Dr. Johnson's would-be libertines, but one assumes for different reasons. Mandeville's book is no longer a *succès de scandale*, but nor is its current popularity purely academic. The revival of interest in Mandeville can be attributed to the resurgence of the old debate on the morality of capitalism, graphically expressed in the subtitle of his work: 'Private Vices, Publick Benefits'.

Indeed, the debate has penetrated to the centre of the political arena, particularly in Britain, where the Thatcher government endorsed the philosophy of self-enrichment, and its leader, in a 'sermon' delivered to the gathering at the annual assembly of the Church of Scotland in 1988,[2] tried to reconcile this philosophy with a narrowly interpreted Christian morality. It could be argued that there is more than a superficial resemblance between certain features of Walpole's England and the self-confident financial capitalism of the nineteen-eighties; that the image of Mandeville as the Walpolean ideologue, defender of the new moneyed classes and the utility of vices is not very different from the Mandeville to whom neo-libertarians of various shades make direct or indirect reference by revamping the theory of 'unintended consequences' as the paramount justification for market society.[3]

The debate on the morality of capitalism appears still more topical now that the historical experience of 'realized socialism' seems to be exhausted, at the least for the foreseeable future. As Habermas has recently written, nowadays socialism can hardly be regarded as a *goal*; it is only feasible to conceptualize it as the 'radically reformist self-criticism of a capitalist society': a largely moral attitude towards the regulative mechanisms and asymmetries of power and wealth in modern complex society; a normative criticism which has its material foundation in the 'universalization of interests through institutions for the formation of public opinion and the political will'.[4] However, the apparently un-challenged supremacy of 'realized capitalism' on a world scale, the generalized acceptance of market mechanisms as the most efficient regulation of economic relationships in both developed and developing countries, and the effective withering away of the issue of the forms of property from the ideological debate, do not by themselves guarantee a wholehearted acceptance of the values prevalent in a market society. The debate on capitalism and its ethics goes on, and in this debate Mandeville, and many other eighteenth- and nineteenth-century authors, have been wheeled in to underpin modern theories and modern capitalism as a whole.

In one of his recent essays, A.O. Hirschman has skilfully drawn a *tableau idéologique* centred on four rival views of 'market society', each associated to one, or more than one, particular social thinker of the last 250 years.[5] The intention of Hirschman's analysis is heuristic, and not crudely ideological. He carefully characterizes the four different views of his *tableau* as ideal-types, allowing for a certain latitude in the classifi-cation of individual authors. Each of the four 'rival views' is identified on the basis of their general attitude towards market society/capitalism, and on the kind of ills and advantages which are associated to the nature and development of this particular social formation. Not surprisingly, Hirschman finds that the various views are not in absolute opposition, but often tend to complement each other. The methodological conclusion which he draws from his analytical exercise is that social scientists should be more concerned with the complexities of social reality than with the prediction power of their theories, and that this descriptive and 'complicative' approach is perhaps to be preferred to the simplifying tautologies of normal social science.

Hirschman's dissection and criticism of the most common perceptions of the dynamic of market society is part of his sustained attack against the vice of excessive parsimony which he considers to have adversely affected the modern social sciences, and economic thought in particular. In another essay in the same collection, he gives a number of examples of the failure of traditional economic concepts to match up and illuminate the complexity of human motivations.[6] Here he tries to show the fundamental inadequacy of an economist's model of human psychology—the interest-only-driven man—by stressing the importance of some features often disregarded by economists. On the one hand, Hirschman points at two basic 'human endowments', self-evaluation and communication/persuasion, which he thinks are generally underestimated, since economists tend to concentrate on first order preferences, neglecting metapreferences, and on the simple market mechanism of *exit* (stopping buying something) rather than *voice* (expressing dissatisfaction with either a product or a service).[7] On the other hand, Hirschman enlarges upon two fundamental 'tensions' in human nature and behaviour—the one between instrumental and expressive modes of behaviour, and the other between the self and others—to which economists seem to pay little attention by exclusively concentrating on instrumental action and self-centred behaviour.

In arguing that certain explanations of an economic type are parasitic on hermeneutical premises, Iain Hampsher-Monk's essay in the present collection seems to me to advance a similar kind of criticism towards the excessive simplification of traditional economic discourse. My intention in this paper is to point to yet another kind of simplification commonly made in histories of social theory. By analyzing Mandeville's reception from the mid-eighteenth century onwards, I hope to show, albeit indirectly, that views of capitalism are often not only partial in their prediction, as suggested by Hirschman's *tableau*, but fundamentally different. In other words, I wish to suggest that a debate on the morality of capitalism which spans several centuries is a debate without an object.

There is perhaps a second note of methodological caution to be drawn from the following account of Mandeville's reception, and this concerns the academic discussion of the links between the emergence of *homo oeconomicus* and the formation of a separate economic discourse. Louis Dumont,[8] amongst others, has stressed the importance of the axiom of 'the natural harmony of interests' as the conceptual pre-condition for the autonomy of the economic language. He singles out Adam Smith's *Wealth of Nations*, and the Mandevillean influence, as the real landmark in the history of economic thought. This is an extremely simplified view, since the distinctive characters of the economic discourse cannot be meaningfully encapsulated in a single, though intellectual powerful, axiom. Nor can the formation of a discipline be reduced to a conceptual exercise, ignoring altogether the institutional aspects of the process. To single out the idea of 'the natural harmony of interests' as the milestone of modern economic thinking unduly stresses one particular aspect in the emergence of this discursive practice, forcing its historiographical reconstruction into the uncongenial strait-jacket of ideology.[9]

Before entering *in medias res*, let me make a final methodological point. This is neither a reception study nor an attempt systematically to compare Mandeville's intentions with latter-day interpretations. I am mainly concerned with the *readings*, not the *writing*, of the *Fable*, and in particular with those authors who have read it as a contribution to social analysis.[10] This often implies taking Mandeville out of context, and treating his text as a cipher, partly divested of the historical background in which it was written. I am not suggesting that this is an appropriate method for intellectual history; my aim is only to sketch in broad outlines the reasons why Mandeville's work in turn has been included in the *sanctioned* history of social theorizing or marginalised on its *periphery*.[11]

Eighteenth-century fame

Although the *Fable* is probably as well known now as it was in the eighteenth century, there seems to have been an intervening period of near neglect between 1818 and 1914, when no new edition, either in English or in translation, was printed.[12] This raises two interrelated questions. Firstly, why, after a century of neglect, was Mandeville's reputation revived? Secondly, and perhaps more importantly, why indeed was Mandeville's work so little read during the nineteenth century? But let us start from the beginning, from its eighteenth-century success.

Adam Smith caught both Mandeville's originality and representativeness when he cited his work as the most recent version of the licentious system of morals, and when in a letter to the *Edinburgh Review* he drew attention to Rousseau's indebtedness to the second volume of the *Fable of the Bees*.[13] In fact Smith's interpretation suggests that Mandeville's satirical defence of vice had become the eighteenth-century standard version of *immoralism*, and that his shrewd conventionalist account of the origin of moral language and behaviour was a challenge not only to rationalist philosophers of morals, but particularly to the supporters of sentimentalism or any other naturalistic theory of morality. On the other hand, Smith's opinion confirms that Mandeville's often original and highly imaginative account of the evolutionary development of social institutions from their rude beginnings to civilized forms had become a stimulating source-book for those very same authors who opposed his general theory from a naturalistic perspective.

With hindsight, Mandeville's importance in the eighteenth century is assured by his contribution to at least three important developments which can be summarized in the graphic idea of the emergence of the *homo oeconomicus*. Mandeville's moral discourse, when interpreted as a satire of the rigoristic conceptions of vice and virtue, could be taken as the unashamed endorsement of utilitarianism. His insistence on self-interest as the driving force of human behaviour may be considered as akin to modern individualism and its related moral and social theories. Moreover, the paradoxical presentation of his theories—calculated, more often than not, to *épater les moralistes*—can also be construed as the typical, counter-intuitive way in which the social sciences transform our commonsensical perception of the world.[14] These three components of Mandeville's writings and thought form what has been described as the Mandevillean Moment, although it is probably true that this *moment* did not really begin until the century was nearing its end, and that its beginnings coincided with the waning of Mandeville's fame.[15]

Paradoxical knowledge

The satirical form of Mandeville's work is certainly one of the reasons for the post-eighteenth-century fluctuations in his reputation as a social thinker. As many of the psychological, social, and anthropological intuitions scattered throughout the *Fable* were appropriated by other authors, who then gave them a systematic treatment, more congenial to the development of a scientific approach, so this naturally affected the popularity of the *Fable*, which, one presumes, came increasingly to be viewed as a mere literary curiosity. And yet, the issues which have been most influential for his posthumous reputation are those connected firstly with the waning of the paradoxical force of his arguments and then with later changes of perspective in the study of modern capitalist society. I will examine these latter in turn, beginning with the question of paradox.

It was characteristic of Mandeville's satirical writings to favour this form for the presentation of his arguments. And the subtitle of the *Fable*, 'private vices, public benefits', is obviously a most concise statement of this and of his presumed social utilitarianism. However, the paradox of the statement is not as self-evident as we have usually been led to believe. In fact, it is neither surprising nor contradictory to state that there is some form of connection between private vices and public benefits.

Mandeville's wording, linking the two parts of the sentence with an inconspicuous comma, does not suggest that this connection is a necessary one, nor, one may argue, does he view it in strictly causal terms. Moreover, in his general statement Mandeville was careful to talk of 'benefits' and not of 'virtues'. He never really stated that the pursuing of selfish interests in private life would result in either the virtuousness of the public as a whole, or in the strengthening of civic virtues. These were conclusions left to his opponents to draw; for they purported to believe that public benefits could only be the result of, or synonymous with, public virtues. Thus the paradoxical nature of Mandeville's statement must first be understood within the context of the prevailing conceptions of virtue of the time: the religious and the classical republican.[16] The question then is to ascertain the particular sense in which Mandeville's paradox was a criticism of these conceptions, and whether, as I tend to believe, the transformation in the common understanding of virtue blunted the epistemological value of his paradox.

However, the fact is that most of Mandeville's contemporaries denied that there really was a paradox. In their view, Mandeville had simply made use of skilful sophisms, based either on prejudices against Christianity and virtue, or on a definition of virtue influenced by a misconceived rigorism. In either case Mandeville's position was seen as supporting a nominalistic theory of moral distinctions which would only encourage and legitimize licentiousness.

It is this apparent fascination with rigorism that Hutcheson attacked in order to refute Mandeville's main thesis on the beneficial effects of vice. One counter-example he advanced against the many cited in the *Fable* was that of the beer industry, which Hutcheson commonsensically believed to be better supported by people who drank with moderation, and who therefore had a reasonable life expectancy, than by immoderate drinkers, who ran the risk of dying young.[17] This kind of reasoning amounted to a rejection of Mandeville's paradox on two counts: it refused to consider any superfluous consumption as tantamount to vice; and it envisaged the possibility that the development of commercial exchanges could be founded on social moderation (in this context perceived as a 'virtue' in itself). But this criticism missed the point on which Mandeville's analysis was based or, at least, it avoided confronting his paradox in full. In his discussion of luxury, probably the single most important 'vice' in the whole of the *Fable*, Mandeville had indeed admitted the absurdity of a strict definition, in which anything above the level of subsistence should be considered as luxury,[18] and therefore a vice.

But he maintained his objection to a more lax definition of luxury on the grounds that this would provide an opening to hypocrisy and extreme subjectivism. In other words without a precise, verifiable limit between necessity and luxury, it seems to have been quite impossible for Mandeville to imagine how the artificial establishment of morality could have occurred; he seems to have regarded the absence of an 'objective' language of morals as a perilous condition, which was always in danger of reverting to an Hobbesian state of nature.[19]

But if Mandeville was not prepared to renounce his rigoristic definition of morality (judged in terms of the 'intentions' of the subject), he was however willing to consider things rather differently when discussing the public effects of private morality. In the case of luxury, his argument ran in two directions. On the one hand, he stressed that the dangers of indulgence to the fortunes of private individuals did not directly concern the public as a whole, who, in a commercial society, could only gain from the mobility of goods, money, and, to a certain extent, property. On the other, he believed that a general indulgence in a luxurious life was of no immediate consequence to the military fortunes of the polity; for these no longer depended, as had seemingly been the case in ancient republics, on the courage and resilience of its citizen-soldiers, but on public wealth, which mainly determined the capacity of the polity to arm and support its navy and its soldiers. Mandeville's argument was not based on a simple utilitarian calculus of the effects of the actions of private individuals, but on the dislocation of private morality from the sphere of public utility. In Mandeville's system, this disjunction between 'private' and 'public' is made even more significant by the fact that, contrary to what he believed to be the case in ancient static societies, modern commercial societies seemed to him to require two entirely distinct sets of criteria with which to judge the appropriateness of actions in the two respective domains.[20]

Thus, the paradox expressed by 'private vices, public benefits' was not a simple one. Its precise meaning is only intelligible when related to those languages and conceptions which had posited a necessary connection between public and private morality. Mandeville's illustration of his paradox was mainly meant as the rejection of the ideals of classical republicanism. Only with great difficulty could the latter be reconciled to the dangers presented by luxury, since it considered stability of property and the bearing of arms as constituent parts of the citizens' identity.[21] The fortunes of individual citizens were intrinsically connected to the public interest: it was therefore difficult to imagine how the whole could remain

stable and powerful if its parts were continuously under threat of losing
their identity. But Mandeville's 'paradox' was also based on the a priori
rejection of traditional Christian ethics, which advocated, as classical
republicanism had done, a necessary link between private and public
morality. In the 'Introduction' to the *Fable* Mandeville had made clear
that he was referring only to people in a state of nature and therefore
outside that of 'divine grace'.[22] In this he may well have been influenced by Augustinianism, or more particularly by the rigorist position
expounded by the Jansenists, who had distinguished between the morality
of the man in a state of grace and that of the *honnête homme*. Yet, if
these elements have some similarity, the overall effect is rather different. In assuming that commerce had strengthened elements of human
psychology which could not be controlled or tamed, but only skilfully
manipulated, it can be argued that Mandeville was self-consciously
undermining a purely rigoristic morality. This was the conclusion to
which Hume and Smith arrived. Hume's essay on luxury, later significantly renamed 'Of Refinement in the Arts',[23] was a perfectly balanced
exposition of how the debate on luxury presented both a philosophical
and a political aspect. Although he considered Mandeville's arguments to
be untenable on a philosophical level, he implicitly endorsed them at a
more practical and political level. Indeed, when Hume maintained that
'those who prove or attempt to prove, that such refinements rather tend
to increase industry, civility, and arts, regulate anew our moral as well as
political sentiments', he was certainly—though perhaps unwillingly—
explaining the logic of Mandeville's paradoxical arguments.[24] However,
where Mandeville seemed to fail, and where his critics in part triumphed,
was in the recognition of the effects which the changes in public morality
had on the standards of private morality itself. Such changes could be
more easily accounted for by sentimentalist theories of morals than by
straight conventionalism. This movement away from rigoristic definitions
of the good life necessarily affected the general reception of Mandeville's
arguments. In moral terms, these seemed to lose their paradoxical force
and epistemological value: they had now come to be seen as either
common-sense or simple nonsense. Dr. Johnson, for instance, justified
luxury on 'strong' moral grounds by comparing the effects it had on the
idleness or industry of the poor with the opposite effects induced by
charity.[25] Luxury, at the beginning of the century generally considered a
vice (from the point of view of the intentions of the agent), had within a
few decades been transformed into a virtue (from a consequentialist point
of view).

The moral divide

Yet, to many eighteenth-century authors there was still something unacceptable in Mandeville's analysis. It was not only that he had schizophrenically established two entirely distinct moral criteria: but, by insisting on the close relationship between vices and benefits, he had represented commercial society as driven by strong passions and excess as a whole. This was the basis for the second part of Hutcheson's criticisms, since he preferred to believe that moderation, in the passions and in consumption, was a more solid base for commercial society. A belief, eventually shared by many important Enlightenment figures, which can be identified in three separate manifestations: firstly, in the form of the empirical observation that moderate passions and the moderate satisfaction of needs may adequately support the development of commercial society and commercial institutions; then in the adherence to a morality of propriety intended as a justification of the urge towards bettering one's life, without necessarily emphasizing crude and unbridled self-interest; and finally, in a more normative approach, which relied on the direct effect of moral and political education on the habits and *moeurs* of the people. This soft-line approach, adopted both in order to comprehend and to justify a society mainly based on exchange relationships, was indeed remarkably successful. If it did not seem to guarantee the full implementation of a peaceful and ultimately fair society, at least it helped to shape social self-consciousness along the lines of apparent morality and decency (a position often bordering on self-righteousness and hypocrisy, as its opponents were eager to point out). Although this vision of commercial society had borrowed some of its ammunition from the arguments advanced in the *Fable* it remained at logger-heads with the Mandevillean hard-line, which emphasized instead the role of envy and excessive consumption as the inner sources of civilization and commercial success. In Mandeville's view, moderation would inevitably dry up the motivations which were the unintended causes of the public benefits enjoyed in rich and powerful countries.[26]

By the end of the eighteenth century Mandeville's analyses and paradoxes had been assimilated and partly moralized, but they were not yet entirely reconcilable with the newly formed vision of the *homo oeconomicus*. A footnote in Malthus' 1818 appendix to his *Essay on Population* seems intriguingly to prove the point.[27] Malthus wrote the 1818 appendix to confute two fundamental objections which had often been moved, in his view rather unfairly, against his theories. One of the objections was directed against his denial of the poor's *right* to support. In his reply, Malthus developed an argument which mainly rested on the assumption—which he believed he had definitively proved—that the growth of population exceeded that of the generally available resources. In such circumstances no one could claim to have a right to sustenance. Such a right, being impossible to implement, was ultimately self-contradictory. If it was true that in individual instances it was just and beneficial to renounce superfluous consumption for the direct gratification of the more immediate needs of the poor, so Malthus' argument ran, it was very different when it came to the generalization of this kind of behaviour. Far from resulting in a more equitable division of goods, the right to sustenance would produce the disquieting effect of reducing humanity to 'the most wretched and universal poverty'. He observed that it was God's nature itself which, in making the passion of self-love stronger than benevolence, had indicated the best way in which to preserve the human race: 'by this wise provision the most ignorant are led to promote the general happiness, an end which they would have totally failed to attain, if the moving principle of their conduct had been benevolence.'[28] The only circumstances in which benevolence might be considered the best general course of action was in a state of perfect knowledge, which naturally could never be achieved by human agents. To this, by then very Smithian argument, Malthus appended a footnote to the effect of distancing himself from any kind of association with Mandeville's 'system of morals', which he described as 'absolutely false, and directly contrary to the just definition of virtue'. According to Malthus, Mandeville's only skill lay in concocting 'misnomers'. But to us, it is evident that Mandeville's fundamental distinction between private morality and questions of public interest had by then become common currency, even though his dissection of prevalent morality was being simultaneously dismissed, with no moral qualms, as a mere play of words.

Production and consumption

As we have seen, the nineteenth-century decline in Mandeville's reputation is partly linked to the fact that the justification of commercial society in terms of utility was no longer seen as purely shocking and paradoxical. There were legitimate ways—empirical, moral, and partly theological—in which the arguments for the propriety of selfish actions could be construed. As Hirschman has suggested, the very concept of interest assumed an almost tautological form: that one could not but pursue one's own interest.[29] This made selfish behaviour predictable and therefore more readily consonant to the pursuit of the common good.

But if Adam Smith was right in his judgement on the many insights to be found in Mandeville's analysis of commercial societies (in his 'science of man' more than in his 'moral theory'), the nineteenth-century's neglect is not yet fully explained. Part of the answer to our problem may lie in another feature of Mandeville's work, in the fact that the majority of his observations pertained to the world of consumption, while later authors, beginning with Smith himself, became progressively more interested in questions of production. In its simplicity such an answer seems quite convincing and in no particular need of great elaboration. I will therefore try to illustrate it by examining some possible objections, starting with the question of the division of labour. It may in fact seem strange to maintain that Mandeville contributed little to the study of the productive aspects of modern commercial societies, when it is generally acknowledged that he was one of the first authors to stress the importance of the division of labour. But to this apparent contradiction there is a solution.

When in his discussion of the production of surplus-value, the object of Book I, Part IV of *Capital*, Marx referred to the question of the division of labour, and to Smith's particular treatment of the issue, he also mentioned Smith's debt to Mandeville:

> The famous passage . . . , which begins with the words, 'observe the accommodation of the most common artificer or day-labourer in a civilized and thriving country', etc., and then proceeds to depict what an enormous number and variety of industries contribute to the satisfaction of the needs of an ordinary worker, is copied almost word for word from the 'Remarks' added by B. de Mandeville to his *Fable of the Bees, or Private Vices, Publick Benefits.*[30]

Marx therefore thought that Smith and Mandeville possessed a similar conception of the division of labour: a conception which he himself criticized. For, he felt that, in speaking of the division of labour and of its positive effect on the productivity of human work, Smith had conflated two different notions: on the one hand, what might be called the 'social' division of labour; and on the other, the division of labour in 'manufacture'. By social division of labour Marx meant the general division of skills and of productive sectors in society; by division of labour in manufacture, he referred to the more particular organization of work to be found within a single unit of production. In Marx's view, this distinction had escaped Smith mainly because he had dismissed it as merely subjective: the superficial view of an observer who immediately 'sees' the division of labour when it is 'performed on one spot', and is less aware of the same phenomenon when it implies 'the spreading-out of the work over great areas' and the involvement of a 'great number of people employed in each branch of labour'. For Marx the distinction was a real one; it resulted in entirely different relationships between the producer and his products and between the producers themselves. The bond between independent workers who had different social specializations consisted in the fact that they produced 'commodities' which were exchanged. By contrast, the labour of individual specialized workers within a workshop produced 'no' commodity. Only the final product of the labour of all the specialized workers involved was a commodity. The general laws which regulated the two kinds of division of labour were also different.

> Within the workshop, the iron law of proportionality subjects definite numbers of workers to definite functions, in the society outside the workshop, the play of chance and caprice results in a motley pattern of distribution of the producers and their means of production among various branches of social labour.[31]

The 'anarchy' of the social division of labour is thus opposed to the 'despotism' of the manufacturing division of labour; the combination and mutual conditioning of these two systems of organization of labour is a constituent feature of what Marx considered the capitalist mode of production. Earlier forms of society did not present such a contrast; they had crystallized and regulated the spontaneous development and differentiation of trades with specific laws, while the division of labour in manufacture occurred only sporadically and on a minimal scale.

From this brief summary of Marx's view of the question, it should be evident that the issue was not an academic one, but had far reaching consequences for his social theory. More generally—and more pertinent to the argument of this paper—it would seem that the rapid progress of industrialization had added a new dimension to the question of the division of labour, changing the emphasis from the consumer-centred view presented by Mandeville and partly by Smith to the producer-centred perspective advanced by Marx and other nineteenth-century sociologists and economists.[32]

The habit of capitalism

Nineteenth-century shifts in the perception of post-feudal society from consumption to production, and from commerce to industrialization, are thus in part responsible for Mandeville's depreciation. Similarly, early twentieth-century preoccupations with the 'spirit of capitalism' were not in tune with Mandeville's sociology of excess. This has seldom been noticed; more often, admittedly with some reason, the opposite view has been taken, and Mandeville has been considered an early supporter of the 'spirit of capitalism'.[33]

But, particularly amongst German scholars, early discussions on the 'spirit of capitalism' revolved around the possibility of distinguishing it, clearly and at a subjective level, from simple greed or money-getting. Many of the turn-of-the-century seminal studies dedicated to the argument were, in various degrees, opposed to the view that capitalism had simply originated through the diffusion of self-interested and avaricious behaviour (or, although this does not concern us here, were opposed to the materialistic interpretation of the formation of the capitalist mode of production). This new approach, which for want of a better name we shall call the *Ethical Thesis*,[34] contended for a strong, direct link between economic behaviour and ethical (particularly religious) motivations; and it considered the 'spirit of capitalism' to be an historical product of modern times. Mandeville's *Petticoat Thesis*,[35] on the other hand, presented commercial society as the product of the uninhibited, and often whimsical, pursuit of human passions and needs, which raised production through an increase in demand. Moreover, this thesis aimed to scoff at contemporary suggestions that religion had great relevance for the behaviour of individuals or the fortunes of nations.

The 'a-historical' and secular approach here attributed to Mandeville could be said to epitomize the kind of position that German historical sociologists (especially Weber) both found uninteresting and wanted to refute. They were particularly insistent that support for the new economic ethos could be found in several currents of post-medieval religious and theological thought. Weber's *Protestant Thesis* was primarily intended as an answer to the paradox of accumulation, or of how it was possible that an irrational and self-contradictory psychology—secular and anti-hedonistic, based on the inversion of the natural relationship between needs and work—could have universal and extensive pragmatical implications. In religion, and particularly in the practical significance of Puritan and Calvinist conceptions of vocation, asceticism, and predestination, Weber saw a favourable ethical terrain for the diffusion of the capitalist economic ethos: a perfectly rational (in the sense of instrumental) conduct had developed on irrational premises. However, as Jacob Viner has shown in his unfinished work on religious thought and economic society,[36] there is no particular reason why early modern theological justifications of economic behaviour should be held to be the *cause* of economic behaviour itself, rather than—as he argued for the dispute between Jansenists and Jesuits—as attempts to respond to the challenges of a world in rapid transformation, where human conduct and motivations could no longer be explained or simply determined by religious sentiments and beliefs. Viner's alternative thesis, which stresses the importance of the overall process of 'secularization' in the modern world, can be regarded as a modern and more general formulation of the *Petticoat Thesis*. Moreover, we should consider this alternative explanation of the accumulation paradox as the dominant position throughout the eighteenth century. Instead of concentrating on the 'spirit of capitalism', the secularization thesis stresses the importance of the *Habit of Capitalism*; and following Hume, this thesis can be said to hold that:

> there is no craving or demand of the human mind more constant and insatiable than that for exercise and employment . . . Deprive a man of all business and serious occupation, he runs restless from one amusement to another . . . if the employment you give him be lucrative, especially if the profit be attached to every particular exertion of industry, he has gain so often in his eye, that he acquires, by degrees, a passion for it, and knows no such pleasure as that of seeing the daily encrease of his fortune. And this is the reason why trade encreases frugality, and why, among merchants, there is the same overplus of misers above prodigals, as, among the possessors of land, there is the contrary.[37]

Thus we have seen that on the issue of the ethical foundations of the spirit of accumulation Mandeville's work, like most of the eighteenth-century literature which took a secular view of the economic effects of luxury, was for the German scholars part of the problem rather than the solution. The arguments advanced in the *Fable* were considered either as lacking great originality (by Sombart) or in direct contrast to the *Ethical Thesis* (by Weber). In the process, we have come across two questions which are central to the remainder of our discussion on the 'spirit of capitalism'. For rationality and frugality, certainly the two most important features of the spirit of capitalism as defined by the German literature to which I have made reference, do not play any relevant part in Mandeville's analysis.

Sombart defined the 'spirit of capitalism' as the complex product of the 'spirit of enterprise' and the 'bourgeois spirit'. By spirit of enterprise he meant the combination of greed for gold and money, and the inclination towards adventure and organizative exploits. By bourgeois spirit he instead referred to more specific social qualities embodied both in the ideal middle-class virtues of thriftiness, frugality, moderation, honesty, and respectability, and in the art of reducing everything to quantities, ordering them according to income and expenditure: in other words, the *art of calculation*. By imposing so many limitations on greed and money-getting, Sombart's representation of the spirit of capitalism necessarily reduced these 'natural' propensities to a rather subordinate role. But according to Weber this did not go far enough. He maintained that greed and the love of gain should not be considered as an intrinsic part of the spirit of capitalism, but as natural forces which needed to be controlled and rationalized. He felt that Sombart's sloppy definition of the spirit of capitalism was confusing; it added nothing to the general understanding of either the specific features of modern capitalism or the reasons for its unique development in western societies. The reverse was also true. Weber thought that Sombart's—but also Brentano's and Simmel's—definition of the spirit of capitalism was unsatisfactory because it was founded on what he considered a rather inaccurate classification of modern western capitalism. It was not the simple kind of monetary economy that Brentano and Simmel implied. Its characterization could not be worked out eclectically, as Sombart had done, because this would obscure the differences with previous forms of capitalism—a system which had existed at other times in various parts of the world. In Weber's view, modern capitalism comprises a complex system of interrelated institutions and economic agents whose actions are oriented towards gain in a *rational* and *continuous* way. Weber's emphasis was on long-term profitability rather than speculative enterprises. What characterizes the general ethos of capitalist economy is not the heroic spirit of enterprise, nor the irrational love of money, but the rational pursuit—or simple expectation—of economic gain.[38]

It is now perhaps clear why a thoroughgoing Mandevillean version of the 'spirit of capitalism' did not appeal to any of the contenders in that early twentieth-century debate. In the *Fable* there was too little rationality and no virtue or asceticism. Whenever Mandeville brought frugality into the picture it was to play down its alleged role in the flourishing of commerce and trade. 'Remark O'[39] is an impressive attack on frugality, which is perceived as the obvious course of action for individuals and families, but as having ruinous consequences for the economy of a country as a whole. According to Mandeville, frugality is merely the product of necessity: as a virtue it is hardly ever practised. In economic society at large, what is usually attributed to frugality is rather the combined effect of avarice and prodigality: 'equally necessary to society'. To the suggestion of 'moderate men' that virtuous frugality could single-handedly achieve the same results as those produced by these two 'vices', Mandeville answered that

> frugality is like honesty, a mean starving virtue. (. . .) Prodigality has a thousand inventions to keep people from sitting still, that frugality would never think of; and as this must consume a prodigious wealth, so avarice again knows innumerable tricks to rake it together, which frugality would scorn to make use of.[40]

Conclusions

Although Mandeville's work had in many ways become marginal to the theoretical preoccupations which underlined more recent studies of the development of commercial society into fully-grown industrial capital-ism, it is possible that such preoccupations indirectly contributed to his successive revaluation. The first new edition of the *Fable* published this century appeared—perhaps significantly—in German in 1914. How-ever, with the publication of Kaye's edition in 1924, the discussion of Mandeville's work has acquired a distinctive scholarly flavour. And yet, this revaluation of Mandeville was also generated by new shifts in social theorizing. It is not entirely surprising that several modern authors have appreciated the *Fable* for precisely those reasons which for a century had made it less topical.

In his general restatement of mercantilism and of its policies, Keynes pictured Mandeville as one of the 'brave army of heretics' who had resisted the logic of unfettered *laissez-faire,* and formulated early versions of the theory of under-consumption.[41] Mandeville's identification of luxury and prodigality as the direct causes of the increase in employment and general wealth was seen as a coherent exposition of the theory that the expansion of effective demand would create more employment. But as

Joan Robinson has noted, this is probably a forced interpretation of his theories, for they cannot be adequately compared with more technical and scientific-minded argumentations found in Keynesian economics:

> That the luxury of the rich gives employment to the poor was something pretty obvious. In an under-developed country, as Mandeville's England was, there is a plentiful reserve of labour in agriculture to supply lackeys and handicraftsmen who can draw sustenance from luxury expenditure.[42]

However, even though we may assume that Keynes' treatment of Mandeville is instrumental and cavalier, this does not affect the hypothesis here advanced that by the twenties and thirties, when the attention of prominent social theorists began increasingly to be focused on the relevance of consumption in modern industrial society, Mandeville's theories were given a new airing. A similar change can be detected on the question of rationalism. Today, the single most influential piece of social theory attributed to Mandeville is without doubt that of 'unintended consequences', which is generally understood to be the complex process, transcending the immediate intentionality of the agents, through which society is produced and re-produced. Mandeville's role in putting forward this theory was first recognized by Robert Merton.[43] A modern commentator has gone to some length to show that there is indeed more than a passing similarity between the original theory and sociological functionalism as a whole. For Mandeville's

> reflections can accurately be said to embody the habit of mind now called functionalism, here understood as the notion that aspects of social behaviour may best be explained in terms of their contribution to the maintenance of a social system, irrespective of what social actors may think that they are doing.[44]

But the theorist who has most convincingly and passionately argued for the originality and absolute centrality of the idea of unintended consequences in modern social thinking is certainly F.A. Hayek.[45] He has adopted a different perspective from the functionalist, and from deterministic approaches at large. Hayek regards Mandeville as the first in a conspicuous line of modern social theorists who have deployed an *individualist* and *evolutionary* conception of social institutions. These are believed to be selected and transformed piecemeal by the combined actions of individuals, following their free inclination, which inadvertently result in the establishment of the most efficient of these institutions. This position, adopted by Hayek himself, and characterized by an almost obsessive insistence on self-interested actions against rational design, is said to have had epoch-making consequences for the development of the modern social sciences. At the same time, Hayek insists that this evolutionary approach—identified with Popper's critical rationalism and more generally with 'original' liberalism—is opposed to the various versions of constructive rationalism, and that these two philosophies are particularly at odds on a political level.

In Mandeville's case these resounding, though perhaps intriguing, claims constitute something of an overstatement. In short, there is no clear evidence for maintaining that Mandeville thought of the principle of 'unintended consequences' with any methodological coherence. If he had, it would be difficult to reconcile it with other features of his writings. For, on the one hand, he insisted that morality and society at large are artificial creations which keep in check Man's a-social characteristics:

> I hope the reader knows that by society I understand a body politick, in which man either subdued by superioɪ force, or by persuasion drawn from his savage state, is become a disciplin'd creature, that can find his own ends in labouring for others, and where under one head or other form of government each member is rendered subservient to the whole, and all of them by cunning management are made to act as one.[46]

On the other hand, Mandeville frequently alluded to the figure of the 'skilful politician' as an important element in social regulation. This, only partly a metaphorical figure, can certainly been understood in a general anthropological sense: the expression of the haphazard and naturally selective accumulation of the experiences of countless generations; but it must also be taken in a more narrow political sense, as the rational, intentional intervention of public authority in the administration of the public good.

The interpretation of Mandeville's conception of unintended consequences becomes particularly difficult when one tries to find a sufficiently clear formulation of it in his writings. Two different things are often confused: Mandeville's generally sceptical and counter-intuitive method of argumentation; and the specific exposition of several instances in which society naturally achieves self-regulation. The *Fable*'s initial paradox and most of its satirical elucidations should be seen as an example of the former. That private vices result in public benefits is no principle of social regulation, unless one intends to justify it on a providentialist ground. As we have already seen, in Mandeville's work this paradox was mainly intended to point to the fact that social and economic life functioned autonomously from the conventional rules of moral judgement. Mandeville's was a *negative* argument, against the 'ought' of the moralists. To this end he deployed a series of traditional sceptical *topoi*, emphasizing the presence of 'evil'—both moral and physical—in nature, and drawing on the ideas of chance and fortune, as indicators of the high degree of flexibility—particularly moral flexibility —required for social agents to operate successfully.

Instead, Mandeville's discussion of social mobility and of the natural equilibrium between the professions should be included in the group of his positive contributions to what is now meant by 'unintended consequences'. But this was not Mandeville's only conception of the rules of social organization. To cite only a few examples in which he clearly departed from a theory of spontaneous order, we may refer to his belief that the skilful use of taxation was expedient to direct consumption in order to maintain a favourable balance of commerce; that politicians and legislators should ensure that manual workers would earn enough to live on, but not so much that they become 'lazy and insolent'; that brothels should be subject to public control or even—and this was not said entirely humourously—to public ownership.

The Hayekian notion of 'unintended consequences' cannot be found in Mandeville,[47] but in his writings there is enough material to appeal to those who view economic and social *dirigisme* with scepticism. There is also a great deal more for those who do not think that 'rationalism', 'moderation', and 'good conscience' are amongst the dominant features of modern western capitalism. But the problem for his modern readers and interpreters is that from this point of view there is too much, and, at the same time, too little. Too much of the eighteenth century, and too little of today's predicaments. Or, to put it in another way, what level of structural analysis is necessary for us to consider Mandeville's 'capitalism' comparable to our 'capitalism'?

Notes

1. This essay is the 'unintended consequence' of a conversation on Mandeville I had a few years ago with Professor Donald Winch, to whom I am indebted for suggesting the *problem* of Mandeville's posthumous reputation. I am also most grateful to the participants of

the seminar I originally gave at the History of Ideas Unit of the Research School of Social Sciences (ANU), and to those of the symposium held at Exeter University in November 1990. The editors' comments have greatly helped to shape the final version. The responsibility for its content is naturally only mine.

2. A short version of Mrs. Thatcher's speech is reproduced in *The Times*, 21 May 1988.

3. There are superficial similarities between the two periods, but I think that both images of Mandeville do little justice to the complexities of his work and intentions.

4. J. Habermas, 'What does Socialism mean Today? The rectifying revolution and the need for new thinking on the Left', *New Left Review* 183 (September-October, 1990), p. 21.

5. A.O. Hirschman, 'Rival Views of Market Society', in *Rival Views of Market Society and Other Essays* (New York, 1986).

6. Id., 'Against Parsimony: Three easy ways of complicating some categories of economic discourse', in *Rival Views*.

7. Id., *Exit, Voice, and Loyalty. Responses to decline in firms, organizations, and states* (Cambridge, Mass., 1970).

8. L. Dumont, *From Mandeville to Marx. The genesis and triumph of economic ideology* (Chicago, 1977); id., *Essays on Individualism. Modern ideology in anthropological perspective* (Chicago, 1986), ch.3.

9. The historical literature on the origin of Political Economy is vast. During the last decade many studies have showed the complexity of the process of formation of the economic discourse and the variety of languages and traditions which have contributed to it; but the temptation remains to look for a single epistemological break. As for certain ideological aspects of the idea of 'unintended consequences', Hirschman has explored the issue in 'Deux Cents Ans de Rhétorique Réactionnaire: le cas de l'effet pervers', *Annales. Économies, Sociétés, Civilisations* 44 (1989), pp. 67–86 (also published in English in volume X of *The Tanner Lectures on Human Values* (Salt Lake City, 1989)).

10. Throughout my argument the focus will be on the *intentione lectorum*, and my main concern with the *uses* to which the *Fable* has been put, but occasionally I shall take issue with the kind of interpretations given of Mandeville's text and its original meaning.

11. The distinction between *Histoire sanctionnée* and *Histoire périmée* is due to Gaston Bachelard, in particular *L'Activité Rationaliste de la Physique Contemporaine* (Paris, 1951). Keith Tribe has made good use of it in his perceptive analysis of Smith's position in the 'histories' of economic discourse: *Genealogies of Capitalism* (London, 1981), ch. 4.

12. In 1705 Bernard Mandeville published a long satirical poem of which

the *Fable*, whose first edition appeared nine years later, is an extended commentary. But it was only with the second enlarged edition, in 1723, that the work made an impact. The Grand Jury of Middlesex denounced the book as blasphemous and subversive and tried to have it banned. However, the *Fable* went through another two editions, and Mandeville also added a second volume in the form of a dialogue. After his death, the book was published a further four times in Britain (two of these editions appeared in Edinburgh), and up until the beginning of the nineteenth century there had been six translations into French and German. The *Fable* was published again, in German, in 1914, and only ten years later the now classic Kaye's edition appeared in print: *The Fable of the Bees; Or private vices, publick benefits*, ed. F.B. Kaye, 2 vols (Oxford, 1924).

13. Adam Smith, *The Theory of Moral Sentiments*, ed. D.D. Raphael and A.L. Macfie (Oxford, 1976), pp. 308–14; 'A Letter to the Authors of the *Edinburgh Review*', in *Essays on Philosophical Subjects*, ed. W.P.D. Wightman and J.C. Bryce (Oxford, 1980), pp. 250–4.

14. On the rise of the *homo oeconomicus* as a political agent, see A.O. Hirschman, *The Passions and the Interests. Political arguments for capitalism before its triumph* (Princeton, 1977); Dumont, *From Mandeville*; and M.L. Myers, *The Soul of Modern Economic Man. Ideas of self-interest. Thomas Hobbes to Adam Smith* (Chicago, 1983). On Mandeville and social sciences: E.J. Hundert, 'Bernard Mandeville and the Rhetoric of Social Sciences', *Journal of the History of the Behavioural Sciences* 22 (1986); and T.A. Horne, *The Social Thought of Bernard Mandeville* (London, 1978). For a discussion of paradox in the social sciences, see the essay 'Morality and the Social Sciences: a Durable Tension', in A.O. Hirschman, *Essays in Trespassing* (Cambridge, 1981). The three aspects of Mandeville's thought here emphasized are decipherable only *with hindsight*. They are a simplification of his intentions and of the historical significance of his arguments. Several interpretative problems which have grown up around the figure of Mandeville (utilitarian or rigorist, economic liberal or mercantilist) have very often proved to be the result of the philosophical love for clear cut definitions. These have only a very limited application in the case of authors like Mandeville, whose argumentative strategies are often dictated by a satirical bent, and who belong to the sceptical tradition of Montaigne and Bayle. For a more historically minded reconstruction of Mandeville's position in the eighteenth-century political and social debate, cf. M.M. Goldsmith, *Private Vices, Public Benefits. Bernard Mandeville's social and political thought* (Cambridge, 1985). On the role of satire in his work, cf. E.J. Hundert, 'A Satire of Self-Disclosure: from Hegel

through Rameau to the Augustans', *Journal of the History of Ideas* 47 (1986), pp. 235–48, and D. Castiglione, 'Mandeville Moralized', *Annali della Fondazione Luigi Einaudi* 12 (1983), pp. 239–90.

15. J.G.A. Pocock maintains that there is no real 'Mandevillean moment' in the eighteenth century: 'Authority and Property: The question of liberal origins', in *Virtue, Commerce, and History* (Cambridge, 1985), p. 70; in another essay in the same collection, 'The Mobility of Property and the Rise of Eighteenth-Century Sociology', he advances a distinction, which I use below, between a 'hard' and a 'soft' line in the legitimation of commercial society.

16. Naturally, I am here simplifying, for there were many versions both of religious and republican morality. Goldsmith, *Private Vices*, rightly points out that the main butt of Mandeville's attack was the particular blend of Christian and civic morality advanced by Steele in the *Tatler*.

17. F. Hutcheson, *Reflections upon Laughter and Remarks upon the 'Fable of the Bees'*, in *Opera Minora* (reprinted, Hildesheim, 1971), pp. 144–56.

18. Mandeville, *Fable*, 'Remark L', vol. 1, pp. 107–23.

19. In his introduction to a recent Italian translation of the first volume of the *Fable*, Tito Magri expounds upon this point. He correctly notices that Mandeville's moral theory cannot be considered rigorist, but also that rigorism seems to be the only adequate language for a conventionalist conception of morality: B. Mandeville, *La Favola delle Api*, ed. T. Magri (Bari, 1987), pp. xxxii–xxxiv.

20. Magri has suggested that the distinction between two kinds of societies (commercial and pre-commercial), to which different moral and epistemological criteria are applied, is one of Mandeville's most original contributions to social thought. My argument on 'private' and 'public' morality in Mandeville needs to be read within the more general context of Magri's distinction: 'Introduzione', in Mandeville, *Favola*, pp. vi–xv.

21. The centrality of the material aspects of virtues to the classical republican tradition until the eighteenth century has been argued by J.G.A. Pocock, particularly in his *The Machiavellian Moment. Florentine political thought and the Atlantic republican tradition* (Princeton, 1975).

22. Mandeville, *Fable*, vol. I, p. 40.

23. D. Hume, *Essays Moral, Political, and Literary*, ed. T.H. Green and T.H. Grose (London, 1898), vol. 1, pp. 299–309.

24. D. Hume, *Enquiry concerning the Principles of Morals*, in *Enquiries*, ed. L.A. Selby-Bigge, third edition revised by P.H. Nidditch (Oxford, 1975), p. 181. On the logic of Mandeville's paradoxes about commercial society, and on the way in which he influenced Hume and Smith,

see T.A. Horne, 'Envy and Commercial Society. Mandeville and Smith on "Private Vices, Public Benefits"', *Political Theory* 9 (1981), pp. 551–69; M.M. Goldsmith, 'Liberty, Luxury, and the Pursuit of Happiness', in A. Pagden (ed.), *Languages of Politics in Early Modern Europe* (Cambridge, 1987); D. Castiglione, 'Considering Things Minutely: Reflections on Mandeville and the eighteenth-century science of man', *History of Political Thought* 7 (1986), pp. 463–88.

25. J. Boswell, *The Life of Johnson*, ed. R.W. Chapman, revised by J.D. Fleeman (Oxford, 1970), pp. 755–6 and 947–8.

26. The 'spiralling appetites, opportunities, and ambitions' fuelled during the eighteenth century, and the intellectual strategies adopted for the evaluation of this 'march of civilization' are explored in Roy Porter's study of Thomas Trotter in this collection. Mandeville, who was also a physician (of the 'hysterical diseases') can be said to represent the opposite line of thought to Trotter's. In his *Treatise of the Hypocondriack and Hysterick Diseases*, Mandeville seems to suggest that the only cure for such diseases is for the patients to understand their nature and to accept their conditions: the malady to cure is not civilization, but the very 'discontent of civilization', which, according to Porter, is at the centre of Trotter's own work.

27. T.R. Malthus, *An Essay on the Principle of Population* (London, 1826), vol. II, p. 454.

28. Ibid. On Malthus' 'natural theology', see D.N. Winch, *Malthus* (Oxford, 1987), pp. 32–5 and 101–3. On other instances in which he makes use of the argument from 'unintended consequences', see J.W. Burrow, *Whigs and Liberals. Continuity and change in English political thought* (Oxford, 1988), pp. 59–60.

29. A.O. Hirschman, 'The Concept of Interest: From euphemism to tautology', in *Rival Views*.

30. K. Marx, *Capital*, ed. E. Mandel (Harmondsworth, 1976), vol. 1, p. 475, fn. 33.

31. Ibid., p. 476.

32. I should perhaps make clear that in linking Mandeville and Smith on the consumer-centred vision of the division of labour, I am not implying that Smith was also marginal to the interests of the nineteenth-century authors. *The Wealth of Nations* was a very different book from the *Fable*, it contained other parts which showed a shift of interest towards production, and it had been 'rewritten' and canonized by Ricardo and Malthus as *the* classical text of modern Political Economy (Tribe, *Genealogies*, pp. 147–52). But it must also be emphasized that Marx's was a strong producer-centred view. This is also shown in his treatment of the process of *valorization*, which he regards as entirely confined to the sphere of production. A similar

point could be made about the relationship between Mandeville's vision of commercial society and Veblen's. As A.O. Lovejoy has acutely suggested (*Reflections on Human Nature* (Baltimore, 1961), pp. 208–15), there are many similarities between their social theories, their insistence on the importance of sumptuous consumption in the regulation of society, and their emphasis of 'envy' and 'emulation' as the driving forces towards accumulation. But Veblen's perception of modernity is associated with the industrial world: a productive, continuously changing, comprehensive system, made up of numerous organs and functions mutually conditioning one another. This is a world very different from the rather irrational monetary economy, mainly based on conspicuous leisure, commerce, speculative business, and—in Veblen's own words—the gambling propensity, which comprises Mandeville's 'modern' world. (T. Veblen, *The Theory of the Leisure Class* (New York, 1934), particularly chs 8, 9, and 11).

33. As Maurice Goldsmith has justly argued, there is a sense in which it could be said that 'Mandeville . . . invented the "spirit of capitalism"' ('Mandeville and the Spirit of Capitalism', *Journal of British Studies* 17 (1977), p. 81). However my point is different. What I argue below is that Mandeville's 'spirit of capitalism' is different from the one 'invented' by the turn-of-the-century German sociologists who made the issue popular.

34. The works with which I am here mainly concerned are M. Weber, *Die Protestantische Ethik und der Geist des Kapitalismus* (1904–05) (*The Protestant Ethic and the Spirit of Capitalism*, trans. New York, 1958); W. Sombart, *Der moderne Kapitalismus* (1902); id., *Der Bourgeois* (1913) (*The Quintessence of Capitalism*, ed. M. Epstein, trans. New York, 1967); L. Brentano, *Der wirtshaftende Mensch in der Geschichte* (1913); G. Simmel, *Philosophie des Geldes* (1900) (*The Philosophy of Money*, trans. London, 1978); E. Troeltsch, *Die Bedeutung des Protestantismus für die Entstehung der modernen Welt* (1906) (*Protestantism and Progress: a Historical Study of the Relation of Protestantism to the Modern World*, ed. W. Montgomery, trans. London and New York, 1912).

35. I call Mandeville's the 'Petticoat Thesis' with reference to the *Fable*, vol. 1, p. 356, where he maintains that the 'capricious invention of hoop'd and quilted petticoat' has done more that the Reformation to enrich the Protestant countries above the rest. The point is reinforced by the index entry, which reads: 'Reformation (the) of less moment to trade than hoop'd petticoat' (vol. 1, p. 378).

36. J. Viner, *Religious Thought and Economic Society: Four chapters of an unfinished work*, ed. J. Melitz and D.N. Winch, in *History of Political Economy* 10 (1978), chs 3 and 4.

37. Hume, 'Of Interest', in *Essays*, vol. 1, p. 325.
38. Cf. Weber's 'Preliminary Observation' to his *Protestant Ethic*.
39. Mandeville, *Fable*, vol. 1, pp. 181–98.
40. Ibid., pp. 104–5. The expression 'moderate men' is Mandeville's own, and can be found in the same passage.
41. J.M. Keynes, *General Theory* (London, 1936), ch. 23, vii.
42. J. Robinson, *Economic Philosophy* (Harmondsworth, 1968), p. 20.
43. R.K. Merton, 'The Unanticipated Consequences of Purposive Social Action', *American Sociological Review* I (1936), pp. 894–904.
44. J.A.W. Gunn, 'Mandeville and Wither: Individualism and the workings of Providence', in I. Primer (ed.), *Mandeville Studies* (The Hague, 1975).
45. F.A. Hayek, 'Dr. Bernard Mandeville', *Proceedings of the British Academy* 52 (1966), pp. 125–41, and several other essays in *Studies in Philosophy, Politics and Economics* (London, 1967).
46. Mandeville, *Fable*, vol. 1, p. 347.
47. It is true that Hayek has only maintained that Mandeville 'asked the right question' and 'probably never fully understood what was his main discovery' ('Dr. Bernard Mandeville', p. 127); but my contention is that the lack of methodological coherence in eighteenth-century authors undermines Hayek's vision of the early development of the social sciences. Moreover, it is probably true that the logical status of the concept of 'unintended consequences' is not as clear as Hayek seems to think. See, for instance, R. Boudon, *The Unintended Consequences of Social Action* (New York, 1982); M. Polanyi, *The Logic of Liberty* (London, 1951), pp. 154 ff.; and R. Brown, *The Nature of Social Laws. Machiavelli to Mill* (Cambridge, 1984), pp. 66–9.

Addicted to Modernity: Nervousness in the Early Consumer Society

Roy Porter

Georgian England, contemporary commentators agreed, was undergoing rapid, accelerating, indeed dizzying change: rapid population rise, wealth accumulation, commercialization, urbanization, mechanization, industrialization, a communications revolution—in short, all the elements of modernization. People were on the move, on the make, wanting more out of life and wanting it fast. From Mandeville onwards, boosters galore cheered the birth of what has been called the 'first consumer society'. But they were matched by a counterpoint of Jeremiahs traumatized by the shock of the new, lamenting the world that was being lost: honest traditions, simplicity, hospitality, stability—all were being swept away by the floodwaters of luxury and artificiality, ephemerality and corruption, bewailed *laudatores temporis acti* from Jeremy Collier at the beginning of the century, through 'Estimate' Brown in the middle, to counter-revolutionaries and Evangelicals at its close. London was Babylon, Britain a Bedlam; wickedness, sinfulness, villainy, vice and greed stained this age of acquisitiveness.[1]

All this, of course, had endlessly been heard before. Yet in this crescendo of criticism, one traditional strain was becoming more audible, more insistent than previously, the expression of social criticism in the language of medicine; doctors were becoming more prominent as pathologists of their own society.[2] And, according to their diagnosis, the nation was not—or, at least, was not merely—sinful and vicious: rather, it had to be understood as morbidly self-destructive and self-enslaving: the acquisitive society was the addictive society. The new relationships being created between producers and the environments they were forging for themselves—environments not just physical but social, cultural and psychological—were generating spiral upon spiral of desire and demand.

New scenarios of propensities and possibilities were being called into being, which, in their turn, were engulfing, mastering, their own authors. Dreamworlds were turning into Gothic nightmares, creators became creatures of their own fantasies; in the modern metropolis, at the masquerade, in the speculative paper-money world of the Exchange, in the new industrial landscape of the pit, the furnace and the factory, man was making monsters which he couldn't control. In the great *fin-de-siècle* Revolution whose contagion started in France, progress seemed to be devouring its own children.

Of course, as David Spadafora has argued in his recent study of Georgian ideas of progress, the emphasis by critics on kaleidoscopic fluidity, on process, so conspicuous in such critiques, had itself been integral to, and a welcome dimension of, Enlightenment naturalistic meliorism.[3] Man was a being of indefinite potential, his nature was his history, enacted through dynamic interplay with his surroundings. Had not Locke—and Sterne!—imaged the infant as a *tabula rasa*, a blank sheet of paper, whose character was to be formed through the inter-action of his sense perceptions with external stimuli? Thus man was the offspring of his education; programmed by his experiences, he in turn imposed himself upon the external milieu. Through the dialectic of nature and nurture, man thereby transformed external reality and was in turn moulded by it. It was this progressive view of change which spurred Enlightenment social engineering philosophies—notably Bentham's utilitarianism—to conjure up proto-Skinnerian visions of beneficial conditioning through positive reinforcement, culminating in the utopian vision of man's redemption through wholesale environmental manipulation, envisaged by Robert Owen's *New View of Society*: a New Heaven at New Lanark.[4]

What is distinctive, however, about the bleaker assessments of man's self-transformative odyssey advanced in the eighteenth century is their stress upon the pathology, indeed psychopathology, of progress. Man might be making himself, but, by trangressing norms and traditions, he was making himself sick. By remoulding his milieu and lifestyle to match his imagination, by multiplying his wants, his urges, his ambitions, man the overreacher was also fixing a dependency upon insatiable appetites. This vision of *homo faber* forging for himself such an armoury of prosthetics—clothes, fire, property, rhetoric, the law, and so forth—that eventually he grew so constitutionally enfeebled as to be incapable of doing without reliance upon such illusory, or, at least, incidental crutches was, of course, advanced most indignantly by Rousseau, who, mounting a moral and political high-horse, denounced the headlong rush from natural, noble freedom into radical chains.[5] A comparable diagnosis— though maybe not cure—was offered in Britain at the beginning of the nineteenth century by the doctor, Thomas Trotter, only in the language of medicine.

A baker's son, Trotter was born in 1760 in Melrose, Roxburghshire.[6] At seventeen, he went to study medicine at Edinburgh University,[7] leaving, however, after two years to become a surgeon's mate in the Navy, and seeing active service in the War of American Independence, where began his lifelong concern with scurvy.[8] Trotter returned to Edinburgh, writing in 1788 his M. D. dissertation, *De Ebrietate* ('On Drunkenness'),[9] before resuming his career in the Navy medical service. Serving at Haslar, the vast naval hospital near Portsmouth, and then as physician to the Channel Fleet, he proved an energetic reformer. Angered by the indifference to health questions displayed by the naval top-brass, Trotter warmly espoused the grievances of the common sailor, above all in the three volumes of *Medicina Nautica: An Essay on the Diseases of Seamen* (1797–1803).[10]

Just turned forty, Trotter then settled as a medical practitioner in Newcastle, pursuing interests both literary and scientific,[11] and publishing there his two most important works: the *Essay . . . on Drunkenness* (1804), and the *View of the Nervous Temperament* (1807), which between them advanced Trotter's vision of social pathology.

Drunkenness, he argued, was a great social evil,[12] but little understood, because it had largely been left to well-meaning but inept parsons and moralists. In truth, the *Essay* claimed, it was properly the province of the 'discerning physician',[13] for inebriety was 'strictly speaking . . . a disease'.[14] Indeed, Trotter regarded it quite specifically as a mental disorder—'the habit of drunkenness is a disease of the mind'[15]—to be placed within the nosological class of the Vesaniae (insanity) as established by his great Edinburgh mentor, William Cullen, where it had the closest affinities to amentia (idiotism), insania, and mania, though melancholia was itself often the melancholy consequence of habitual intoxication.[16]

In the *Essay . . . on Drunkenness*, Trotter proceeded to investigate the disease's 'phenomena and symptoms', plotting the Sot's Progress from stimulus to 'indirect debility', 'from pleasure to pain, from the purest perceptions of intellect to the last confusion of thought', which 'ends, by bringing [man] to a level with the brutes'.[17] He thereby laid bare the cardinal paradox of 'vinolency': prolonged potations proved counterproductive; imbibed as a stimulant, alcohol was subject to the law of diminishing returns: 'like all human enjoyments, the exhilarating powers of wine lose their fine zest and high relish, by being too frequently indulged'.[18] For Trotter, such a conclusion was not just a moral truism, but a somewhat Brunonian medical judgment about the operations of the nervous system, incorporating the insight of the unorthodox Edinburgh medical teacher, John Brown, that, without perpetual external stimulus, life itself would falter.[19]

Trotter proceeded to examine the chemistry, the physiology, and finally the pathology of 'temulency'.[20] Its short-term damage included apoplexy, epilepsy, hysterics and convulsions.[21] In the long run, those who pursued 'habitual intoxication' were susceptible to brain-fever, pleurisy, rheumatism, inflammations of the stomach and the bowels, ophthalmia, carbuncles, hepatitis, gout, schirrus, jaundice, dyspepsia, dropsy, tabes, and other wasting disorders, palpitations, diabetes, palsy, ulcers, madness, melancholy, impotence, and premature old age.[22]

From his medical viewpoint—specifically as one who had studied large captive populations of sufferers trapped in the 'total institution' of ships-of-the-line—Trotter was led to insist that habitual drinking could be properly understood not in isolation with the individual patient, but only in its wider context of socio-cultural pressures. Alcohol abuse had to be situated amongst all the other stimulants and intoxicants readily available and increasingly consumed in the emergent consumer society: opiates, tobacco, tea, coffee, cordials, and (not least) medicines. Above all, it was necessary to grasp the growing social accentuation of consumption. The Ancients, he remarked, were frugal and modest in their habits; in his day, by contrast, honour demanded that gentlemen drank each other under the table—even statesmen had to be three-bottle men.[23] Nor was the fair sex any better, being equally addicted, if usually secretively, to brandy-based cordials, laudanum and volatile spirits, to say nothing of their inordinate swallowing of the slow poison of hyson tea.[24] The consequence, he bemoaned, was sickness:[25]

> The last century has been remarkable for the increase of a class of diseases, but little known in former times, and what had slightly engaged the study of physicians prior to that period. They have been designated in common language, by the terms NERVOUS; SPASMODIC; BILIOUS; INDIGESTION; STOMACH COMPLAINTS; LOW SPIRITS; VAPOURS, etc.

To understand this social pathology, Trotter felt obliged to propose a comprehensive historical sociology of health and sickness in the emergent consumer society, or, in other words, to move from the restricted topic of the *Essay . . . on Drunkenness* to the wider frame of the *View of the Nervous Temperament* (1807).

What was the balance sheet of progress?—a question ceaselessly debated throughout the Enlightenment, above all by Montesquieu and Rousseau in France, and by the Scots 'conjectural historians' with whom Trotter must have become *au fait* while in Edinburgh. In this context, the *View of the Nervous Temperament* examined what Trotter himself called man's advance from 'rudeness to refinement'. History, Trotter believed, bore testimony to epochal transformations. Man had developed the useful and the fine arts; through science and technology he had maximized his control over Nature; the ensuing economic progress had multiplied wealth and leisure; social organization had become more sophisticated, manners and morals more refined. Modern society boasted affluence, comforts and personal liberty, offering enticing opportunities and kindling enhanced expectations. Above all—and possibly reflecting the personal experience of a Scottish country boy who had moved to Edinburgh—Trotter emphasized the transformative role of the great commercial town in accelerating the circulation of wealth, goods and fashions, and creating an emulative environment of narcissism and competitiveness.[26]

But what were the deeper consequences of such developments for human nature and happiness, for man's permanent well-being, psychic and physical? There was, of course, an optimistic option. 'Every age of the world has increased, and still increases, the real wealth, the happiness, the knowledge, and perhaps the virtue, of the human race': thus Gibbon closed the third volume of his *Decline and Fall of the Roman Empire*.[27] Trotter read Gibbon, but advanced a clean contrary interpretation of this epochal transition. Echoing the outraged Rousseau rather than the suave Gibbon, Trotter looked back to the Patriarchs of the Old Testament, to the more elemental civilizations of Antiquity, and even to Tacitus' gothic barbarians—and, one may surmise, to the rural Scotland of his childhood—and discovered peoples marked by a noble 'simplicity'.[28] 'Our rude ancestors', he claimed, were sturdy, hardy, independent; they suffered few ills, because they had few needs: 'where the savage feels one want, the civilized being has a thousand'.[29] Above all, they 'had few bodily disorders', and none were 'brought to the grave by excess or debauch'.[30] It might be conceded of the 'primitive', Trotter admitted, that 'his enjoyments are limited'; nevertheless 'his cares, his pains, and his diseases are few' (a view echoed today, and perhaps no less tendentiously, in anthropologists' studies of the Kalahari bushmen).[31]

In Trotter's evaluation, the march of civilization, bringing with it claustrophobic urbanization, indoors existence, 'refined life',[32] and sedentary occupations—or none at all![33]—spelt the demise of independence and the spread of discontents and disorders, fuelled by spiralling appetites, opportunities, and ambitions. 'In a state of progressive improvement and civilization', mankind had quit 'hunting and fishing for the town': he 'forsakes a mode of life that had been presented to him by nature, and in adopting a new situation he becomes the creature of art'.[34] But the mirage of progress had fomented a spirit of inquietude, a restless, insatiable quest for intenser experiences, new gratifications, wilder excitements. Surplus wealth had brought idleness, indolence and consequent 'low spirits';[35] these in turn had spurred fresh cravings for 'debilitating pleasures'[36] and 'excessive stimuli'.[37] Indulgence in luxuries begat the evils of excess;[38] and the cultivation by the 'voluptuary' of subtler tastes and exquisite sensitivities brought in their train an increased susceptibility to pain: under the pressures of 'inordinate stimulation', stoicism yielded to sensibility.[39]

By consequence of these morbid cravings for novel stimuli, polite society developed needs for sedatives, to deaden the pains of the discontents of civilization—not least the 'hysteria' and 'hypochondriacism' resulting from the interplay of hothouse life-styles with ultra-febrile imaginations.[40] The civilizing process thus created insatiable needs, both for 'inordinate stimulation'[41] and for narcotics, all spurred by the allure of the new and the empire of fashion. More specifically—and here Trotter seems particularly to echo his contemporary, Thomas Beddoes[42]—the artifices of modish living—over-sophisticated diet,[43] stifling rooms, such pernicious fashions as tight-lacing, late rising, and lack of exercise—necessarily bred ill-health, ailments and invalidism, and so led automatically (given the new supersensitivity to pain) to the gulping of ever greater quantities of medicines and analgesics. Since many of these were both harmful and addictive, in turn they further destroyed the stomach and the nervous organization, debilitating the constitution, causing secondary sickness, and so inducing a yet further spirals of medication to counteract iatrogenic maladies.

All in all, judged Trotter, the so-called growth of freedom of choice in modern society was utterly illusory. New pleasures rapidly wore out, trapping the voluptuary on a treadmill, for, as had been suggested in the

Essay . . . on Drunkenness, 'the exhilarating powers . . . lose their fine zest and high relish, by being too frequently indulged'.[44] Thus modern man was enslaving himself to his own great expectations, to his vices and self-induced physical and mental weaknesses. The nation that supposedly 'ruled the waves' had degenerated, bemoaned Trotter, into a 'nation of slaves'.[45] In its currently morbid manifestations, civilization itself had become a mode of disease.

So, suffering from that very 'nervous temperament' which the civilizing process had created and even coveted, civilized man grew unhealthy. To revive jaded appetites, high society resorted to such stimuli as ardent spirits; to ease their pains and calm their jangled nerves, the highly-strung swallowed sedatives; but all these in turn merely gave new twists to the screw of sickness. Medicines proper had the same deplorable side-effects, and gave a further dimension to addiction. For, argued Trotter,[46]

> All nervous persons are uncommonly fond of drugs; and they are the chief consumers of advertised remedies, which they conceal from their medical friends. Among some well-meaning people, this inordinate desire for medicine has frequently become of itself a disease. With many of them, physic, to be useful, must be clothed in mystery; and the moment a discovery is made of the composition, the confidence is lost. Medical attendants have too often brought this punishment on themselves. Were they unanimous in combating the prejudices of mankind, by candour and openness of conduct, by a fair avowal of the imperfections of their art, and the honest concession that articles of Materia Medica form but a small portion of its resources, they would not so frequently see their commands disregarded, or learn that their compounds have been thrown out of a window. This is the only way in which I can account for so many persons of good sense and discernment, consigning themselves and families into the hands of impudent and illiterate quacks.

And all the while, Trotter emphasized, echoing Lockean theories of habit- and character-formation through education and environment, these pathological facets of civilization were becoming integral to human nature itself, embossed upon the collective mind, and descending through the generations, as acquired characteristics. Far from being fixed, human nature was the product of self-development. And civilized man, a delicate, hothouse plant, was above all, Trotter insisted, a *'creature of habit'*.[47] He could be the victim of the 'nervous temperament' precisely because he was the *'creator* of his own *temperament'*—self-made man with a vengeance![48] 'In the present stage of society', he underlined in his *Essay*, 'human kind are almost taken out of the hands of Nature; and a custom called *fashion* . . . now rules everything.'[49]

Within this process, the disposition to drunkenness, in the individual, the community and the race, was both a symptom and a spur. Despite all the obvious macho associations, the craving for strong liquor betokened an effeminate, decadent stage, for 'natural appetite requires no such stimulants'.[50] Trotter was not such a primitivist as to decry stimulants entirely. But—as with ardent spirits and hyson tea—he feared they were in essence harmful; and he deplored the fact that such stimulants as wine, safe and even beneficial if wisely deployed, had been reduced to necessities. Soda water likewise, which ought to be used strictly medicinally, had become a habitual beverage. They were sorry times when opium, God's greatest gift to the physician for the relief of acute pain, had become, in the shape of the laudanum phial, an item in every fashionable lady's reticule. Lay people dosed themselves with powerful medicines as though they were sweets.[51] In fact, Trotter concluded, Britain was being swamped with 'narcotics'. 'These include', he argued,[52]

> ardent spirits, opium, and all those articles commonly called anodynes, hypnotics, paregories, &c. such as lactuca, bang, belladonna, hyosciamus, laurus cerafus, cicuta, &c. Of the effects of ardent spirits, in producing stomach and nervous complaints, I have treated largely in my Essay on Drunkenness, to which I refer the reader. All the articles now enumerated, act very much alike on the human body. In small quantities, they induce vigor, activity and strength, and an increase of muscular power throughout the frame; at the same time are felt serenity, pleasure and courage of mind. In larger doses they bring on sleep, stupor and delirium; and when carried to the utmost quantity, insensibility, apoplexy and death. It is of little moment in this inquiry, whether narcotics ought to be considered as directly or indirectly sedative. They are forbid in all inflammatory diseases, where they certainly do harm in the first stage: they generally occasion constipation, but hyosciamus has a laxative quality. When long continued, they are known to weaken the nervous system in a surprizing degree; disposing to amentia, epilepsy, palsy, tremors, convulsions, melancholy, madness, etc.

Thus, in both individual and society, there was a vortex of desire and dissatisfaction. Drawing upon the Brunonian analysis of excitability,

Trotter asserted that each dose of artificial stimulant perhaps produced the expected sensations, but merely temporarily, and their powers to excite were rapidly exhausted. Hence they needed to be consumed in ever larger quantities, greater concentrations, or in adulterated forms—and Trotter was a ferocious critic of the adulterating practices of the great brewers and the quack doctors.[53] Finally, more potent stimulants had to be found. Time was when the rich had satisfied their cravings in wine; now, enervated by 'luxury and refinement'[54] and racked by 'diseased sensibility',[55] they abandoned themselves to such fortified liquors as port and brandy. Formerly the poor had quaffed home brews; now they downed rum and gin, or, no less perniciously, ales adulterated by unscrupulous brewers who added addictive bitters and even opiates.

Thus 'polished society' was so acting as to 'bring on its own dotage' and 'dig its own grave'.[56] Trotter was, of course, far from the first to point to the ambivalent consequences of the transition from 'rudeness to refinement'.[57] A host of contemporary critics, from the authoritarian right to the populist left, offered their versions of pastoral, evoking golden ages when life was simpler, healthier, happier. Advocacy of plain living had long been the doctors' stock-in-trade, from George Cheyne's *English Malady* (1733),[58] which urged a return to grains, greens and milk, to Trotter's slightly senior Edinburgh-trained contemporary, the quackish sex-therapist, James Graham, who accused over-sophistication of causing impotence and depopulation, and demanded an end to alcohol consumption and a return to water, fresh air, and hard beds.[59] Trotter's picture of the maladies of rich and poor alike in Newcastle closely parallels Beddoes' contemporary bludgeoning of the Bristolians. Cheyne had suggested that perhaps a third of all the maladies of the Quality were nervous; echoing him, Trotter thought that such disorders constituted 'by far the largest proportion of the whole which come under the treatment of the physician'—a sign that in an open, opportunity, consumer society, even diseases were being democratized.[60]

But if Trotter's account of the diseases of civilization was not original, his formulations are important, because of his perceptive, if tendentious, emphasis upon the symbiosis of physical and psychological dependency, both in the individual (increasingly hooked on his stimulants, be they alcohol or medicines), and also in that 'creature of habit and imitation',[61] civilized man at large, 'wallowing in wealth and rioting in indulgence',[62] enslaved to fashion and fantasy. Physical stimuli, such as alcohol, excited the senses; these in turn registered their effects upon the nervous system, producing the 'nervous temperament'; this temperament

affected the psyche; and in turn the imagination begat fresh desires
triggering new chain-reactions of cravings. 'Are not habits of drunkenness', asked Trotter, 'more often produced by mental affections than
corporeal diseases? I apprehend few people will doubt the truth of this.'[63]
Convinced thus of psychological enslavement, it was natural that Trotter
should be the first analyst clearly to formulate the idea of habitual
drunkenness as a mental illness, and to generalize this into a vision of
modernity as a disorder.

Unlike Rousseau at his more provocative, Trotter was never an out-
and-out primitivist, advocating a return to Nature. Indeed, he thought
that certain pockets of hardy manhood still survived uncorrupted. A well-
disciplined British warship, manned by doughty tars and commanded by
dreadnought officers, was one exception, and he was confident that
Britain would defeat Napoleon, for the process of effeminization—the
reduction of men to 'manikins'[64]—cultural decadence, the evolution of
the nervous diathesis, had proceeded further in foppish France.[65] Hence
he was no mere nostalgia monger, and it was the abuses of civilization,
not civilization itself, that he deplored. But he was in no doubt as to the
measures needed both for the individual and for the polity at large:[66]

> Great Britain has outstripped rival states in her commercial
> greatness: let us therefore endeavour to preserve that ascendancy,
> which is so essential to our welfare in the convulsed condition of
> Europe, by the only means that can do it effectually. That is, by
> recurring to simplicity of living and manners, so as to check
> the increasingly prevalence of nervous disorders; which, if not
> restrained soon, must inevitably sap our physical strength of
> constitution; make us an easy conquest to our invaders; and
> ultimately convert us into a nation of slaves and idiots.

Trotter, in short, is a social critic whose works deserve study as signs of
the time. As noted above, he can be taken as symptomatic of a growing
tendency, in a secularizing age of science, to express social ills in the
language of a kind of 'social medicine': the figure of the doctor was
perhaps assuming greater prominence as the authorized critic of social
trends.[67]

More significantly, Trotter's analysis of his own society as suffering
from the evils of over-stimulus produced by food, alcohol, stimulants and
narcotics reinforces the claims of early industrial Britain to be regarded,
not just as a commercial society, but specifically as a consumer society.
For it can be argued that the label 'consumer society' should not be

exclusively reserved for the age of the Model T Ford—the age of genuine 'mass production' of absolutely standardized goods—but has an authentic applicability to an earlier order characterized by the mobilization of consumerist expectations—a psychology of stimulus—much as Trotter depicts.

Not least, Trotter is a perceptive psychologist and physiologist of habit. Of course, as a medical man, his focus is mainly upon the personal motors influencing the formation of habits—he hardly addresses himself to the 'hidden persuaders' promoting consumption in the commercial society. Nevertheless, his insightful account of alcohol addiction, applied more widely to the habituation of desires for a range of other potent commodities, offers a powerful model for a vision of a modern age becoming inexorably socialized into compulsive, if not compulsory, consumerism.

Notes

1. For eighteenth-century commentary and criticism, see J. Sekora, *Luxury* (Baltimore, 1977). The claim that eighteenth-century England saw a consumer revolution can be found in Neil McKendrick, 'The Birth of a Consumer Society: The commercialization of eighteenth-century England', in Neil McKendrick, John Brewer and J.H. Plumb, *The Birth of a Consumer Society: The Commercialization of Eighteenth-Century England* (1982), p. vii. This claim has been disputed: for evaluation, see Roy Porter, 'Introduction', in John Brewer and Roy Porter (eds), *Consumption and the World of Goods* (1993).

2. I am not trying to suggest that medicine had never before offered metaphors of social criticism. Given the prevalence, ever since the Greeks, of emblems of the 'body politic' that would be absurd. It may be true, however, that, with the rise of the medical profession in the eighteenth century, medical men began to assume a more prominent part in social commentary—a role culminating in the critique of 'degenerationism' in the *fin de siècle*. The subject of the analysis of social pathology deserves further study. See, however, Barbara Spackman, *Decadent Genealogies. The Rhetoric of Sickness from Baudelaire to D'Annunzio* (Ithaca, 1989).

3. David Spadafora, *The Idea of Progress in Eighteenth-Century Britain* (New Haven, 1990); J. Passmore, *The Perfectibility of Man* (1971).

4. For wider Enlightenment ideas of human potential, see Peter Gay, 'The Enlightenment as Medicine and as Cure', in W.H. Barber (ed.), *The Age of the Enlightenment: Studies Presented to Theodore Besterman* (Edinburgh, 1967); id., *The Enlightenment: An Interpretation*, 2 vols

(New York, 1967–9); Roy Porter, *The Enlightenment* (1990).

5. On Rousseau, see Ronald Grimsley, *The Philosophy of Rousseau* (Oxford, 1973).
6. For Trotter, see Roy Porter, 'Introduction', to *Thomas Trotter: An Essay on Drunkenness* (1988; 1st edn. 1804).
7. The best accounts of Trotter's life are Ian Porter, 'Thomas Trotter, M.D., Naval Physician', *Medical History* 7 (1963), pp. 155–64; Sir Humphry Rolleston, 'Thomas Trotter, M.D.', in *Contributions to Medical and Biological Research Dedicated to Sir William Osler, In Honour of His Seventieth Birthday, by His Pupils and Co-Workers* (New York, 1919) (perceptive yet unreliable on points of detail). Hardly any manuscript material seems to have survived.
8. See T. Trotter, *Observations on the Scurvy: with a Review of the Theories Lately Advanced on that Disease; and the Opinions of Dr. Milman Refuted From Practice* (Edinburgh, 1786. 2nd edn. 1792); Kenneth Carpenter, *The History of Scurvy and Vitamin C* (Cambridge, 1986).
9. Thomas Trotter, *De Ebrietate, Eiusque Effectibus in Corpus Humanum* (Edinburgh, 1788). A copy of this is to be found in Edinburgh University Library.
10. T. Trotter, *Medicina Nautica; and Essay on the Diseases of Seamen; Comprehending the History of Health in His Majesty's Fleet under . . . Earl Howe (with an Appendix Containing Communications on the New Doctrine of Contagion and Yellow Fever, By American Physicians, etc)* 3 vols (1797–9). Copious extracts from this work have been printed, with a brief commentary, in C. Lloyd (ed.), *The Health of Seamen. Selections from the Works of Dr James Lind, Sir Gilbert Blane and Dr Thomas Trotter* (1965), pp. 217–316.
11. T. Trotter, *Sea Weeds. Poems Written on Various Occasions Chiefly During a Naval Life* (1829).
12. For the place of drinking within pre-industrial society see A.L. Simon, *Bottlescrew Days. Wine Drinking in England During the Eighteenth Century* (1926); J.A. Spring and D.H. Buss, 'Three Centuries of Alcohol in the British Diet', *Nature* 219 (1977), pp. 567–72; M.M. Glatt, 'The English Drink Problem: Its rise and decline through the ages', *The British Journal of Addiction* 4 (1958), pp. 51–67; H.G. Graham, *The Social Life of Scotland in the Eighteenth Century* (1969); Keith V. Thomas, *Religion and the Decline of Magic* (1971), p. 17; P. Clark, *The English Ale House* (1983). For the gin craze see J. Watney, *Mother's Ruin* (1976); D.M. George, *London Life in the Eighteenth Century* (Harmondsworth, 1966); T.G. Coffey, 'Beer Street: Gin Lane: Some views of eighteenth-century drinking', *Quarterly Journal for the Study of Alcoholism* 34 (1966), pp. 662–92; Lord

Kinross, 'Prohibition in Britain', *History Today* 9 (1959), pp. 493–9.

13. Thomas Trotter, *An Essay, Medical, Philosophical and Chemical, on Drunkenness and its Effects on the Human Body* (1804), p. 6.

14. Trotter, *Essay . . . on Drunkenness*, p. 8.

15. Ibid., pp. 8, 179. For similar formulations, see ibid., pp. 128, 182 ('the habit of intoxication belongs to the mind'), 26 (drunkenness is 'a species of insanity'), and 186 ('are not habits of drunkenness more often produced by mental affections than corporeal diseases?'). For further discussion, see Roy Porter, 'The Drinking Man's Disease: The "pre-history" of alcoholism in Georgian Britain', *British Journal of Addiction* 80 (1985), pp. 385–96. For histories of the idea of alcoholism, and Trotter's part therein, see W.F. Bynum, 'Chronic Alcoholism in the First Half of the Nineteenth Century', *Bulletin of the History of Medicine* 42 (1968), pp. 160–85, esp. p. 162; J. Hirsch, 'Enlightened Eighteenth-Century Views of the Alcohol Problem', *Journal of the History of Medicine* 4 (1949), pp. 230–6; H.G. Levine, 'The Discovery of Addiction: Changing conceptions of habitual drunkenness in America', *Journal of the Study of Alcoholism* 39 (1978), pp. 143–74; John Romano, 'Early Contributions to the Study of Delirium Tremens', *Annals of Medical History* 3 (1941), pp. 128–39; J.-C. Sournia, *Histoire de l'Alcoolisme* (Paris, 1986). For Erasmus Darwin see E. Darwin, *Zoonomia; or, the Laws of Organic Life*, 2 vols (1794–6). Darwin explicitly termed 'drunkenness' a disease (in his classification it was number I. 1. 2. 2, a disease of 'irritation').

16. Trotter, *Essay . . . on Drunkenness*, p. 11.

17. Ibid., p. 16.

18. Ibid., p. 29.

19. For exposition of John Brown's view that life itself should be understood as a matter of constant, external stimulus, see W.F. Bynum and Roy Porter (eds), *Brunonianism in Britain and Europe* (1988).

20. Trotter, *Essay . . . on Drunkenness*, p. 33.

21. Ibid., pp. 98, 105.

22. Ibid., pp. 109–35.

23. Ibid., p. 165.

24. Ibid., pp. 154, 174.

25. T.Trotter, *A View of the Nervous Temperament, A Practical Enquiry into the Increasing Prevalence, Prevention, and Treatment of those Diseases Commonly Called Nervous, Bilious, Stomach and Liver Complaints; Indigestion; Low Spirits; Gout etc.* (1807), p. xv.

26. For the Scottish historical sociology of progress, see Gladys Bryson, *Man and Society: The Scottish inquiry of the eighteenth century* (Princeton, 1945). For Trotter's own account of the shift from stable rural environment to the vertigo of the city, see Trotter, *View of the*

Nervous Temperament, pp. 26 ff., where he notes how, when 'the human being in a state of progressive improvement and civilization, quits his earthen-floored, straw-clad cottage on the skirts of the forest, or a creek of the ocean, where his time had been spent in hunting and fishing, for the town, where he is to turn himself to trade and manufacture, he necessarily undergoes a prodigious change of circumstances'.

27. Edward Gibbon, *The Decline and Fall of the Roman Empire*, ed. J.B. Bury, 7 vols (n.d.), Vol. iv, p. 169.
28. Trotter, *View of the Nervous Temperament*, p. viii.
29. Ibid., p. 220.
30. Ibid., p. 20.
31. Ibid. p. 29. For modern interpretations of the healthiness of 'primitive' peoples, see Mark Nathan Cohen, *Health and the Rise of Civilization* (New Haven, 1989).
32. Trotter, *View of the Nervous Temperament*, p. 35.
33. Ibid., p. 22.
34. Ibid., p. 70.
35. Ibid., p. 27.
36. Ibid., p. 48.
37. Ibid., p.142.
38. Ibid., p.135; for context see Sekora, *Luxury*.
39. Trotter, *View of the Nervous Temperament*, p. 27; see p. 69 for a discussion of the modern voluptuary.
40. Ibid., p. 39.
41. Ibid., p. 31.
42. See Roy Porter, 'Reforming the Patient. Thomas Beddoes and medical practice', in Roger French and Andrew Wear (eds), *British Medicine in an Age of Reform* (1991); id., 'Plutus or Hygeia? Thomas Beddoes and medical ethics', in Robert Baker, Dorothy Porter and Roy Porter (eds), *The Codification of Medical Morality in the Eighteenth and Nineteenth Centuries*, vol. i (forthcoming); id., *Doctor of Society: Thomas Beddoes and the sick trade in late Enlightenment England* (1991); id., 'Consumption: Disease of the consumer society?' in Brewer and Porter (eds), *Consumption and the World of Goods*.
43. Trotter, *View of the Nervous Temperament*, p. 24.
44. Trotter, *Essay . . . on Drunkenness*, p. 29.
45. Trotter, *View of the Nervous Temperament*, p. xi.
46. Ibid., p. 104.
47. Ibid., p. 31.
48. Ibid., p. 34.
49. Trotter, *Essay . . . on Drunkenness*, p. 153.
50. Ibid., p. 155.

51. Ibid., p. 38; *id.*, *View of the Nervous Temperament*, p. 312. See V. Berridge and G. Edwards, *Opium and the People* (New Haven, 1982).
52. Trotter, *View of the Nervous Temperament*, p. 133.
53. Id., *Essay . . . on Drunkenness*, p. 103.
54. Id., *View of the Nervous Temperament*, p. 135.
55. Ibid., p. 90.
56. Ibid., p. 106.
57. Ibid., p. 143.
58. G. Cheyne, *The English Malady; or, A Treatise of Nervous Diseases* (1733); Roy Porter, 'Civilization and Disease: Medical ideology in the Enlightenment', in J. Black and J. Gregory (eds), *Culture, Politics and Society in Britain 1660–1800* (Manchester, 1991); H.R. Viets, 'George Cheyne, 1673–1743', *Bulletin of the History of Medicine* 23 (1949), pp. 435–52.
59. Roy Porter, 'The Sexual Politics of James Graham', *British Journal for Eighteenth-Century Studies* 5 (1982), pp. 201–6.
60. Trotter, *View of the Nervous Temperament*, pp. xvi–xvii.
61. Ibid., p. 233.
62. Ibid., p. 257.
63. Trotter, *Essay . . . on Drunkenness*, p. 186.
64. Ibid., p. 41. Trotter's discussion is a veiled attack on the growth, as he sees it, of homosexuality as a manifestation of effeminacy.
65. Trotter, *View of the Nervous Temperament*, p. 153.
66. Ibid., p. xi.
67. I have tried to explore this phenomenon in Porter, *Doctor of Society*. Like Beddoes, Trotter is offering personal health illumination for the educated reader. His frame of reference is more that of consciousness-raising self help than the 'public health' consciousness of the era of Chadwick. For parallels see W. Coleman, 'Health and Hygiene in the *Encyclopédie*: A medical doctrine for the bourgeoisie', *Journal of the History of Medicine and Allied Sciences* 29 (1974), pp. 399–421: id., 'The People's Health: Medical themes in eighteenth-century French popular medicine', *Bulletin of the History of Medicine* 51 (1977), pp. 55–74.

Bourgeois Production and Realist Styles of Art

Robert W. Witkin

By the early part of the fifteenth century, it was already established as an aesthetic principle that artists should seek to make their representations life-like or 'perceptually real'. In the visual arts this consisted of a coherent attempt to simulate the optical values obtained in natural perception, to make paintings and sculptures which represent objects and events much as they appear to the eye in ordinary perception, that is, as substantial and as existing in a real and continuous space. An art with such a motive has existed in very few cultures, principally those of classical Greece and Rome and the Italian and Flemish city states of the Renaissance through to 1900. Furthermore, it was only in the European Renaissance traditions that it was ever really perfected. For sociologists and art historians alike, there appear to be parallels among the societies in which this kind of 'perceptual-realist' art develops. It is easy to see that they are urban cultures with developed middle classes, with merchants, artisans and commercial relations of a more or less sophisticated kind; that they tend to democratic political structures, the progressive erosion of the power of aristocracies and priesthoods; that they develop worldly, relativistic and anthropocentric philosophies, for example the Sophism of the Greeks or the Humanism of the Renaissance thinkers. In short, these societies appear to conform to some general notion of a bourgeois social order, societies dominated by practical men of affairs. A simple equation then emerges. Classical bourgeois societies in which there is a high level of individuation give rise to perceptual-realist styles of art in which the everyday objects and events of sensible reality are made objects of special perceptual attention.

Notwithstanding the close identity that has so often been drawn between bourgeois production and realist styles of art, there are some very real difficulties in theorizing the link. Why is a perceptual-realism necessary to bourgeois culture? Are we dealing with a loose 'fit' or propounding a causal nexus? Should we speak of both bourgeois culture and perceptual-realism in the singular or the plural? If the latter, do we need to conceive of perceptual realism in developmental terms and as corresponding to different stages in the development of bourgeois society? It is possible to have some sympathy with historians of art such as Gombrich,[1] who has dismissed the thesis asserting the necessity of a connection between the two as 'superficially plausible' or Baxandall,[2] who refers to it as 'facile'. Faced with the rich and detailed evidence of the works themselves, such historians are often loathe to accept that so crude a sociological generalization can effectively account for the complex and varied developments that go to make the history of styles of art.

However crude the generalization, the equation of bourgeois relations of production with perceptual-realist styles of art remains, nevertheless, one of the most fruitful hypotheses for a sociology of art that seeks to tackle what Gombrich[3] has labelled, 'the riddle of style'. Furthermore, it is not a hypothesis restricted to the visual arts. The emergence of the novel in the eighteenth century with its realist characterization and attention to individual biography has been directly linked by a number of theorists to the development of bourgeois society and bourgeois social relations. Ian Watt's study *The Rise of the Novel*[4] states the argument fully for the early novels such as *Robinson Crusoe, Moll Flanders* and so forth. George Lukacs, in his seminal study *The Theory of the Novel*,[5] analysed the novel as a 'bourgeois epic'. The form of the novel, with its 'problematic hero' embarked upon a search for transcendental values in a degraded world mirrored, for Lukacs, the very structure of bourgeois life and bourgeois relations in which it was grounded. Similar reasoning can be found in the work of Rene Girard).[6] Lucien Goldmann draws upon both to build his sociology of the novel,[7] arguing that, as a form, the relations among its constitutive elements is homologous with the conditions of a life dominated by capitalist markets, by exchange values and so forth. The most influential thinkers of the Frankfurt School, writers such as Adorno,[8] Benjamin[9] and Marcuse,[10] have theorized the link between the development of commodity production in late capitalist societies and the departure from the realism they associate with the nineteenth-century capitalist order.

In the present paper, however, I shall confine myself to a consideration of the argument in connection with the visual arts. In particular, I shall be concerned to explore the link between the aesthetic structure of works of art and the structure of social relations in so-called bourgeois societies. A sociology of art is necessarily concerned with the inscribing of society in pictures. There is a need to distinguish, however, between inscription at the level of the content of pictures and inscription at the level of form or aesthetic structure. I shall therefore begin with a thumbnail sketch of recent theorizing about the bourgeois character of realist art, one that is admittedly highly selective but which raises issues that have been important in recent polemical debates about the relationship between art and society. I shall then go on to discuss the Hauser thesis in order to develop a critical exposition of the concepts of individuation in society and of 'naturalistic representation' in paintings. While I shall offer a critique of both these concepts as developed by Hauser, I shall nevertheless argue that suitably re-formulated in a more genuinely sociological way, they do provide the best way of exploring the identity between the morphology of perceptual-realist styles of art and that of bourgeois social relations.

John Berger[11] has looked at the inscription of capitalist and mercantile values in the content of paintings, arguing that such paintings are essentially about the things rich people own or possess or seek to possess. Even the technique of oil painting itself, with its superior possibilities for representing flesh tones, is seen by Berger as supplying the representational needs of the materialist and possessive culture of the Renaissance mercantile class in whose time it was invented. The Gainsborough painting in the National Gallery of *Mr. and Mrs. Andrews*, shows the couple richly attired and with the man sporting a gun under his arm, standing together beneath a tree, while the landscape opens up before them. In case we are inclined to suppose that this is a picture about the beauty of an English landscape, Berger hangs a 'trespassers will be prosecuted' sign around the tree. In the famous painting of the *Regents* by Hals, Berger invites us to see in the 'dissolute' faces of the sitters, the truth of a social relation between them and the impoverished old man who is painting them and who is dependent upon their cold charity. For Berger, social relations and social values are somehow literally transcribed in these pictures and can be read directly. The argument is that we are all members of a similar society, a capitalist society in which exchange values and commercial and exploitative relations predominate and that therefore we can recognize the content of these pictures without having their meaning mystified by art historians glossing them in terms of aesthetic criteria. Not surprisingly such a view has attracted serious criticism.[12] Of course, Berger does not take his own argument about literal transcription as entirely adequate to the task of analyzing works of art since he wishes to except the masterpieces of painters such as Vermeer from this kind of ideological reading and he is not free from what his left critics would call 'bourgeois aesthetic sensibility'.

On the whole Berger leaves the all-important question of style in art alone and therefore sidesteps some of the issues which are central to this paper. However, one Marxist writer who does attempt to approach the question of styles of representation is Hadjinacolaou.[13] The major European styles (the Baroque, Mannerism, neo-classicism and so forth) correspond, in Hadjinacolaou's notion, to 'visual ideologies' which he sees as realizing the interests of distinct class fractions and as inscribing bourgeois social relations. Hadjinacolaou does not give space to even a residual aesthetic sensibility nor does he feel the need to raise any of the issues concerning the *development* of representation which are discussed by Hauser and by major figures in the German art historical tradition, most noticeably Riegl,[14] Panofsky[15] and Wolfflin.[16] Of course, the in-scribing of bourgeois social relations in pictures has been approached in quite a different way. T.J. Clark, in his studies of Courbet[17] and of art and politics in nineteenth-century France,[18] provides a meticulous and detailed interpretive reconstruction of the life-world of the artists, their relations and concerns considered in relation to the specific content of the pictures as well as the ways in which they are painted. It is just this kind of careful interpretive reconstruction of the mind-set and social milieu of the artist engaged upon real artistic projects that is missing from Berger's polemical analysis.

Baxandall's[19] careful attempt to transcribe social relations into works of art in his study of painting in fifteenth-century Italy starts from the opposite viewpoint. The society was very different from our own, works of art were produced in the context of relations with patrons and constrained by contracts that were in no sense comparable to the way such works are produced now and the painters in producing their pictures were able to presuppose a kind of visual and visualizing experience in their audience which we simply do not possess. Baxandall is in no doubt that we do not see these paintings as they were seen by the artists' contemporaries. Furthermore, Baxandall makes no attempt to inscribe social relations, of the kind in which Berger is interested, into the con-tent of paintings. Instead, he seeks to identify important social skills necessarily acquired by people in the fifteenth-century city cultures in which such art was produced, social skills important to a nascent bourgeois and mercantile society, such as gauging the depths of barrels, dancing, and also visualizing the holy stories under the guidance of sustained and elaborate preaching. It is these skills (developed in the emerging Italian city cultures) in visualizing and organizing experience, in mathematical operations and in the habits of thought in everyday life, that come to be reflected in paintings, in the danced character of a Botticelli and so forth. Now, inscription here refers not so much to the actual content of paintings as to the aesthetic structure of the work and it is an important contribution of Baxandall's work to have seen that the habits of mind engendered in a given social context are necessarily reflected in the way an artist organizes his or her aesthetic means.

However, it is no accident that Baxandall's argument is developed in relation to the art of the *quatrocento*. It would appear that such an approach might meet with some real difficulty if we tried to use it on the art of the early Middle Ages, that is to pursue the formal motifs and aesthetic structure of these works in the world of everyday material experience. I do not mean that such an approach would be incorrect or would lack relevance, merely that it would meet with certain difficulties. For one thing we are inclined to look upon this earlier art as ceremonial and hieratic, as highly formalized and stylized and as admitting little that is not dictated by tradition. There appears to be a certain unbridgeable gulf between this art and the detail and personality of everyday life. It is from the fifteenth century onwards, in European art, that we are increasingly confident in making assertions about the inscribing of social relations at the level of both the content of paintings and also, as Baxandall does, at the level of their aesthetic structure.

In short, it is when art develops in the direction of a perceptual-realism and society in the direction of individualism, democratic political relations and urban modes of production, that it appears easier to perform this transcription from ordinary social life into pictures. Arnold Hauser's monumental *Social History of Art*[20] approaches the problem of inscription at a much higher level of generality. Hauser divides the world's art into two large classes, that of formalized and geometrized art, on the one hand, and that of naturalistic (I prefer perceptual-realist) representational art, on the other. It is clear that the greater part of the world's art belongs in the former category, that is in the class of formalized, geometrized art—the art of antiquity, of archaic civilizations as well as of primitive societies and even twentieth-century art. Perceptual-realist art, on the other hand, occurs in very few traditions. Hauser sees formalized, geometrized art as the art of hieratic, authoritarian and aristocratic societies. It is an art which inscribes the impersonal order, the formal and hierarchical socio-political relations that transcend individuals, in the aesthetic structure, in the mode of representation, the structure of aesthetic means. By contrast, perceptual-realist art is the art of a bourgeois and individuated society, with democratic political relations and a strong mercantile class. It is an art which accords to individual experience, to the world of everyday things as they appear to the senses, a priority over impersonal and transcendental forces. Just as the things of everyday life gradually come to predominate in perceptual-realist pictures, so modes of depiction come to be equally individualized and we are more inclined to differentiate aesthetically between the works of one master and another and to perceive some cultural significance in these aesthetic differences.

We can conceive of the link between bourgeois society and perceptual-realist styles of art at three distinct levels:

1. The Content. Works of art in a bourgeois society become increasingly concerned with the depiction of the ordinary objects, events, people and relations that are the stuff of bourgeois social life. In and through their depiction of everyday reality, such works come to express or reflect bourgeois values. The artist, caught up in bourgeois life, reproduces both the forms and the contents of this involvement in aesthetic works. The studies of art historians such as T.J. Clark[21] elegantly testify to this.

2. The Social Relations of Art-making. At another level we can speak of there being an identity or correlation between the social relations of art-making and the social relations of bourgeois production. Like artisans and merchants in the wider society, the bourgeois artist becomes an own-account worker developing his creations for sale on the market. In the very practice of his profession he enjoys the same entrepreneurial freedom that other bourgeois producers have.

3. Representational Codes. Bourgeois realism also concerns the correspondence between bourgeois modes of production and the 'representational codes' governing aesthetic production, codes which have yielded the 'styles' of aesthetic works, those that have been labelled 'classical', 'mannerist', 'baroque', 'romantic', 'Gothic' and so forth.

It is this third level, that of the representational codes governing the development of styles of art, which provides the theoretical focus here. Hauser's thesis delineates two broad stylistic tendencies in art, or, in my terms, two representational codes, a perceptual-realist code (he refers to 'naturalistic' modes of representation) and a formalist code (he speaks of geometrized or stylized modes of representation).

Perceptual-realist versus formalist styles of art

Hauser uses the term 'naturalistic' to refer to modes of representation that aim at capturing the real appearance of objects and events as they are experienced by individuals in everyday life. In a purely perceptual sense such an art aims at simulating, in a visual representation, the optical values that would obtain if the represented world was viewed in real life. More than this, however, such an art seeks to capture the sensuous import of the individual's material encounters in the world, to show objects and events not only as they might actually appear to the eye but also, in and through that optical truth, to convey their larger significance in the materially grounded and lived experience of the individual subject. Such an art simulates real life and liveliness, depicts bodies as substantial, as fully supported and occupying real space. Such an art is concerned with the dynamism and relativity of experience occurring in real situations in real time and makes available to perception the inner psychological reality of individual personalities.

Hauser contrasts 'naturalistic' representation with styles of art that are highly formalized and 'abstract', 'geometrized' styles. Such styles are the very antithesis of naturalism in that they aim at representing, not the real empirical world that is lived and experienced by individuals but an idealized and superordinate world that transcends the experience of individuals, an art dealing only in the 'typical' and the 'emblematic', a one-sidedly spiritualistic art emptied of real sensuous content. People and objects are represented in such an art but never in a fully sensuous form as they appear in everyday life. Rather they are represented in global and schematic forms. They are often portrayed as devoid of body and substance, sometimes as insubstantial and unsupported as though suspended in mid-air (as in some early medieval Christian representations). The interior of a house or of an animal such as fish may be shown through its outer form as though the latter was transparent. The two-dimensional and planar quality of representations applies both to objects and people and to space itself. Objects are portrayed as being not in a space, through which they can freely move, but of a space. In 'formalist' art, the space of the representation is the space of the relief or surface itself. Moreover, a representation may combine views of an object that could not possibly share the same visual plane in real life. For example, ancient Egyptian art represents the head and legs of figures in profile while the eyes and torso face front. The importance of figures may be represented by their relative sizes and by certain expressive features, such as the eyes, which may be greatly exaggerated. If 'naturalistic art' (Hauser's term) aims at representing the concrete reality of the real and situated experience of individuals, formalistic and 'geometrized' art aims at representing the 'eternal', the 'unchanging' order that transcends the accidents of particular events. It is an art centred on the collectivity and its continuity rather than on the individual in his or her transience and mutability, on the people in general, rather than on particular persons, on kingship rather than on the particular person of the king. It emphasizes the traditional and the enduring and eschews innovation and change.

Nor are these mutually exclusive categories. For Hauser, the art forms of any period results from a continuous accommodation between these two orientations, with now one dominant and now the other. Each style in art is seen by Hauser as a resolution, more or less unstable, in a recurring dialectics of style which has, at the level of its superstructure, naturalism and formalism as its thesis and antithesis, and at the level of its base, the opposition between individuating and de-individuating social structures.

Naturalistic modes of representation which valorize the ordinary details of everyday life, are said to arise in societies which have a high level of individuation, personal freedom and initiative in everyday life, with democratic political institutions, developed middle classes and an urban way of life.

> The urban and financial conditions of life which force man out of his static world of custom and tradition into a more dynamic reality, into a world of constantly changing persons and situations, also explain why man now acquires a new interest in the things of his immediate environment. For this environment is now the real scene of his life, it is with this environment that he has to prove his worth; but to do so he must know its every detail. This every detail of daily life becomes an object of observation and description; not only human beings but also animals and trees, not only living nature, but also the home and the furniture in the home, costumes and tools, become themes of artistic interest in themselves (vol. 1, p. 240).

By contrast, non-naturalistic styles are said to predominate in societies which have an autocratic and hieratic structure, a formalistic and bureaucratic administrative system (Hauser frequently fuses two massively different sets of conditions into a single principle without explanation or justification), a low level of individuation, and a predominantly agrarian way of life. Rigidity, authoritarianism, and a life-denying traditionalism are what characterizes such societies in Hauser's view.

> The uniform conception of the art of the period dominated by the geometric style corresponds to an equally uniform sociological characteristic, which exerts a determining influence on this whole age, despite individual variation, namely the tendency towards a homogeneous organization of the economy, towards an autocratic form of government and a bureaucratic outlook in the whole of society, an outline dominated by cultus and religion, as opposed both to the still unorganized, primitively individualistic nomadic existence of the hunters and to the differentiated, consciously individualistic social life of the ancient and modern bourgeoisie, based on the idea of competition (vol. 1, p. 13).

It should be noted here that Worringer, many years earlier, had contrasted geometrized and formalistic art with naturalistic art in his book *Abstraction and Empathy*.[22] He had argued that abstract and formalized styles were associated with a fear of nature and a profound ambivalence towards all natural phenomena. By contrast, naturalism was seen as the product of societies which were basically at ease with nature and the environment and so empathized with the natural order. A similar set of assumptions concerning the psychological foundations of the styles prevails in Hauser's work, although, in the latter, they are qualified in a somewhat more sophisticated way.

A critique of Hauser's concept of 'individuation'

Hauser nowhere acknowledges any indebtedness to Durkheim in this work (his name does not even appear in the index for any of the four volumes), and yet there is no doubting the close kinship between Hauser's project and the themes of Durkheim in the *Division of Labour*[23] and *The Elementary Forms of the Religious Life*.[24] Notwithstanding this kinship, Hauser's approach is fundamentally different from that of Durkheim in key respects, as I seek to demonstrate below. Durkheim argued that the greater the degree of social differentiation arising from the division of labour in society, the more the locus of moral authority, of initiative and social order devolves from the superordinate and collective level to the individual, or rather, to the society of individuals involved in co-operative relations with one another. At the same time, precisely because co-operation with others means developing and preserving the very systems of social relationships upon which actors depend in order to play their roles, socio-political relations are necessarily democratic in character. Furthermore, the moral rules and the moral authority which sanctions them are increasingly seen to originate in the practical social world that is constituted by co-operating individuals acting on their own initiative and jointly responsible for making their world and not in a transcendental order peopled by powerful deities. The consciousness of such individuals becomes intensely worldly and anthropocentric.

In societies where there is a lack of social differentiation (i.e. a poorly developed division of labour) and a low level of individuation as a consequence, moral authority appears to the subject as a transcendental force arising from outside himself or herself, a categorical imperative handed down like the tablets of stone and over which the individual neither singly, nor in co-operation with others, has discretion. Quite simply, if there is a low level of individuation the moral principles guiding action cannot appear to the subject as originating within himself. He does not experience himself as morally autonomous nor does he attribute such moral autonomy to others like himself. The psychologist Jean Piaget, in his book *The Moral Judgement of the Child*,[25] drew consciously on this thesis to explore the difference between the attitude towards moral rules in older and younger children. He claimed that the younger children, in their playing of games, such as the game of marbles, did not develop a truly differentiated form of play in which each player has to take account of the play of the other in formulating a counter-play. At the same time, the children actually thought of the rules of a game as somehow sacrosanct, handed down from on high, by fathers, grandfathers or God, and that they were unchangeable. The older children, by contrast, did develop fully differentiated play and took into account all the moves of the other players in formulating their play. They treated the rules of the game as changeable by democratic agreement and saw the purpose of the rules, and of changing the rules, as that of improving the game. In short, their mode of developing the game was democratic, their consciousness of the rules was practical and realistic. A similar argument concerning the development of consciousness in the game and in play can be found in G.H. Mead's analysis of the development of the self-concept in *Mind, Self and Society*.[26]

We can see an echo of this aspect of Durkheimian thought in Hauser's theoretical argument when he seeks to explain the emergence of dualistic thought and formalist representation in the neolithic age. He presupposes an earlier naturalism associated with a monistic, 'primitively individualistic' society of hunter-gatherers.

> In the final analysis, the neolithic change of style is determined . . . by the replacement of the monistic, magic-dominated conception of the world by the dualistic philosophy of animism, that is, by a conception of the world that is itself dependent on the new type of economy . . . It is the dualism that came into the world with the animistic creed and has since found expression in hundreds of philosophical systems, which is expressed in the opposition of the idea and reality, soul and body, spirit and form and from which it is no longer possible to separate our conception of art (vol. 1, p. 12).

This dualism has its roots in the transition from what Hauser sees as the purely consumptive and parasitical economy of hunters and gatherers to the productive and consumptive economy of the cattle breeders and crop farmers. The demands of settled agriculture in terms of planning, planting seasons, provisions for winter, administration of communities, the accumulation, distribution and control of resources, property and so forth, not to mention the arrangements that must be made for its defence, all give rise to a complex social order which mediates encounters with nature and the natural world. Furthermore, the division of the society into primary producers on the one hand, and the guardians and custodians of that social order (the priests and nobles etc.), on the other, itself gives rise to the dualism of spirit and matter. Art is harnessed to this spiritual world, which is but the veiled form of the mediating social order, the province of priests and aristocrats, and is pressed into representing the power and majesty of this order and glorifying its claims on life. Because it is an art centred on the (transcendental) mediating social order it is an art devoted to the impersonal and the eternal, not to the personal and the transient.

If Hauser's model approximates to that of Durkheim in certain respects, it diverges from it at others, most notably in the development of the concept of individuation. For Durkheim individuation is not the acquiring of freedom from the imposition of moral constraints and social controls by the society. On the contrary, as with Freud, individuation occurs through a process of socialization in which society is internalized in personalities. The 'individual' in the classical sociological sense of that term is thus constituted through the introjection of the social whole or totality, and it is this introjection (achieved, according to Durkheim and Freud, through the pressure of one generation on the next and, according to Piaget and Mead, through the pressure of one generation on itself) that is constitutive of the absolutely particular personality with its particular location in social relations and its particular viewpoint. An 'individual', so conceived, is not apart from or distinct from society but, rather, is the society manifest in one of its parts or facets, drawing its very particularity from the social system of which it is an element. The 'individual' and 'society' remain entirely correlative terms in Durkheim. In this way he is able to explain the continuity of moral obligation and constraint in modern industrial societies. Individuation in this sense can, therefore, be sharply distinguished from 'egotism', which is often called by the same name. The latter arises from a lack of, or break in, continuity between the person and the social whole. Because Durkheim's concept of individuation turns on this continuity between the individual and society, his analysis focuses upon the social conditions under which this continuity is either reinforced or undermined, hence the work on *Suicide*,[27] which explores different types of discontinuity between the individual and society. One advantage of such an approach is that it opens the way to conceptualizing more clearly the link between representational codes and social structure.

As the locus of control over action and social relations moves from the collective community to the society of co-operating individuals, the members of that society increasingly experience the world in terms of (their own) action, construction and making. The world in its social forms is seen as 'produced' through 'making' and as understood through a simulation of its 'making', a simulation which, like scientific experiment, yields insight into the machinery of its construction. This constructive and productive activity must be continuously supplied at an ideological level with representations which are adequate to its needs, representations in which the world is refracted through particular points of view, representations which reflect the continuity between the universal and the particular, the society and the individual. One class of such representations takes the form of perceptual-realist works of art and literature. It should be possible, making use of such a theory of individuation, to specify more closely the social conditions which give rise to perceptual-realist codes of representation. To that extent, it should also be possible (ultimately) to delineate more clearly the points at which bourgeois society approaches these social conditions and the points at which it departs from them. Such delineation would require the construction of a theory that relates the structural development of societies in general, and bourgeois societies in particular, to the morphology of aesthetic codes.

That Hauser's massive work does not achieve these theoretical results is due, in my view, to his treatment of the pivotal concept of the individual. For all its parallels with Durkheim's work, Hauser's idea of the individual is far less sociologistic. It is an essentially romantic concept. Hauser's individual is endowed by nature with all the qualities, characteristics and potential to realize himself or herself in the world. It is the individual rather than the society that is primary. In cooperating with others in society, the individual may lose his power, be repressed or oppressed by authority, by transcendental forces, by social institutions which come to mediate his encounters with the material world, which denature him; and this process will reflect itself in the development of equally denatured and formalistic styles of art which fetishize the structure of authority, of social convention and tradition. However, Hauser does not treat the social order as primary, as actually constitutive of the individual, as constituting the particularity of the individual in which it is itself refracted.

As a result, the means are not there for going beyond the static generalization of a link between bourgeois society and art at the level of content and developing a dynamic theory, identifying developmental processes at the level of social relations in a given type of society with developmental processes at the level of representational codes or aesthetic styles. Instead, Hauser offers a view of society as a recurring battle between individuating and de-individuating forces. Styles of representation, now more formalistic, now more realistic, reflect the state of this battle at a given historical moment. His historical method appears to involve identifying an important stylistic development, for example the transition from the High Renaissance style to that of the Mannerists, delineating its composite formal tendencies and then searching the historical record for events that would account for this stylistic development in terms of the advance or retreat of authoritarian or institutional pressures upon the individual. Quite apart from the fact that the method itself is questionable—having identified historical events that constrain the individual there is no attempt to demonstrate that the same or similar type of constraint was not operating at other times when the stylistic results were very different—Hauser's dialectics of style, grounded, as they are, in the eternal battle between authority and freedom, provide no basis for theorizing the social development and progress that is nevertheless assumed by the author. The result is a theoretical sterility in which empirical styles of art are seen as incorporating all those tendencies which enable them to face both ways at once. Thus, in writing of ancient Egyptian art, Hauser says:

> One must feel the living forces of experimenting individualism and expansive naturalism behind the traditional forms, forces which flow from the urban outlook on life and destroy the stationary culture of the Neolithic age; but one must not on any account allow oneself to be led by this impression to under-estimate the spirit of conservatism at work in the history of the Ancient East (vol.1, p. 24).

At a theoretical level, Hauser confounds two quite distinct sets of oppositions in his concept of 'individuation'. One of them is indicated by his strong preference for words like 'nature', 'naturalistic' and so forth. It is the opposition between the natural world of sense experience and material encounters, on the one hand, and the supra-natural spiritual world of ideal values, on the other. Hauser always writes as though natural and sensuous experience is inseparable from the notion of the individual and individuality. Anything spiritual, de-natured or supra-natural is seen as necessarily 'collective' (as distinct from 'individual') in origin. However, there is little reason for believing (and Hauser provides none) that a consciousness that is 'collective' rather than 'individuated' must necessarily be de-natured or lacking in practical and sensuous materiality. On the contrary, there is every reason to believe, on the evidence of the vital and sensuous art of many so-called 'primitive' societies which appear to have a heightened collective consciousness— one that is vivified in collective rituals—that the opposite is the case.

The failure to uncouple the opposition ideal/material from the opposition individual/collective has important consequences for the thesis as a whole. The difficulties are plainly visible at the beginning and at the end of the thesis, that is, in Hauser's account of both pre-historic art and of modern art. Hauser views the art of the cave-dwellers as being essentially naturalistic and he argues that it is the product of societies of hunters and gatherers that he characterizes as individualistic, albeit 'primitively individualistic'. It is here that Hauser reveals that his concept of individualism is essentially a regression to the formulation that was thoroughly discredited by the nineteenth-century sociologists, notably Durkheim and Marx. In Durkheim's *Division of Labour*, individuation was seen as a function of the division of labour and the associated heightening of social differentiation. In the context of such an argument, societies with a very low degree of division of labour and a low level of social differentiation, also have a very low level of individuation. A typology consistent with this viewpoint would place the Paleolithic societies on the lowest rung of the ladder of individuation and would claim that the *conscience collective* would be as highly developed in such societies as the sense of self and of individuality would be poorly developed. Hauser's need to make the opposite claim seems to arise because of his view that the art of these hunters was naturalistic, a problem to which I shall return below. Prior to that, however, we need to jump to the other end of the social history of art and consider Hauser's treatment of modern art.

Perhaps the most remarkable aspect of Hauser's treatment of modern art is the lack of attention it receives from him in this work. The radical break with the Renaissance traditions of 'naturalistic' representation which occurred in the work of the Cubists, the Futurists and other avant-garde movements is very little discussed in the final chapter devoted to the modern period and actually titled 'The Film Age'. Of course, these movements are mentioned and it is possible to piece together something of Hauser's views about modern art but only with a great deal of infilling. In order to be consistent with the view, advanced throughout his social history of art, which ties geometrized and non-naturalistic styles of art to a de-individuated society, the modern age has to be seen as one in which individualism is undermined and the individual alienated.

In a number of passages, Hauser draws parallels between modern art and the art of the Mannerists of the late sixteenth century. The stylized art of the Mannerists, the almost surreal quality of an El Greco, the distortions of a Parmigianino are, for Hauser, a distant precursor of the twentieth-century revolution in art. In his two-volume study *Mannerism,*[28] there is a lengthy discussion of Mannerism in relation to modern art. In that discussion Hauser describes the social condition in terms of a growing and suffocating 'institutionalization' and a progressive 'alienation' of the individual who finds his compass of action and being restricted by, and subordinated to, the new superordinate productive order within which he figures, more or less as a cog. The arguments here are reminiscent of those of the sociologist Georg Simmel in his essay 'The Metropolis and Mental Life'.[29] It is altogether a modern critique of social relations as these have developed from the end of the nineteenth century through the twentieth. It is not at all clear that the backwards extra-polation of these ideas to the *Zeitgeist* of the late fifteenth century can serve as anything other than a dubious and fanciful analogy.

More serious for the Hauser thesis, however, is the fact that the de-individuating forces referred to here are no longer those of the aristocracy and the priesthood but of the rational (and bureaucratic) institutions of a modern society and have a different meaning as a con-sequence. These forces are marked, theoretically, not by the opposition individual/collective but by the opposition individual/egoistic. Hence, without acknowledging the theoretical implications, Hauser has shifted the entire ground of the thesis. Instead of individuality being sacrificed to the collective symbols and transcendental ideals of an hieratic society we are now dealing with an intensive withdrawal into the self, an alienation of the self which Hauser clearly identifies with bureaucratized institutions and the psychology and culture of narcissism. This new twist in the argument necessarily implies a heightening of the personal ego not a diminishing of it. Some of Hauser's insights here are interesting both in their application to Mannerism and to modern art but the weakness of his concept of individuation leaves them disembodied with no secure foundation in a coherent sociological theory.

A critique of Hauser's concept of naturalistic representation

If Hauser's concept of individuation is theoretically unsound, similar doubts can be expressed about the other pillar of the Hauser thesis, namely the concept of a naturalistic mode of representation (I prefer the term 'perceptual-realist modes of representation'). Hauser's difficulties here are also most evident at either end of his history of artistic styles. Just as there is little justification for regarding the Paleolithic cave dwellers as individualists, so there is equally little justification for regarding their art as in any sense comparable to the so-called naturalistic styles of art that emerged in the European Renaissance and which reached their fullest development in the nineteenth century. Precisely because this art is the product of a fully natured and sensuous consciousness and yet is thoroughly collective in orientation, it is quite distinct, stylistically, from the art of what are called 'bourgeois realists'. In the latter tradition, objects and bodies are constructed architectonically from the skeleton. So, too, is the space and the structured relations among them within that space. The whole construction presupposes a particular viewpoint and the subjective projection of the viewer. Nothing like that occurs in the case of the cave paintings. Although the paintings of bisons and horses appear to be 'realistically' modelled, they were in fact constructed very differently from Renaissance paintings and for very different purposes. They were often painted in the darkest recesses of the caves and could only be seen by the flickering light of torches. They were not constructed architectonically as Renaissance pictures were. The artists often made use of the suggestive shapes and contours of the cave walls and rocks, adding the outer 'skin', as it were, to forms (felt as) incipiently present in the walls themselves. Nor was any kind of consistent scale observed, and animals painted on a very large scale are sometimes placed in close proximity to animals painted on a diminutive scale. Furthermore, representations are often superimposed upon earlier paintings with overlap still visible and, where there is not room to complete a representation of an animal on the surface of the rock, it may be completed on the back side of the rock which is not visible. Just as there is considerable variation of scale, so, too, there is a complete lack of consideration for any particular viewpoint. Representations are even indifferent to the basic vertical which constrains the upright observer. Paintings of animals appear to lie in all spatial orientations including the diagonal and are more or less indifferent to the body of the observer. That is certainly not true of later, highly formalized art which, for all its geometrized schematism, certainly does conform to consistent rules concerning all these relations. Giedion, in his monumental work on Paleolithic art,[30] has argued that the space of these paintings is not even an optical space but is, rather, an acoustic space. Certainly, this would make sense in the context of the 'magical' purposes for which this art was undoubtedly created. The acoustic space is an all-round space, a space that does not favour one set of directions. It is pre-eminently, perhaps, the space of the hunters. The function of this art appears to have been to 'conjure' the presence of the animals upon which these hunters depended. Perhaps they were experienced, not as representations of animals, but as magically controlled 'incarnations'. In any case, Giedion is himself in no doubt that these works should not be seen as naturalistic.

There is also a difficulty in applying the term 'naturalistic' consistently to the art of the Renaissance traditions. The concept of an art which sought to capture a 'real' moment or situation without embellishment or idealization of any kind appears only at the end of this period, in the nineteenth century. It is possible, of course, to construct a developmental theory of the evolution of bourgeois society from the Renaissance to the modern day, to note the important stages in this development and to consider what relationship these have to postulated stages in the development of realist styles of art. However, this is precisely what Hauser does not do. His work is littered throughout with insights that remain theoretically unsecured. His thesis requires the closest attention to be paid to certain key transitions such as the transition from the realist perspective that characterized the writings of Balzac, or of the nineteenth-century realist painters, and the 'naturalism' of writers such as Zola or the impressionist painters. This transition is of key importance in the development of modern art and needs to be anchored to an understanding of the development of modern social relations in what was still a bourgeois society. In the penultimate chapter of the final volume, a chapter devoted to impressionism, Hauser demonstrates his peculiar mixture of substantive insight and theoretic confusion when commenting upon the achievements of the impressionists.

> If one interprets naturalism as meaning progress from the general to the particular, from the typical to the individual, from the abstract idea to the concrete, temporally and spatially conditioned experience, then the impressionistic reproduction of reality, with its emphasis on the instantaneous and the unique, is an important achievement of naturalism . . . But by detaching the optical elements of experience from the conceptual and elaborating the autonomy of the visual, impressionism departs from all art as practiced hitherto, and thereby from naturalism as well. . . This neutralization and reduction of the motif to its bare material essentials can be considered as an expression of the anti-romantic outlook of the time and seen as the trivialization and stripping bare of all the heroic and stately qualities of the subject-matter of art, but it can also be regarded as a departure from reality . . . as a loss from the naturalistic point of view (vol. 4, p. 160).

The troubled response that Hauser makes to modern art, the commitment to viewing modernist forms as reactionary, is more or less inevitable given his basic assumptions about naturalism. They also recall, in some respects, the attitude towards modern art and literature expressed by Lukacs in *The Meaning of Contemporary Realism*.[31] Lukacs' attitude, however, is grounded in a strong commitment to a theory of individuation which acknowledges the character of a genuine realism to be that which expresses the totality in the absolutely particular. The characters of a Balzac novel may each be unique but each is also profoundly typical of the society as a whole, of the bourgeois order that resonates in his or her being. It is a view fully consonant with the classical sociological viewpoint, in which the social whole is implicit in, and constitutive of, the life process of individuals. The realist picture or literary description in which the whole is seen from a particular point of view, that is, in one of its aspects or facets, is thus in an homologous or corresponding relationship to a society in which the social is implicit in each of its constituent individuals.

The morphology of social relations and the morphology of aesthetic codes

The term 'realism' is probably one of the most abused in the current literature where it has assumed a particular significance in relation to the literature on modernity and post-modernity. A number of writers use the term as if its meaning was somehow self-evident and unproblematical; as if, for example, a painting by Leonardo might be thought of as realist in the same sense as a painting by Courbet or Manet or a T.V. soap such as 'Eastenders' or 'Brookside'. The term serves such writers as a kind of monochrome background against which they can set off the character-istics of what they see to be the departure from realism in modern culture. There is, however, a world of difference between the so-called realism of a quattrocento painter and an artist of the nineteenth century. The difference concerns not only the content of such works, what they are about, but also their modes of symbolizing, their aesthetic structures. Moreover, while an artist such as Alberti may have appealed to the facts of experience in his treatise on painting, it was in the context of aesthetic motives of a fundamentally different kind from those which inspired nineteenth-century artists. What would Alberti have made of the Romantic notion that gave primacy to self-expression or the Realist idea that art should be faithful to the ordinary and prosaic facts of everyday life?

However, while it is true that a sociological understanding of realism must explore these fundamental differences, it is also the case that it must recognize a certain underlying invariance in the disparate styles emerging in European art between 1400 and 1900. All of these different styles were broadly constrained by a set of principles governing the mode of depiction, a perceptual-realist presentational code. While the code was variously realized in different styles of art and with different degrees of distortion, it remained a powerful set of constraints governing the production of works of art for five centuries. At a technical level, perceptual-realism was based on three developments:

1. Linear Perspective. By adapting the optical principle whereby parallel lines converge to one of an infinite number of points on the horizon, artists were able to project three-dimensional spaces on two-dimensional surfaces. The conquest of one-point perspective drawing was already well advanced in the early fifteenth century when Bruneleschi published his technical treatise on the subject in 1425. The development of linear perspective meant that the optical values describing objects and relations could be represented systematically in terms of their relations with one another. Thus a figure or object's size in a picture was not an intrinsic attribute of the figure considered in isolation but was a function of its relations to other figures and objects and to the viewpoint of the observer. The figure was larger if nearer, smaller if more distant, more distinct if in the foreground and so forth. Such a system which represents a coherent and 'objective' structuring of optical relations is best fitted to represent cultural values that are also a function of interactions within some shared and universalistically and systematically ordered rational space, be it political or social. It seems reasonable to hypothesize an isomorphism between the morphology of social relations and that of the presentational or aesthetic forms through which such relations are brought to mind.

2. Chiaroscuro. The mastery of consistent variations in light and shade which occur as objects are variously oriented in respect of a unified light source permits of realistic modelling of objects and surfaces. Here, too, we have to see this as rendering optical values in terms of their relations within a unified and objective visual field. They vary in light or darkness in accordance with whether they are turned towards or away from a unified light source. This is another aspect of the same homology referred to above—that is, chiaroscuro permits of a more rational mode of depicting values as a function of the system of relations in which they are involved.

3. Colour Interaction. The mastery of the micro-structure of colour in objects and the colour interactions and colour harmonies distributed throughout the total surface of a picture was another important step in the production of perceptual-realism. Colour has always been important in the depiction of symbolic values and in the expression of the sensuous and the emotional dimension of experience. The growing mastery of the complex micro-structure of colourific relations provided a third link between aesthetic structure and the nascent structure of bourgeois societies.

To the extent that the hegemony of such a unitary, rational, and (in the Durkheimian sense) necessarily individuated social order, means that values defining sensuous relations and modes of being are specified in terms of it, then such a system must necessarily be supplied with representations which reproduce its systematic and individuated relations, which are perceptual-realist in character. Art is necessarily concerned with modes of being and with sensuous relations in the world. Perceptual-realist art reflects the 'capture' of such values by the rational productive order.

Abstract and tentative as these suggestions are, they are intended not so much as a solution to the problems raised as a brief statement of a line of thinking about the problem of individuation in the context of the critique of Hauser's key concepts. If I have been critical throughout of Hauser's treatment of the concepts of 'individuation' and of 'naturalistic representation', it has been from the standpoint of an admirer, of one who retains a continuing interest in the Hauser project and a conviction that, despite its critics or because of them, such a project may be brought to fruition.

Notes

1. E.H. Gombrich, 'The Social History of Art', in *Meditations on a Hobby Horse* (Oxford, 1975).
2. M. Baxandall, *Painting and Experience in Fifteenth-Century Italy: A primer in the social history of pictorial style* (Oxford, 1972), p. 152.
3. E.H. Gombrich, *Art and Illusion* (Oxford, 1977).
4. Ian Watt, *The Rise of the Novel* (1953).
5. George Lukacs, *The Theory of the Novel* (1978).
6. Rene Girard, *Deceit Desire and the Novel* (1976).
7. Lucien Goldmann, *Towards a Sociology of the Novel* (1975).
8. T. Adorno, *Aesthetic Theory* (1984).
9. Walter Benjamin, *Illuminations* (1970).
10. H Marcuse, 'On the Affirmative Character of Culture', in *Negations, Essays in Critical Theory* (Boston, 1968).
11. John Berger, *Ways of Seeing* (1972).
12. Peter Fuller, *Seeing Through Berger* (1988).
13. N. Hadjinacolaou, *Art History and Class Struggle* (1973).
14. M. Podro, *The Critical Historians of Art* (New Haven, 1982).
15. E. Panofsky, *Meaning in the Visual Arts* (Harmondsworth, 1970).
16. H. Wolfflin, *Principles of Art History* (1932).
17. T.J. Clark, *Image of the People: Gustave Courbet and the 1848 revolution* (1973).

18. Id., *The Absolute Bourgeois: Artists and politics in France, 1848–1851* (1973).
19. Baxandall, *Painting and Experience*.
20. Arnold Hauser, *The Social History of Art*, 4 vols (new edn., 1989).
21. Clark, *Image of the People*; id., *Absolute Bourgeois*.
22. W. Worringer, *Abstraction and Empathy* (1963).
23. E. Durkheim, *The Division of Labour* (1964).
24. Id., *The Elementary Forms of the Religious Life* (1976).
25. J. Piaget, *The Moral Judgement of the Child* (1968).
26. G.H. Mead, *Mind, Self and Society* (1967).
27. E. Durkheim, *Suicide* (1952).
28. A. Hauser, *Mannerism*, 2 vols (1965).
29. G. Simmel, 'The Metropolis and Mental Life', in K. Wolff (ed.), *The Sociology of Georg Simmel* (Glencoe, Illinois, 1950).
30. S. Giedion, *The Eternal Present*, 2 vols (1962–4).
31. G. Lukacs, *The Meaning of Contemporary Realism* (1963).

Setting-up the Seen

Philip Corrigan

I propose to organize my response to earlier essays in this collection, especially in Section III, in three parts—initially to 'converse' with Roy Porter and Dario Castiglione, then with Robert Witkin, and to conclude, reflectively, with Stephen Mennell. But before doing so, I wish to draw attention to two important contexts for my argument. Though only briefly summarized (since I have explored them elsewhere)[1] readers are encouraged to consider further their implications for what follows.

The first concerns a conundrum of historiography and social studies, to which Raymond Williams drew attention as part of his general 'critique of the categories'. Disciplines in the academy validate themselves by tacit or explicit appeals to tradition (the canon, art-history) and/or fundamental universal laws (Science) and/or formal universal categories (Literature), the key quality of which is that they must be empty but valid. That is they can in and of themselves say precisely nothing about any particular case: in theory, knowledge that something is, say, a work of art, does not imply any concrete information about that particular work.[2] (In this critique, Williams 'forgets' that this impertinence is genderically constructed, so that some bodies are radically othered as essence because their gender/sexuality/race or ethnicity is not normal. This pertinent embodiment of difference I return to later.)

However, Williams argued again and again,[3] such disciplines (and the practices they inform) are just as constantly redefining, and so changing, the traditions, laws, and formal categories they establish, precisely by specifications—in arguments about origins, provenance, identity, meaning, and value in relationship to the canon of art-history (what *is* art?), for example. Framing devices of disciplinary validity are thus really, in

217

practice, sustained by debate, argument, mistakes, parody, and the like; that is, by social struggles over social signs!

The second context is provided by Christopher Caudwell in his essay on 'Consciousness', where he clearly delineated the following, sharply contrasting, self-image of the bourgeois masculine mind:

> The closed world of sociology. Here, once again, the bourgeois surveys a world from outside, and since his mind is not deter-mined by it, though he lives in it, the social concepts in his mind are eternal (the laws of appetite, supply and demand, justice, free trade, etc.). These concepts therefore function . . . as laws regulating the free clash of individuals and not as products of certain stages of that clash. Consequently, as in the famous mercantile examples, if two men meet on a desert island, their transactions strangely enough always and inevitably produce bourgeois economics . . . and this is taken as a proof of the validity of the bourgeois concepts. It follows from this that although the bourgeois can give a fairly accurate picture . . . it is a static picture . . . Yet change manifestly occurs and therefore some force must be invoked from an outside world to produce these changes . . . spheres anterior . . . or posterior to the sociological will be used in explaining the change.[4]

I provide this 'framing device' for my response since I believe this way of seeing offers an advance upon how histories of the European and Scottish Enlightenments[5] and social or sociological histories are currently 'thought' (i.e. practised) in this book and elsewhere.

A further general remark is also required. As always: words matter. 'Culture' is a very complex term, as are 'production' and 'consumption'. Marx refused the validity of any determining theory based on consump-tion, 'commercial', 'trade' or exchange relations: the latter signs indicate a further set of signifieds beyond the immediately real (which is not to deny their 'power', as Foucault's work showed). But, crucially, there were and are other signifieds (briefly, those of the dialexis of power/difference) —namely those of differential embodiment, forms of life, coercively-encouraged dress and address—which Marx's historical sociology never fully recognizes.

This does not, to repeat, deny the realities (as historical experiences) of consumption as facts of life and ways of appropriating continuities within change and changes within continuity (see, for example, Defoe on 'fashion' in the late seventeenth and early eighteenth centuries). To see (live) consumption as a way of seeing, that is a cosmology, is to join in a language-game in which some forms of 'The Good Life' are good and demonstrated by the possession of goods (as Weber argued). Immediately the fusion, and confusion, of health and wealth needs to be stressed, particularly when we speak of being/doing well. But who 'did well' differed within single categories (ranks, estates, levels, types) and between them.

Nevertheless Marx rightly argues two quite exceptional critiques of these surface understandings (which are now, curiously, celebrated in some versions of post-modernism). First, there is no 'society' (as in, for example, 'consumer society') to be abstracted from 'individuals', since individuals are ensembles of both social relations and, in modernity (i.e. by 1885, *globally*), the contradictions of capitalism. Second, production relations define people's life-chances insofar as only a majority forced to work in order to live can 'supply' the 'demands' of capitalism. If 'force' is thought too strong, then let me translate 'force' (as Marx did in 1845) as willed—that is 'coercively encouraged'. But again this cosmology ignores how within those coercively encouraged to labour there are at least two divisions: women compared with men are differently coerced (notably into 'domesticity' and 'privacy': the great unmentioned proletariat here is that of domestic servants) and some women are differently situated, and maximally oppressed, at the place of paid work (whether in England or in the English Empire).

So any 'consumption' (and, to use the late twentieth-century anachronism, 'consumerism') is likely to distract attention from differential determinations displaced from the 'conspicuousness' of consuming. Though facts of consumption are in and of themselves part of the way of noticing and differentiating ways (including, chances) of life itself, such explanations, typically, tend to relate to the consumer, to persons and groups. That is, they blame problems of the (surface) social on characteristics of the people concerned. The diseases (note, here and in what follows, the root meaning of dis-ease) of the social (also known as 'commercial civilization') are displayed as disorders of some people (albeit of the majority). 'Blaming the victim(s)' has a very long history, especially with regard to women, colonials, and others.[6] 'Commercial society' (site of so many new forms of consumption and denial) was held to be productive of major 'consequences' which were dangerous; *sotto voce*: 'civilization'[7] already had its discontents. But the latter—another trope attended to by Raymond Williams—were rhetorically argued to be understood, in part, as the product of *malcontents*. Social dys-functions were explained away in two ways. They were seen as the result of wrong thinking or

understanding (precisely identified as faulty socialization).[8] Furthermore
the presence of inadequately socialized (read also regulated) individuals
was seen as integral to a value system of socially structured differentiation—the infamous 'splitting' of 'the individual' and 'society'[9] was
reaffirmed.[10]

Social diseases, then, are related to social disorders, to social troubles.
Of course 'trouble' often starts when individuals are de-individualized as
groups and communities of interest, polarized from some others and
solidarized amongst themselves. Consider the settings visualized by the
articles under discussion. The site of such 'trouble' is sometimes the
market (e.g. shops), very rarely the art gallery, and very often the pub,
since this is one area of 'the public' that is always on the edge of
excess, threatening radical de-subordination for some, mainly males.[11]
Consumption thus relates to the modern problematic of *excess*: some of
X is 'good', too much of X is 'bad'. This problematic is associated
specifically with an emergent middle class, who identified themselves
against both the 'best' (the aristocracy and gentry) and the 'rest'
(the population, the populace). In this problematic 'the best' set an
unreformed, and hence bad, example to 'the rest'—that is too much
consumption (or consuming too much of X) is A Bad Thing! From this
followed several other modern features of social analysis: too much
democracy (or 'democracy' realized) or too little (apathy!) being a danger
to the state; too much 'desire' (or 'desire' for too much) or its alternative,
inadequate consumption, being a danger to the market. Thus we find that
talk of consumption turns upon a certain—shall we call it—civic ('citizen'
being too dangerous) consumer. 'Civic' here might also contrast with 'the
state' (later, 'public') purchasing of goods and provision of services. To be
civilized was to be able to demonstrate a regulated consumption of goods
and their display—effortlessly so in the 'gentleman of leisure'.

Both Castiglione's Mandeville and Porter's elucidation of Trotter can
be contextualized as symptomatic of the dialexis[12] of uneasiness and
fear[13] which so much recent study has rediscovered. As Roy Porter argues
here and in his other writings[14] (following Foucault)[15] the body emerges
as both bipolar and a persisting social metaphor.[16] Jonathan Clark
has recently noted the importance of locating change in the 'long
eighteenth century' not in ideas or ideologies, nor yet particular thinkers
or politicians, but in 'medicine and the economy'.[17] Porter's stress upon
the way doctors and medicine became part of a general sociology (of
a capitalist economy) is thus neatly confirmed, but at the price of
'forgetting' Who, Whom? Disease—both that of 'too little' and that of

'too much'—must be related to the institutionalization of disciplines into social practices through which white, male ruling classes and their agents thought and handled their own uneasiness with social procedures and organizational forms that caused fear in subject populations and groups, including 'their (owned) women' and the women of other men. I want to emphasize that uneasiness and fear are bodily states, forms of embodied knowledge, both of which are valid ways of experiencing (knowing) a differentiated, radically changing social structure.

As Castiglione shows, Mandeville shared with Trotter an anxiety about the dangers of under- or over-consumption by the population. Consumption was presented in one powerful cosmology as a private (domestic) affair, but Mandeville recognized it as occupying the public domain of the market. Hence the link of 'private vices' with 'public benefits', though of course both vices and benefits, and public and private, applied differently to bodies of different gender. This is confirmed by both Mandeville's 'underground existence' in the nineteenth century and his celebration by Hayek, and others, as 'the first individualist'. Concern with the public character of consumption lessened as emphasis turned, in the construction of 'civilization', to production. But this was only possible through blindness (continued until today) to 'production places' as 'public' sites. Does not every legal system of capitalism regulate or establish such sites as legally *private*? Hence talk of state 'intervention' and of the 'danger' of trades unions—the latter as a 'concern' of the state. Yet at the same time, state forms relating to 'the social' and its construction as an *object* of politics or policy originate in regulating three aspects of the private, even the personal—certainly the person. These are: the contracts of masters with slaves, servile labourers and servants; associations based on the sexual or generational division of labour, largely domestic; restrictions on the free movement of the majority of the population (e.g. in Poor Law settlement regulations). These modes of constructing 'private' realms were extended and regularized during the nineteenth century, culminating in the nightmare vision of electronically-tagged offenders and 'hidden persuaders' found today.

A key concept in the social imagery of the eighteenth and nineteenth centuries was 'realism'—a notoriously ambiguous term in any social vocabulary. Robert Witkin's exploration of the relationship between bourgeois production and artistic style may not seem to raise issues of power and difference. Yet the communist Arnold Hauser was determined to make the connection. Changes in cultural practices and productions and thus changes in ways of seeing, are, Hauser insistently documents,

changes in the ways of life we call a mode of production. In forming the
state, and creating the optimal personal structure for the market, how
you see (and seem) is who you are. The argument could be strengthened
by reference to Gordon Childe's work on numeration, lettering and
figuration (that is, representation, in the broadest sense) and Steinberg's
study of iconic shifts in Christian religious symbolism.[18]

All too often aesthetics is a matter of anaesthetics—that is, 'forgetting'!
Witkin's arguments on representation can be placed within three alternative approaches to the same problem. Firstly, that set of social theorists
who propose a social linguistics. They argue for the impossibility of
seeing, representing, picturing 'the individual' as other than a complex
ensemble of 'social relations' (and 'society' as other than individuals
embodying their differential historical experience of such social
relations). Second, we must observe the absence both of generic forms
of picturing and perception (i.e. social representation) and of the easily
'captured' (on canvas or on film) native other. This ontological thus
epistemological thus representational difference is *showable* and if it is
not shown—whether in Art-History, or Criticism, or Literature—this is a
determinate, systematic, patterned, conscious denial of not just 52% of
our population, but, in world terms, of (say) 80%. Third, even if shown
(portrayed, for example) these representations are not those *of* the
represented and so are morally regressive, violent and evil, insofar as they
simultaneously (i) deny the voice or sign of those de-signed but shown (ii)
divide and marginalize any form by which these groups can represent
themselves differently. In short, the codes (all of them: Naturalism,
Realism, Modernism, Post-Modernism) operate by a standard trope:
including can be denial of importance; comprehensive representation can
be denial (what else is pornography about?).

Whatever the focus or means of representation, the resulting images
(here paintings) are consumed in two importantly different 'senses'. First,
they can be 'eaten up with the eyes [ears]'—to have seen the Mona Lisa or
Van Gogh's Sunflowers is to *behave representationally* with regard to
Art. Second, such objects are—in fact—consumed (check out the latest
Sotheby's sale catalogue); they circulate as 'valuable goods' and are
desired for *that* sort of value.

All the papers considered so far thus provide an example of how that
most 'personal' and 'private' of possessions, 'our' bodies,[19] were not
immune from the comprehensive (re)cartographization of 'the social'
which takes place during the eighteenth and nineteenth centuries.[20] By the
early nineteenth century, political doctors, experts and state servants[21]

identified and offered remedies for social diseases (read also: diseases of the social). Indeed by the end of the nineteenth century poverty, that major negative habit of the idle and undeserving (the poor, of course, not the aristocracy!), is rearticulated as a 'social disease', while 'social legislation' was invented as an antidote to that most un-English epidemic, socialism.[22] Take for example the following quotation from Dr. James Kay (later Sir James Kay-Shuttleworth) in 1860:

> It is impossible either to limit the pernicious influence of pauperism or crime to the wealth and productive power of the country, or to combat them effectually without employing moral transformatory as well as economical repressive forces for their extirpation . . . sanitary measures reach even the moral nature of man. They are part of civilization.[23]

What this social cartography involves is nothing less than the re-arrangement of space and time[24] which eventuates in a radically differentiated and wildly contradictory set of social identifications which impact differently on individuals as individualization *and* emplacement. 'Knowing one's place' is a good example of how the older repertoire of orders and ranks is recontextualized and how order is restored and continued in a disordered society. Like, for example, the disorder of women. There has never been a human society that didn't propose a human type as *subjectively* normal (that from whom the viewpoint flows; those to whom some one(s) should look up) and the rest (Women, Natives, Others?) as totally 'representable' as objects.

The importance of Edinburgh (and the Scottish Enlightenment thinkers),[25] the Philosophical Radicals[26] and political economy[27] (insofar as they can be separated) is that, through them, we can see a new social grammar being formed and so reforming the state. Central to this sociology was an image of the facts, and of the modes of their collection, manipulation, and dissemination about which Edwin Chadwick[28] was uniquely forthcoming, although the belief was quite general. Moral regulation[29] is the term I have employed for many years to describe this complex of 'programmes of power' and 'practices of institutionalization' (involving concomitant establishments of masculine middle-class professional expertise), which turn on the social construction and regulation of knowledge/ignorance.[30] Bodies—as consuming, as dangerously excessive, as pictured—remain affective and somatic sources of a knowledge not caught up in purchases, boozing or being painted, nor in history or historical sociology. This is what 'education' and 'academia' (including *in this volume*) ignore—construct as *an ignorance*. Yet this too (across all the divisions of labour—in production, consumption, and culture) —socially signifies! Equally there is a consistent argument, from the eighteenth to the late twentieth centuries, that solutions to the problems that the facts reveal (all of these terms themselves questionable) will entail *an educational tendency*.[31] This operates through doubled dichotomies which reduce to the quartet of Self: Other; Male: Female.

Stephen Mennell's chapter builds on the work of Norbert Elias, itself much concerned with the process of civilization and the history of the body, but from a different perspective. The danger of rendering active history as passive process is that the scene is depersonalized and the metaphors of the game, implying fairness and participation for all, obscure the real historical experiences of the past, especially those of women, natives and others. Within a largely Eurocentric view these groups risk being unrepresented, let alone considered as sources of social knowledge. Such an approach was brilliantly assailed and deconstructed by Marx in his rejection of 'necessity' and the call for a social revolution that would simultaneously change both objectivity and subjectivity. Much of the recent work on social linguistics has been oriented to the invention of cosmologies, the imagining of worlds. We do not, any longer, have to contemplate necessity. Instead, we have to find the means (ourselves, no less, no more) to transform all the constraints on human capacities in relation to those social forms that hurt more than they help, that de-form us. Our identities need not be affixed by the state or determined by the market, for we are being-and-becoming, as Philip Abrams so persuasively argued. Why, then, do social studies focus on the 'being' and not the 'becoming'?

In all of these arguments for 'new ways of seeing' it is essential to remember our socialscape with *embodied differences*—we are differently formed and informed by and experience differently the constructed social cosmologies I have annotated above. Critique has accentuated class(es), but in remarkably disembodied ways, ignoring how gender, sexuality, race, ethnicity, age and religion (as embodied identities), result in different somatic 'ways of knowing' structures and relations of power/difference. Thus two historians (or historical sociologists) who have shifted our way of seeing—Edward Thompson and Herbert Gutman—both quote Benjamin Franklin on the dangers of 'drinking-up time' in that 'certain place'—the public house.[32] But both fail to see how women were (a) also working (even if unpaid), (b) subject to a differential temporal pattern,[33] and (c) suffered differently the consequences of drink. Nicky Hart has traced these violent consequences and the exclusion of women from the pleasures of the pub, indeed from 'leisure time' as normally, naturally and obviously discussed.[34] Equally I would emphasize that the recently discovered 'joys' and 'pleasures' of shopping are a disappearing gloss on/of the experience of working class women for millennia, difficult to relate to the facts of trying to board the new mini-buses with five bags of shopping, a push-chair and two children.

Lexically, 'my turn', 'your shout', 'want another', 'taking the other half', 'no it's my round' and so on are remarks of an including/excluding conviviality. Pubs and bars remain dangerous sites of a different conviviality, a different lived sociality. But this fantasy (largely male) community should, finally, be located within that bourgeois social mapping where a certain deviance (read also: the deviance of certain persons) is always granted a value—a value related to the consumption of alcohol (and other narcotics and stimulants) and to the productions of an isolated creative (usually male) 'genius'. Writing-under-the-influence has been O.K. if, and only if, it produces Art, Literature, Criticism,[35] History, Law and Medicine.

Notes

1. P. Corrigan and D. Sayer, *The Great Arch* (Oxford, 1985); P. Corrigan, *Social Forms/Human Capacities: Essays in authority and difference* (1990); id., '"Innocent Stupidities"' in G. Fyfe and J. Law (eds), *Picturing Power* (1988); id., *Who, Whom?* (forthcoming).
2. Cf. Corrigan and Sayer, *Great Arch*; id., 'Hindess and Hirst: A critique', *Socialist Register 1978*, pp. 194–214 ; D. Sayer, *Marx's Method* (Hassocks, 1979); id., *Violence of Abstraction* (Oxford, 1987); id., *Capitalism and Modernity* (1990); D. Frisby and D. Sayer, *Society* (1986); A. Wilden, *The Rules are NO Game* (1988).
3. This theme is so persuasive in Williams' work that there is no single source but see: *The Country and the City* (1971); 'Notes on the Sociology of Culture', *Sociology* 10 (1976), pp. 497–506; *Culture* (1981) and *Politics and Letters: Interviews with New Left Review* (1978), especially pp. 307 ff.
4. C. Caudwell, *Further Studies in a Dying Culture* (reprinted, New York, 1971), pp. 170–1. Cf. E.P. Thompson, 'Caudwell', *Socialist Register 1977*, pp. 228–76 .
5. For critical new perspectives on 'Enlightenment' see: P. Hulme and L. Jordanova (eds), *The Enlightenment and its Shadows* (1990); D. Outram, *The Body and the French Revolution: Sex, class and political*

culture (New Haven, 1989); J. B. Landes, *Women and the Public Sphere in the Age of the French Revolution* (Cornell, 1988); V. Jones (ed.), *Women in the Eighteenth Century: Constructions of femininity* (1990); F. Nussbaum and L. Brown (eds), *The New Eighteenth Century: Theory, politics, English literature* (1987) and the works of C. Pateman cited in n. 10. I discuss the fracture of this episteme in 'Power/Difference', *Sociological Review* 39 (1991), pp. 309–34.

6. For examples from the ninth to the twentieth century see Corrigan and Sayer, *Great Arch*; the expulsion of Jews in the thirteenth century and the attempted state genocide of the Rom in the sixteenth century are crucial examples. See above all, Trinh Minh-ha, *Woman, Native, Other* (Bloomington, Indiana, 1989).

7. A. Pagdon, 'The Defence of "Civilization" . . .', *History of the Human Sciences* 1 (1988), pp. 33–45 ; A. Bestor, 'The Evolution of a Socialist Vocabulary', *Journal of the History of Ideas* 9 (1948), pp. 258–302 ; R.W. Balogh, *Love or Greatness: Max Weber and masculine thinking —a feminist inquiry* (1990), especially pp. 1–20.

8. 'We advocate, both for England [which, note, includes/hides Wales] and Ireland, the necessity of a national provision for the training of the young. In the old we cannot hope for much improvement. But the new generation springing up might be modelled to *our* will.' *Westminster Review* January 1837 quoted in E. Halevy, *The Triumph of Reform, 1830–1841* (1923, trans. 1949), pp. 105–6, n. 5 (my emphasis).

9. P. Abrams, *Origins of British Sociology* (Chicago, 1968); id., 'Notes on the Difficulty of Studying the State' [1977], *Journal of Historical Sociology* 1 (1988), pp. 58–89 ; Corrigan, *Social Forms*, chs 1, 3, 4 and 7 and all of Part II.

10. B.S. Green, *Knowing the Poor: A case-study in textual reality construction* (1983); A. Ashforth, 'Reckoning Schemes of Legitimation: On Commissions of Inquiry as power/knowledge forms', *Journal of Historical Sociology* 3 (1990), pp. 1–22; K. Mannheim, *Ideology and Utopia* (1936, trans. 1960), pp. 249 ff.; T.H. Marshall, 'Value Problems of Welfare-Capitalism', *Journal of Social Policy* 1 (1972), pp. 15–32; C. Pateman, *The Sexual Contract* (Cambridge and Oxford, 1988); id., *The Disorder of Women* (Cambridge and Oxford, 1990).

11. B. Harrison, *Drink and the Victorians* (1971).

12. Cf. Corrigan, *Social Forms*, p. 193 for sources regarding this dialexis. I would stress N. Poulantzas, 'The Institutional Materiality of the State', Part 1 of *State/Power/Socialism* (1978).

13. Cf. Corrigan, *Social Forms*, ch. 7 and its application in M. Kearney 'Borders and Boundaries of State and Self at the End of Empire', *Journal of Historical Sociology* 4 (1991), pp. 52–74.

14. R. Porter: 'Body and History', *London Review of Books* 31 August 1989; 'Libertinism and Promiscuity' in J. Miller (ed.), *The Don Giovanni Book* (1990).

15. M. Foucault, *History of Sexuality*, Vol. I *Introduction* (1979), pp. 139 ff.; id., 'My Body, This Paper, This Fire', *Oxford Literary Review* 4[1] (1979). Cf. Corrigan, *Social Forms* chs 5 and 6; id., 'Playing, Contra/Dictions' in H. Giroux and R. Simon (eds), *Popular Culture, Schooling and Everyday Life* (South Hadley, Mass., 1989).

16. A profound critical account of embodiment textuality is given in Outram, *The Body*, especially in chs 1, 4, and 5. Of course the 'dating' of modern uses of 'society' is debated—for two relevant contrasts see J. Bossy, 'Some Elementary Forms of Durkheim', *Past and Present* 95 (1982), pp. 3–18 and E. Wolf, 'Inventing Society', *American Ethnologist* 15(4) (1988).

17. J.C.D. Clark, 'Change and Decay not All Around', *Spectator* 10 November 1990, p. 48.

18. V. Gordon Childe, *Man Makes Himself* (1936); L. Steinberg, *The Sexuality of Christ in Renaissance Art and Modern Oblivion* (1984).

19. R. Cooter, 'The Power of the Body: The early nineteenth century' in B. Barnes and S. Shapin (eds), *Natural Order* (Beckenham, 1979); P. Corrigan 'Race/Ethnicity/Gender/Culture' and R. Simon 'Being Ethnic/Doing Ethnicity: A response to Corrigan' in J. Young (ed.), *Breaking the Mosaic* (Toronto, 1987); B. Turner, *The Body in Society* (Oxford, 1986). But see, contrastingly, *Representations* 14 (1986); P. Connerton, *How Societies Remember* (Cambridge, 1989); J. Gallop, *Thinking through the Body* (Columbia, 1988); P. Brown, *The Body in Society* (Columbia, 1988); Minh-ha, *Women, Native, Other*; T. Laqueur, *Making Sex* (Cambridge, Mass., 1990).

20. B. Bailyn, 'The Challenge of Modern Historiography', *American Historical Review* 87 (1982), pp. 1–24; B. Cohn and N. Dirks, 'Beyond the Fringe', *Journal of Historical Sociology* 1 (1988), pp. 224–9; J.A. Agnew, 'The Devaluation of Space in Social Science' in J.A. Agnew and J.S. Duncan (eds), *The Power of Place* (1989).

21. Insofar as they could be separated: Dr J.P. Kay, for example, was all three—cf. Corrigan 'State Formation' ch. 3 and app. I. It was Kay who argued in 1846: 'The authority of government, especially in a representative system, embodies the national will. There are certain objects too vast, or too complicated, or too important to be intrusted [sic] to voluntary associations; they need the assertion of power.' (*The School in its Relations to the State, Church, and the Congregation*, reprinted in *Four Periods of Public Education* (1862), p. 451).

22. Corrigan and Sayer, *Great Arch*, ch. 7; R. McKibbin, 'Why was there

no Marxism in Great Britain?', reprinted in *The Ideologies of Class* (Oxford, 1990).

23. 'Address', *Transactions of the National Association for the Promotion of Social Science* (1860), p. 92.

24. E.P. Thompson, 'Time, Work-Discipline and Industrial Capitalism', *Past and Present* 38 (1967), pp. 56–97; H.G. Gutman, 'Work, Culture and Society in Industrializing America, 1815–1919', *American Historical Review* 78 (1973), pp. 531–88.

25. See the work of W. Lehman, 1931 to 1971; D. Winch, *Adam Smith's Politics* (Cambridge, 1978).

26. W. Thomas, 'The Philosophic Radicals' in P. Hollis (ed.), *Pressure from Without* (1974).

27. On the dissemination devices of popularization see the articles by S. Checkland in *Economica* 16 (1949), pp. 40–52; A. Fetter in *Journal of Political Economy* 56 (1953), pp. 232–59 and *Economica* 38 (1965), pp. 424–37 ; S. Finer 'The Transmission of Benthamite Ideas 1820–1850' (1959, reprinted in G. Sutherland (ed.), *Studies in the Growth of Nineteenth-Century Government* (1972)); R. Clements in *Economic History Review* 14 (1961), pp. 93–104; and R. Gilmour in *Victorian Studies* 11 (1967), pp. 207–24. For 'contrasting moralities' see A.W. Coats in *Past and Present* 54 (1972), pp. 130–3; E.P. Thompson, *The Making of the English Working Class* (rev. edn Harmondsworth, 1968); J. Mitchell and A. Oakley (eds), *Rights and Wrongs of Women* (Harmondsworth, 1976); B. Taylor, *Eve and the New Jerusalem* (1983); E. Paul, *Moral Revolution and Economic Science* (Westport, Conn., 1979).

28. S. Finer, *The Life and Times of Sir Edwin Chadwick* (1952) is the key book for my whole argument. Chadwick, J.P. Kay, L. Horner and H.S. Tremenheere are studied in P. Corrigan, 'State Formation and Moral Regulation in Nineteenth-Century Britain: Sociological investigations' (University of Durham, Ph.D thesis, 1977), economically summarized in Corrigan and Sayer, *Great Arch*, p. 223, n. 18.

29. Corrigan, *Social Forms*, ch. 3.

30. P. Abrams, 'Notes on the Functions of Ignorance', *Twentieth Century* April 1963; F. Inglis, *The Management of Ignorance* (Oxford, 1985), ch. 1.

31. Corrigan, *Social Forms*, ch. 5; Corrigan and Sayer, *Great Arch*, ch. 6; B. Curtis, *The Building of the Educational State* (Falmer, 1987); J. Purvis, *Hard Lessons* (Cambridge and Oxford, 1990); N. Pearson, *The State and Fine Art* (Milton Keynes, 1982). All the work of Carolyn Steedman and Valerie Walkerdine bears on this point, generalized in Corrigan, 'Institutions and Individuals' (forthcoming).

32. Thompson 'Time', p. 89; Gutman, 'Work, Culture and Society', p. 532

(the latter, concerning 'Saint Monday' needs to be read in the light of both Thompson and P. Corrigan and V. Gillespie, *Class Struggle, Social Literacy and Idle Time* (Noyce, 1979)).

33. T. Haraven, 'Family Time and Historical Time', *Daedalus* 106 (2) (1977), pp. 57–70; F. Paterson, *Out of Place* (Falmer, 1989); E. J. Forman (ed.), *Taking our Time: Feminist perspectives on temporality* (Oxford, 1989).

34. N. Hart, 'Gender and the Rise and Fall of Class Politics', *New Left Review* 175 (1989), pp. 29 ff. reviews the literature on pubs from the early nineteenth to the mid-twentieth centuries, using Harrison, *Drink and Victorians* and others, to draw out its masculinist qualities and the economic consequences for the working-class family. For a contemporary analysis which accentuates the physical as much as the economic violence see *Pubs and Patriarchy* (1986).

35. Williams, 'Notes' sees Art, Literature, and Criticism as features of 'bourgeois specialization and control'. These points are brilliantly illuminated *within imperialism* by J. Ferguson, *The Anti-Politics Machine* (Cambridge, 1990) (especially 'Epilogue') and in the 'Issues and Agendas' section of the *Journal of Historical Sociology* 3[3] and 4[2–3] (1990–1), by M. Taussig, G. Kinsman and E. Wamba dia Wamba respectively.

Index

231

DATE DUE